Activities Manual for ELECTRONICS Principles and Applications

Activities Manual for ELECTRONICS Principles and Applications

Third Edition

Charles A. Schuler
California University of Pennsylvania
California, Pennsylvania

GLENCOE
Macmillan/McGraw-Hill
New York, New York
Columbus, Ohio
Mission Hills, California
Peoria, Illinois

ACKNOWLEDGMENTS

The *Basic Skills in Electricity and Electronics* series was conceived and developed through the talents and energies of many individuals and organizations.

The original, on-site classroom testing of the texts and manuals in this series was conducted at the Burr D. Coe Vocational Technical High School, East Brunswick, New Jersey; Chantilly Secondary School, Chantilly, Virginia; Nashoba Valley Technical High School, Westford, Massachusetts; Platt Regional Vocational Technical High School, Milford, Connecticut; and the Edgar Thomson, Irvin Works of the United States Steel Corporation, Dravosburg, Pennsylvania. Postpublication testing took place at the Alhambra High School, Phoenix, Arizona; St. Helena High School, St. Helena, California; and Addison Trail High School, Addison, Illinois.

Early in the publication life of this series, the appellation "Rainbow Books" was used. The name stuck and has become a point of identification ever since.

In the years since the publication of this series, extensive follow-up studies and research have been conducted. Thousands of instructors, students, school administrators, and industrial trainers have shared their experiences and suggestions with the authors and publishers. To each of these people we extend our thanks and appreciation.

The manuscript for this book was processed electronically.

Activities Manual for Electronics: Principles and Applications
Third Edition

Imprint 1992

Send all inquiries to: Glencoe Division, Macmillan/McGraw-Hill, 936 Eastwind Drive, Westerville, Ohio 43081.

4 5 6 7 8 9 10 11 12 13 14 15 SEM 00 99 98 97 96 95 94 93 92

ISBN 0-07-055593-1

Contents

Editor's Foreword

The McGraw-Hill *Basic Skills in Electricity and Electronics* series has been designed to provide entry-level competencies in a wide range of occupations in the electric and electronic fields. The series consists of coordinated instructional materials designed especially for the career-oriented student. Each major subject area covered in the series is supported by a textbook, an activities manual, and a teacher's manual. All the materials focus on the theory, practices, applications, and experiences necessary for those preparing to enter technical careers.

There are two fundamental considerations in the preparation of materials for such a series: the needs of the learner and the needs of the employer. The materials in this series meet these needs in an expert fashion. The authors and editors have drawn upon their broad teaching and technical experiences to accurately interpret and meet the needs of the student. The needs of business and industry have been identified through questionnaires, surveys, personal interviews, industry publications, government occupational trend reports, and field studies.

The processes used to produce and refine the series have been ongoing. Technological change is rapid and the content has been revised to focus on current trends. Refinements in pedagogy have been defined and implemented based on classroom testing and feedback from students and teachers using the series. Every effort has been made to offer the best possible learning materials.

The widespread acceptance of the *Basic Skills in Electricity and Electronics* series and the positive responses from users confirm the basic soundness in the content and design of these materials as well as their effectiveness as learning tools. Teachers will find the texts and manuals in each of the subject areas logically structured, well-paced, and developed around a framework of modern objectives. Students will find the materials readable, lucidly illustrated, and interesting. They will also find a generous amount of self-study and review materials to help them determine their own progress.

The publisher and editor welcome comments and suggestions from teachers and students using the materials in this series.

Charles A. Schuler
Project Editor

BASIC SKILLS IN ELECTRICITY AND ELECTRONICS
Charles A. Schuler, Project Editor

Books in this series

Introduction to Television Servicing by Wayne C. Brandenburg
Electricity: Principles and Applications by Richard J. Fowler
Communication Electronics by Louis E. Frenzel, Jr.
Instruments and Measurements by Charles M. Gilmore
Microprocessors: Principles and Applications by Charles M. Gilmore
Small Appliance Repair by Phyllis Palmore and Nevin E. André
Electronics: Principles and Applications by Charles A. Schuler
Digital Electronics by Roger L. Tokheim

Preface

This manual provides a wide range of student activities in electronics. Its content runs parallel to the theory presented in the third edition of *Electronics: Principles and Applications.* Students will find that applying theory and working with practical circuits will enhance their understanding and make it easier for them to remember what they are learning. The activities include review tests, problems, experiments, projects, and design work. All the activities have been selected to focus on the kinds of skills and knowledge used by practicing electronic technicians.

The experiments are a very important part of this manual. Their intent is not to have students merely read instruments and record data. Although these functions are essential, they are not the final objective. Each experiment is designed to demonstrate concepts and principles of linear electronic circuits. They also show practical ways in which devices and circuits are used. The data collected has value because it serves as a vehicle for learning. If it merely represents numbers, then it is useless. Students are encouraged to look for meaning in their data, to verify trends, and to solve for values whenever possible.

The activities span the range of modern linear electronic applications. The content progresses from basic concepts in linear electronics to advanced applications such as a switch-mode power supply circuit with feedback for voltage control. Students will learn how to lay out and wire circuits using schematic diagrams. They will apply color codes, read and interpret symbols, and learn about the physical arrangement of components. They will use common instruments to measure electrical quantities, verify proper circuit operation, and interpret their results. They will analyze data and develop a keener insight into circuit behavior. Finally, they will use tools and related equipment to fabricate and debug various projects. All the activities have one central goal: to develop the skills and knowledge needed to pursue a technical career in the field of electronics.

A rich assortment of projects is included to give students tangible evidence of accomplishments in their studies and to get them involved in circuit layout, fabrication, and troubleshooting. The knowledge gained about tools, materials, and components is invaluable to any technician entering the job market. The projects have been carefully selected to be interesting, practical, and reasonable in cost. They have been tested in the author's classes over the years and include a curve tracer, a wideband voltmeter, a booster amplifier, a signal tracer, a function generator, a phase-locked loop signal generator, a wireless microphone, a line voltmeter with memory, a regulated motor-speed controller, a programmable timer, and a triple-output/dual tracking power supply.

Every effort has been made to develop activities that support modern theory and that also have a strong link to current practices. Based on feedback from the earlier editions, it has been possible to improve the activities and relax some of the equipment requirements. I would enjoy hearing from both teachers and students about this third edition.

Charles A. Schuler

Safety

Electric and electronic circuits can be dangerous. Safe practices are necessary to prevent electrical shock, fires, explosions, mechanical damage, and injuries resulting from the improper use of tools.

Perhaps the greatest hazard is electric shock. A current through the human body in excess of 10 milliamperes can paralyze the victim and make it impossible to let go of a "live" conductor or component. Ten milliamperes is a rather small amount of electric flow: it is only *ten one-thousandths* of an ampere. An ordinary flashlight uses more than 100 times that amount of current!

Flashlight cells and batteries are safe to handle because the resistance of human skin is normally high enough to keep the current flow very small. For example, touching an ordinary 1.5-V cell produces a current flow in the microampere range (a microampere is one-millionth of an ampere). This much current is too small to be noticed.

High voltage, on the other hand, can force enough current through the skin to produce a shock. If the current approaches 100 milliamperes or more, the shock can be fatal. Thus, the danger of shock increases with voltage. Those who work with high voltage must be properly trained and equipped.

When human skin is moist or cut, its resistance to the flow of electricity can drop drastically. When this happens, even moderate voltages may cause a serious shock. Experienced technicians know this and they also know that so-called low-voltage equipment may have a high-voltage section or two. In other words, they do not practice two methods of working with circuits: one for high voltage and one for low voltage. They follow safe procedures at all times. They do not assume protective devices are working. They do not assume a circuit is off even though the switch is in the OFF position. They know the switch could be defective.

As your knowledge and experience grows, you will learn many specific safe procedures for dealing with electricity and electronics. In the meantime:

1. Always follow procedures.
2. Use service manuals as often as possible. They often contain specific safety information.
3. Investigate before you act.
4. When in doubt, *do not act.* Ask your instructor or supervisor.

GENERAL SAFETY RULES FOR ELECTRICITY AND ELECTRONICS

Safe practices will protect you and your fellow workers. Study the following rules. Discuss them with others, and ask your instructor about any that you do not understand.

1. Do not work when you are tired or taking medicine that makes you drowsy.
2. Do not work in poor light.
3. Do not work in damp areas or with wet shoes or clothing.
4. Use approved tools, equipment, and protective devices.
5. Avoid wearing rings, bracelets, and similar metal items when working around exposed electric circuits.
6. Never assume that a circuit is off. Double check it with an instrument that you are sure is operational.
7. Some situations require a "buddy system" to guarantee that power will not be turned on while a technician is still working on a circuit.
8. Never tamper with or try to override safety devices such as an interlock (a type of switch that automatically removes power when a door is opened or a panel removed).
9. Keep tools and test equipment clean and in good working condition. Replace insulated probes and leads at the first sign of deterioration.
10. Some devices, such as capacitors, can store a *lethal* charge. They may store this charge for long periods of time. You must be certain these devices are discharged before working around them.
11. Do not remove grounds, and do not use adaptors that defeat the equipment ground.
12. Use only an approved fire extinguisher for electric and electronic equipment. Water can conduct electricity and may severely damage equipment. Carbon dioxide (CO_2) or halogenated-type extinguishers are usually preferred. Foam-type extinguishers may also be desired in some cases. Commercial fire extinguishers are rated for the type of fires for which they are effective. Use only those rated for the proper working conditions.
13. Follow directions when using solvents and other chemicals. They may be toxic, flammable, or may damage certain materials such as plastics.
14. A few materials used in electronic equipment are toxic. Examples include tantalum capacitors and beryllium oxide transistor cases. These devices should not be crushed or abraded, and you should wash your hands thoroughly

after handling them. Other materials (such as heat shrink tubing) may produce irritating fumes if overheated.
15. Certain circuit components affect the safe performance of equipment and systems. Use only exact or approved replacement parts.
16. Use protective clothing and safety glasses when handling high-vacuum devices such as picture tubes and cathode ray tubes.
17. Don't work on equipment before you know proper procedures and are aware of any potential safety hazards.
18. Many accidents have been caused by people rushing and cutting corners. Take the time required to protect yourself and others. Running, horseplay, and practical jokes are strictly forbidden in shops and laboratories. Circuits and equipment must be treated with respect. Learn how they work and the proper way of working on them. Always practice safety; your health and life depend on it.

CHAPTER 1

Introduction

ACTIVITY 1-1
RESEARCH AND DISCUSSION

Complete your answers to the following questions on separate paper. Be prepared to discuss each in class.

1. List five major developments from the history of electronics and include the date for each. Describe the importance of each to everyday life.
2. Examine Fig. 1-1 and classify each circuit as digital or analog.
3. List four major future trends in electronics.

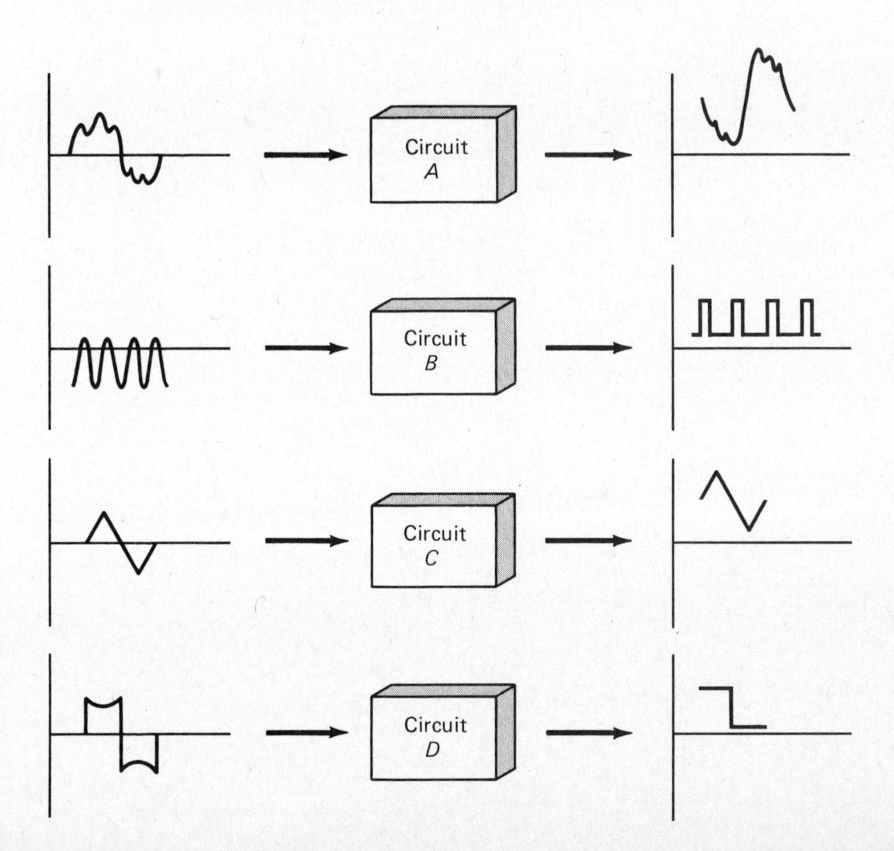

Fig. 1-1 Examples of digital and analog circuits.

ACTIVITY 1-2
MATCHING TEST

Match the terms at the left with the descriptions at the right.

1. Amplifier
2. Analog
3. Attenuator
4. Audio
5. Binary
6. Bit
7. Block diagram
8. DSP
9. Digital
10. Electronics
11. Filter
12. Linear
13. Schematic
14. Signal
15. Troubleshooting

a. shows system functions and signal flows
b. the output is a replica of the input
c. binary digit
d. usually required for component-level troubleshooting
e. increase signal amplitude
f. computer manipulation of the binary representation of an analog signal
g. a useful voltage or current
h. decreases signal amplitude
i. having two states (such as 0 and 1)
j. removes unwanted frequencies
k. pertaining to hearing and sound
l. the study of active devices and applications
m. an infinite number of levels
n. locating malfunctions
o. a fixed number of levels

CHAPTER 2

Semiconductors

ACTIVITY 2-1
TEST: SEMICONDUCTORS

Choose the letter that best completes each statement.

1. Conductors have
   a. Loosely bound valence electrons
   b. Low resistance
   c. A positive temperature coefficient
   d. All of the above
2. Which of the following is *not* a conductor?
   a. Copper
   b. Silicon
   c. Silver
   d. Aluminum
3. How many valence electrons do semiconductors have?
   a. 1
   b. 2
   c. 3
   d. 4
4. At room temperature pure silicon crystals conduct
   a. Very poorly
   b. Moderately
   c. Well
   d. Very well
5. As the temperature increases, the resistance of a conductor will
   a. Not change
   b. Decrease
   c. Increase
   d. Be impossible to predict
6. As the temperature increases, the resistance of a semiconductor will
   a. Not change
   b. Decrease
   c. Increase
   d. Be impossible to predict

7. Germanium semiconductors are not as popular as silicon semiconductors because of their sensitivity to
   a. Heat
   b. Light
   c. Water vapor
   d. Vibration
8. If a silicon crystal is doped with a material having five valence electrons,
   a. A conductor is formed
   b. Its resistance goes up
   c. A P-type semiconductor is formed
   d. An N-type semiconductor is formed
9. A dopant with five valence electrons is called a(n)
   a. Semiconductor
   b. Insulator
   c. Acceptor
   d. Donor
10. If a germanium crystal is doped with a material having three valence electrons,
    a. A conductor is formed
    b. An insulator is formed
    c. A P-type semiconductor is formed
    d. An N-type semiconductor is formed
11. Doping a semiconductor crystal
    a. Decreases its resistance
    b. Increases its resistance
    c. Does not change its resistance
    d. Makes it act as an insulator
12. The direction of electron current is
    a. From negative to positive
    b. From positive to negative
    c. From left to right
    d. Impossible to predict
13. In a P-type semiconductor the *hole* current is
    a. From negative to positive
    b. From positive to negative
    c. From right to left
    d. Impossible to predict
14. In an N-type semiconductor the *minority* carriers are
    a. Valence electrons
    b. Electrons
    c. Holes
    d. Neutrons
15. In a P-type semiconductor the *majority* carriers are
    a. Valence electrons
    b. Electrons
    c. Holes
    d. Protons
16. The major cause of minority carriers is
    a. Heat
    b. Cold
    c. Impurities with three valence electrons
    d. Impurities with five valence electrons

17. Thermal carriers are generated
    a. One hole at a time
    b. One electron at a time
    c. In pairs
    d. By doping

ACTIVITY 2-2
LAB EXPERIMENT: HEAT AND RESISTANCE

PURPOSE

To demonstrate and compare the effect of heat on conductors and semiconductors.

MATERIALS

Qty.		*Qty.*	
1	volt-ohm-milliammeter (VOM) or digital multimeter (DMM)	2	2N4401 transistors or equivalent
1	each of 25-, 60-, 100-, and 200-W 120-V incandescent lamps	1	23-W soldering pencil

INTRODUCTION

Conductors have a positive temperature coefficient. Their resistance increases with temperature. An incandescent-lamp filament operates at a very high temperature. The filament resistance at room temperature can be measured with an ohmmeter. This can be compared with the operating resistance, which is determined by making a calculation.

Semiconductors have a negative temperature coefficient. Their resistance decreases with temperature. Most transistors are made from silicon, which is a semiconductor material. It is possible to measure a decrease in resistance as transistors are heated.

PROCEDURE

1. Copy Table 2-1 onto a separate sheet of paper.

Table 2-1

Lamp Wattage (W)	Cold Resistance (Measured) (Ω)	Hot Resistance (Calculated) (Ω)
200		
100		
60		
25		

2. Use the $R \times 1$ or 2-kΩ range of your meter. Measure the room temperature (cold) resistance of each of the incandescent lamps and record your results in your copy of the table.
3. Calculate the operating (hot) resistance for each lamp and record your results in the table. Use the formula

$$R = \frac{V^2}{P}$$

where R = resistance, Ω
V = voltage, V
P = wattage rating, W

4. The following example is for a 10-W 120-V lamp:

$$R = \frac{V^2}{P} = \frac{120^2}{10} = \frac{14{,}400}{10} = 1.44\ \text{k}\Omega$$

Thus, the hot resistance of the lamp is 1.44 kΩ.

5. Plug in the soldering pencil and put it aside where it is safe. Build the circuit shown in Fig. 2-1. *Note:* There is no connection to the base of transistor Q_1.
6. A battery-operated VOM works best for this part of the experiment. If one is available, set it on its highest ohms range and connect it as shown in Fig. 2-1. The indicated resistance should be high (typically 1 MΩ or greater).

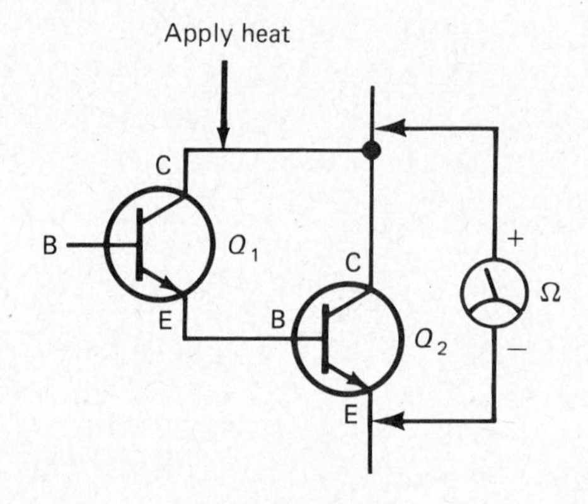

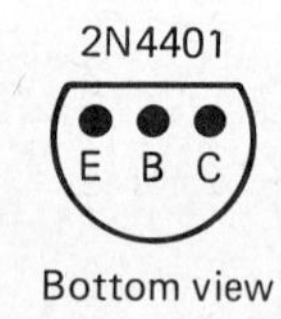

Fig. 2-1 Semiconductor temperature response circuit.

7. If the soldering pencil is hot, touch its tip to the collector (C) lead of transistor Q_1. Make contact about ¼ in. away from the transistor case. Hold the contact for about 5 s and note the ohmmeter response. Remove the soldering pencil and watch the ohmmeter as the transistor cools. If you wait a few minutes, the ohmmeter should eventually return to its initial reading.

DISCUSSION TOPICS

1. How would you compare the temperature coefficients of conductors with those of semiconductors?
2. When an incandescent lamp is first turned on, there is usually a large surge of current. Why?
3. Incandescent-lamp burnouts often occur at the moment the power is turned on. Why?
4. Some manufacturers make semiconductor devices called *thermistors* which have high resistance when they are cold and low resistance when they are hot. Can you think of any uses for these devices?

CHAPTER 3

Junction Diodes

ACTIVITY 3-1
TEST: JUNCTION DIODES

Choose the letter that best completes each statement.

1. In a PN-junction diode, the depletion region is formed by
   a. Applying forward bias across the diode
   b. Heating the diode to a high temperature
   c. Electrons crossing the junction and filling the holes
   d. Current flowing from anode to cathode
2. The depletion region of a PN-junction diode acts as
   a. A good conductor
   b. An insulator
   c. A semiconductor
   d. None of the above
3. With no external bias applied, the depletion region is limited or balanced by
   a. The barrier potential
   b. Temperature
   c. The cathode lead
   d. Zener breakdown
4. In a PN-junction diode, forward bias can
   a. Force the majority carriers to the junction
   b. Collapse the depletion region
   c. Cause conduction from cathode to anode
   d. All of the above
5. Silicon diodes begin conducting at a forward voltage of
   a. 0.15 V
   b. 0.20 V
   c. 0.30 V
   d. 0.60 V
6. Compared with silicon diodes, germanium diodes
   a. Show a greater forward voltage drop
   b. Begin conducting at a higher forward voltage
   c. Are less affected by high temperatures
   d. Show higher leakage current

7. Excessive reverse bias may cause a silicon diode to
   a. Avalanche
   b. Reverse its polarity
   c. Turn off
   d. Become nonlinear
8. Reverse bias forces the minority carriers
   a. Away from the junction
   b. To the junction
   c. To disappear
   d. To form a second depletion region
9. The volt-ampere characteristic curve for a resistor
   a. Is nonlinear
   b. Does not pass through the origin
   c. Shows constantly changing slope
   d. Is a straight line passing through the origin
10. In order for a diode to be forward-biased
   a. The P-type material must be positive with respect to the N-type material
   b. The anode must be positive with respect to the cathode
   c. The current must be flowing against the arrow on the schematic symbol
   d. All of the above

Questions 11 to 14 refer to Fig. 3-1.

11. The volt-ampere characteristic curve shows the behavior of
   a. A conductor
   b. A PN-junction diode
   c. A resistor
   d. None of the above
12. Value *A* represents
   a. The zener voltage
   b. The avalanche voltage of a rectifier diode
   c. Either of the above
   d. None of the above
13. Value *B* represents
   a. Diode leakage current
   b. Barrier voltage
   c. The zener knee
   d. The peak-reverse-voltage rating for a rectifier
14. Value *C* represents
   a. The diode turn-on voltage
   b. Leakage
   c. Breakdown
   d. Minority-carrier action

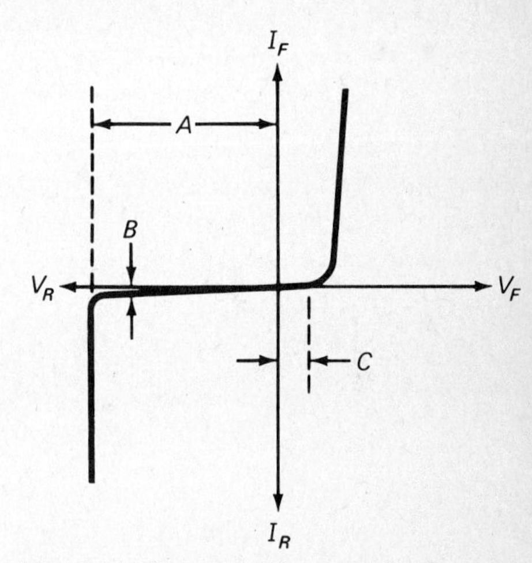

Fig. 3-1 Characteristic curve for Questions 11 through 14.

15. At high temperatures, the forward voltage drop across a diode can be expected to
   a. Be less than it is at low temperatures
   b. Be more than it is at low temperatures
   c. Be zero
   d. Become unpredictable
16. An ohmmeter is connected across a diode both ways, and a rather low resistance reading is obtained both times. The diode is
   a. Open
   b. Shorted
   c. Good but improperly marked
   d. Reversed and polarity

17. An ohmmeter is connected across a diode both ways, and there is only a little difference between its forward resistance and its reverse resistance. The diode is
    a. Defective
    b. Good
    c. Improperly marked
    d. Reversed in polarity
18. If an ohmmeter test reveals a large difference between the forward and reverse resistance of a diode, the diode is
    a. Defective
    b. Good
    c. Improperly marked
    d. Reversed in polarity
19. A good diode is showing low resistance with the ohmmeter connected. The negative lead of the ohmmeter is connected to the diode's
    a. Anode
    b. Cathode
    c. P-type material
    d. All of the above
20. A diode case may have a band at one end to identify
    a. The anode lead
    b. The cathode lead
    c. The zener lead
    d. The rectifier lead
21. The diode schematic symbol uses an arrow to identify the
    a. Majority carriers
    b. Case style
    c. Cathode
    d. Anode
22. Rectifier diodes are used to
    a. Replace panel lamps
    b. Tune coils to resonance
    c. Regulate voltage
    d. Change alternating current into direct current
23. Schottky diodes are used as
    a. Current regulators
    b. Voltage regulators
    c. High-frequency rectifiers
    d. All of the above
24. The diode designed to operate constantly in reverse breakover is
    a. The rectifier diode
    b. The zener diode
    c. The light-emitting diode (LED)
    d. The varicap diode
25. How are diode clippers used?
    a. To limit signal amplitude
    b. To change the shape of a signal
    c. To remove noise from a signal
    d. All of the above
26. What is another name for a dc restorer?
    a. Clipper
    b. Clamp
    c. Limiter
    d. Converter

27. PIN diodes are used as
    a. RF switches and attenuators
    b. High-frequency rectifiers
    c. Optocouplers
    d. All of the above

Complete the following exercises on a separate sheet of paper.

28. Draw the schematic symbol for a rectifier diode. Label the cathode lead and the anode lead. Show the direction of forward current through the diode with an arrow.
29. Draw the schematic symbol for a zener diode. Label the cathode and the anode. Show the direction of current through the diode when it is being used as a regulator.
30. Draw the schematic symbol for a varicap diode. Draw a bias supply across the diode. Use the correct polarity for the diode power as it would be connected in a tuning circuit.
31. Draw the schematic symbol for an LED. Show a bias power supply and a current-limiting resistor as required for normal operation.

ACTIVITY 3-2 LAB EXPERIMENT: SEMICONDUCTOR DIODES

PURPOSE

To become familiar with solid-state diodes, their characteristics, and some of their applications.

MATERIALS

Qty.	
2	multimeters
1	oscilloscope with ÷10 probe
1	0- to 10-V dc power supply
1	RF or audio generator
1	audio or function generator
1	digital frequency counter (optional)
1	47-Ω 2-W resistor
1	270-Ω ½-W resistor
2	1-kΩ ½-W resistors
1	3.3-kΩ ½-W resistor
1	10-kΩ ½-W resistor
1	100-kΩ ½-W resistor
1	1-MΩ ½-W resistor
1	30-mH RF choke
1	500-μH RF choke

Qty.	
1	1N4001 silicon rectifier or equivalent
2	1N914 silicon diodes or equivalent
1	1N541 germanium diode or equivalent
1	1N4733 zener diode or equivalent
1	National NSL5076A LED or equivalent
1	1-μF nonpolarized capacitor
1	0.1-μF capacitor
2	1-nF ceramic capacitors
1	10-pF ceramic capacitor
1	SPST switch

INTRODUCTION

This experiment has been designed to be safe for you, the equipment, and the components, but there are some precautions which should be followed. Do not exceed a power-supply output of 10 V. Most variable dc power supplies can produce more, *so be cautious.* Check your circuit before the power is turned on. Improper connections and improper polarities can result in damage to the circuit. Be sure that the meters are on the correct range and function. Some meters are easy to damage in the current function.

This experiment has been divided into eight parts. Be sure to record all the data before moving on to the next part. If there is not enough time, you can begin again where you left off. If there is a shortage of equipment or parts, different parts of the class can work on different parts of the experiment at the same time. It is not necessary to follow the order given.

PROCEDURE

Part 1

1. Test several diodes with the $R \times 1$ range of your VOM. If you are using a DMM, use the 20-kΩ range. Measure the forward and reverse resistance of each diode. You should find a large difference. Diodes that do not show this difference may be defective and should be called to the attention of your instructor.
2. Identify the cathode lead of each diode. Does the ohmmeter test agree with the lead identification on the diode case? If not, check the polarity of your ohmmeter using a separate voltmeter.
3. If you are using a VOM or vacuum-tube voltmeter (VTVM) copy Table 3-1 onto a separate sheet of paper. If you are using a DMM, change the left-hand column values to 20-kΩ, 200-kΩ, and 2-MΩ and change the right-hand column to indicate a 10-kΩ resistor. Measure the forward resistance R_F of the silicon rectifier diode on each of the three ranges and record these readings in your table.

Table 3-1

Ohmmeter Range	Forward Resistance R_F (Ω)	Measured Resistance of 47-Ω Resistor (Ω)
$R \times 1$		
$R \times 10$		
$R \times 100$		

4. Measure the resistance of the 47-Ω (or 10-kΩ) resistor on all three ranges and record the results in your table.

PROCEDURE

Part 2

1. Construct the circuit shown in Fig. 3-2. Use a VOM or DMM to measure the diode forward current I_F and a VTVM or DMM to measure the diode forward voltage drop V_F. Verify your circuit before turning on the power supply. If in doubt, have your instructor check your wiring.

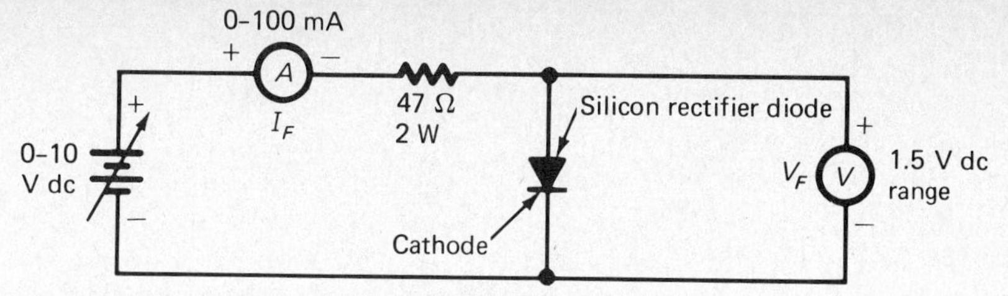

Fig. 3-2 Characteristic circuit for a silicon diode.

2. Copy Table 3-2 onto a separate sheet of paper. Begin with the power supply set at 0 V. Slowly increase its output and observe V_F. Record all data in the table. When all readings have been taken, reduce the power-supply voltage to zero and turn it off.

Table 3-2 Silicon Rectifier Diode

V_F (V)	I_F (mA)
0	
0.1	
0.2	
0.3	
0.4	
0.5	
0.6	
0.7	
0.8	

3. Turn the diode around. This will reverse-bias it. Increase the voltmeter range to 10 or 15 V. If your current meter has a 50-μA range, switch to it. Turn on the power supply and *slowly* increase the voltage output. You should not be able to measure any leakage current in the silicon diode. If there is a small current, determine whether it is caused by the voltmeter. Disconnect the voltmeter from the circuit, and the current flow should be zero. Leakage current in silicon diodes of this type is in the *nanoampere* range and cannot be measured with ordinary meters. If your silicon rectifier does show leakage, notify your instructor, as it may have been damaged.
4. Construct the circuit shown in Fig. 3-3. Be sure to change both the resistor and the diode. Copy Table 3-3 onto a separate sheet of

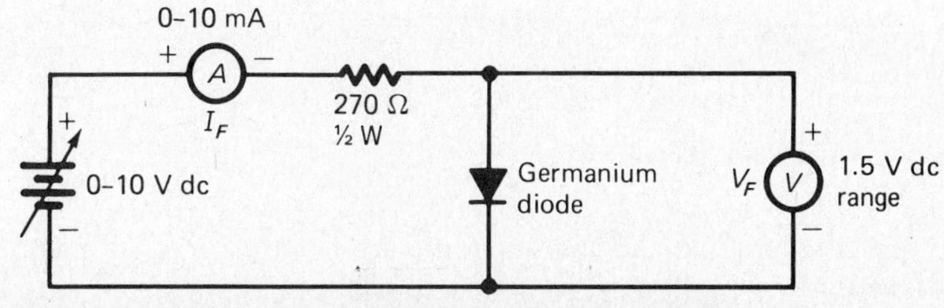

Fig. 3-3 Characteristic circuit for a germanium diode.

paper. Start at 0 V and fill in your table. Reduce the voltage to zero and turn off the supply.

5. Calculate the forward resistance for the silicon diode and the germanium diode at 0.8 V of forward bias. Use Ohm's law

$$R_F = \frac{V_F}{I_F} = \frac{0.8}{I_F \text{ (from table)}}$$

The forward resistance will be much lower for the silicon diode, yet germanium is a better conductor than silicon. Since these facts do not seem to agree, a word about power diodes and small-signal diodes is in order.

Table 3-3 Germanium Diode

V_F (V)	I_F (mA)
0	
0.1	
0.2	
0.3	
0.4	
0.5	
0.6	
0.7	
0.8	
0.9	
1.0	

The silicon rectifier specified for this activity is considered a *power* device. It can handle currents up to 1 A. The germanium diode used is a *small-signal* device. It can handle currents only up to 50 mA. This is related to the size of the semiconductor crystal. If the germanium crystal were as large as the silicon crystal, its forward resistance would be less.

6. Measure the leakage current of the germanium diode. If your current meter has a 50-μA range, switch to it. Increase the range on the voltmeter to 10 or 15 V. Reverse the diode. Turn on the power supply and *slowly* increase the voltage. Do not forget about the loading effect of the voltmeter. Disconnect it from the circuit. You should be able to measure a few *microamperes* of leakage current at 10 V of reverse bias. This is very small, but it is more than could be measured with the silicon rectifier.

PROCEDURE

Part 3

1. Figure 3-4 shows experimental circuits for evaluating the tuning capabilities of a diode. Figure 3-4(a) shows a circuit you can use if you have access to an RF signal generator with coverage up to 2 MHz. If you do not have this equipment, use Fig. 3-4(b), which

uses an audio-signal generator or function generator with coverage to 200 kHz.

The diode is a rectifier type but is used here as a varicap diode. Although varicap diodes are available, the rectifier types do a reasonable job of tuning, as this experiment will demonstrate.

The oscilloscope is used to measure the signal amplitude across the tuned circuit. When the tuned circuit resonates at the same frequency as that developed by the generator, the oscilloscope display will show maximum vertical deflection. Make sure that your oscilloscope has a ÷10 probe to avoid loading effects on the tuned circuit.

2. Build the appropriate circuit from Fig. 3-4. If you are using an RF generator, set it for 1.5 MHz with no modulation. If you are using an audio or function generator, set it for a sine-wave output of 150 kHz. If you have access to a digital frequency counter, connect it across the output of the generator. This equipment is not necessary, but it is convenient to have an accurate display of the generator frequency. Increase the amplitude output of your generator until a useful display appears on the oscilloscope. In this experiment, only the amplitude (height) shown on the screen is important. If a ragged or unstable display is seen, check to make sure that all circuit and equipment grounds are common (connected to the same point).

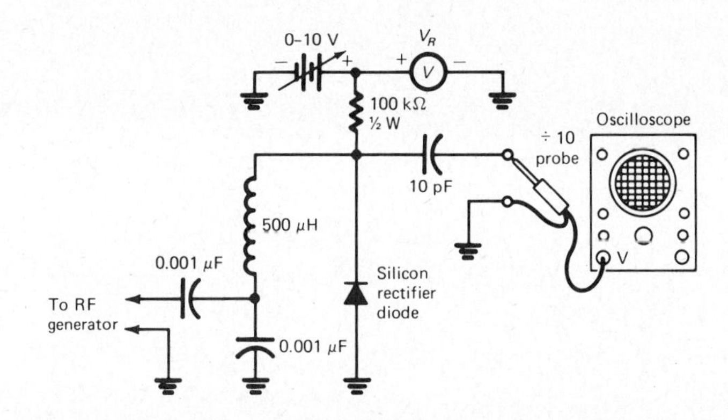

(a) Diode tuning circuit

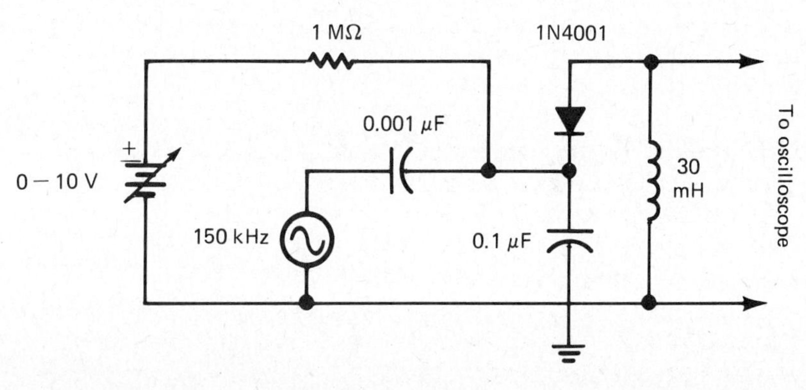

(b) Alternate circuit

Fig. 3-4 Circuits for Part 3.

3. Set the dc power supply to 1 V. This reverse-biases the diode so that V_R is now equal to 1 V. Slowly tune the generator to find the frequency where the oscilloscope display shows maximum vertical size. A definite peak should be found. Ask your instructor for assistance if you cannot find this peak.

4. When the circuit shows peak amplitude, the generator dial (or frequency counter) can be read to find the resonant frequency f_r of the diode-tuned circuit. Copy Table 3-4 onto a separate sheet of paper. If you are using the alternate circuit in Fig. 3-4(*b*), change the right-hand column heading to indicate kilohertz units. Record f_r for V_R = 1 V. Adjust the dc supply for V_R = 2 V and find the new resonant frequency by adjusting the generator frequency. Complete the table.

Table 3-4

V_R (V)	F_r (MHz)
1	
2	
3	
4	
5	
6	
7	
8	
9	
10	

PROCEDURE

Part 4

1. Figure 3-5 shows the circuit to be used for finding the characteristics of a zener diode. Construct the circuit and start with the supply voltage at 0 V (V_S = 0 V). Increase the power-supply voltage to 1 V.

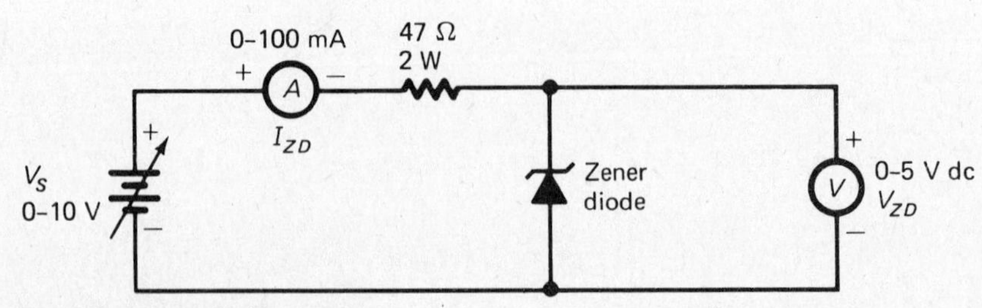

Fig. 3-5 Zener-diode circuit.

2. Copy Table 3-5 and record the zener diode current I_{ZD} and the voltage across the zener diode V_{ZD} in your table. Complete the table.

Table 3-5

V_S (V)	I_{ZD} (mA)	V_{ZD} (V)
0		
1		
2		
3		
4		
5		
6		
7		
8		
9		
10		

PROCEDURE

Part 5

1. Refer to Fig. 3-6. This circuit will be used to test an LED. Construct the circuit shown. Start with the power supply at 0 V. Slowly increase the voltage until approximately 30 mA of current is indicated. Note the brightness of the LED at various current levels between 0 and 30 mA.
2. Turn off the power supply after reducing its output to 0 V.
3. Reverse the LED in the circuit. Turn on the power supply and slowly increase the output to 4 V. Do not exceed 4 V of reverse bias. Note the current and the output of the LED under conditions of reverse bias.

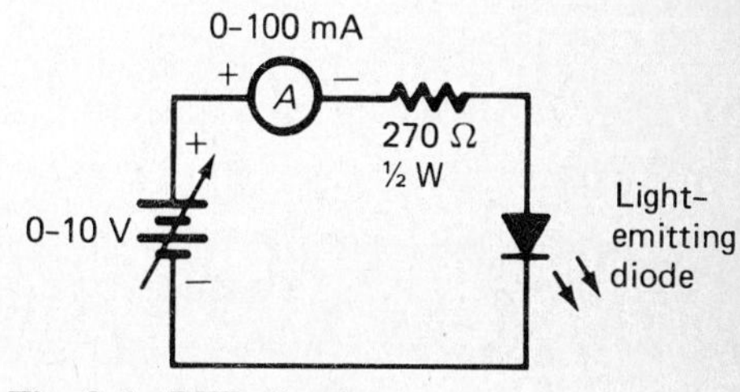

Fig. 3-6 LED circuit.

PROCEDURE

Part 6

1. Build the circuit shown in Fig. 3-7 on the next page. Set your audio generator for a sine-wave output at a frequency of 1 kHz. Connect your oscilloscope probe across the 3.3-kΩ resistor. Be certain that generator and oscilloscope grounds are both connected at the bottom of the circuit. Set the vertical sensitivity of the oscilloscope to around 50 mV/div and the sweep to about 500 μs/div. Slowly increase the output from the generator. What do you see on the oscilloscope as the output waveform approaches 1 V peak-to-peak? Continue increasing the generator output. What happens to the waveform? What is the peak-to-peak amplitude of the waveform?
2. Disconnect the diode on the left. What happens to the waveform? Reconnect the diode on the left, and disconnect the diode on the right. What happens to the waveform?

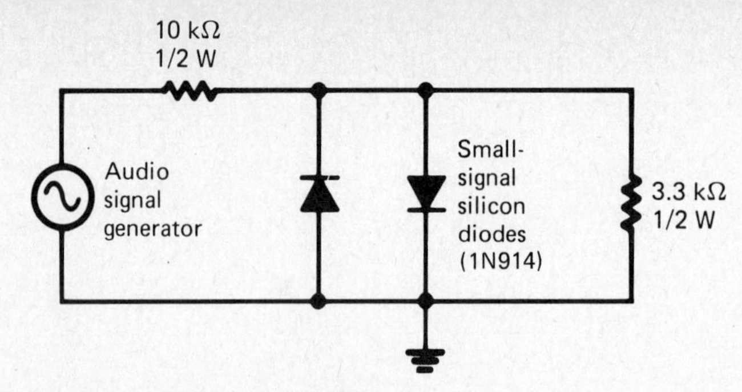

Fig. 3-7 Diode clipper circuit.

PROCEDURE

Part 7

1. Build the circuit shown in Fig. 3-8. Set your audio generator for sine-wave output at a frequency of 1 kHz. Connect your oscilloscope probe across the 10-kΩ resistor. Be certain that the generator and oscilloscope grounds are both connected at the bottom of the circuit. Set the vertical sensitivity of the oscilloscope to 1 V/div and the sweep to 500 μs/div. Set the amplitude of the audio generator for maximum. Set your vertical oscilloscope input switch to ground and center the trace on the screen. Now, set the switch for *dc*. What can you conclude about the waveform on the screen? Verify the dc content of the waveform with your high-impedance meter by connecting it across the 10-kΩ resistor.

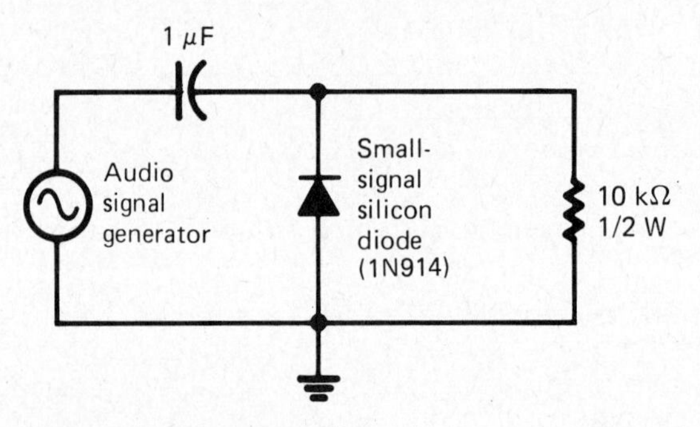

Fig. 3-8 Diode clamp circuit.

2. Disconnect the diode from the circuit. What happens to the waveform? What happens to the dc meter reading? Reconnect the diode but with opposite polarity (the cathode lead should be connected to ground). What happens to the waveform? What is the dc meter reading?

PROCEDURE

Part 8

1. Diode resistance varies greatly with dc bias. This fact allows diodes to be used as switches. Figure 3-9 shows a diode switching circuit. When the SPST switch is open, there is no dc flow through the diode and its resistance is very high. Because of this, the 10-kHz ac signal cannot flow through the diode and the oscilloscope will show a straight line. When the SPST switch is closed, a direct current will flow through the diode and the two 1-kΩ resistors. The direct

current will cause the diode's resistance to decrease, and the 10-kHz ac signal will be seen on the oscilloscope.

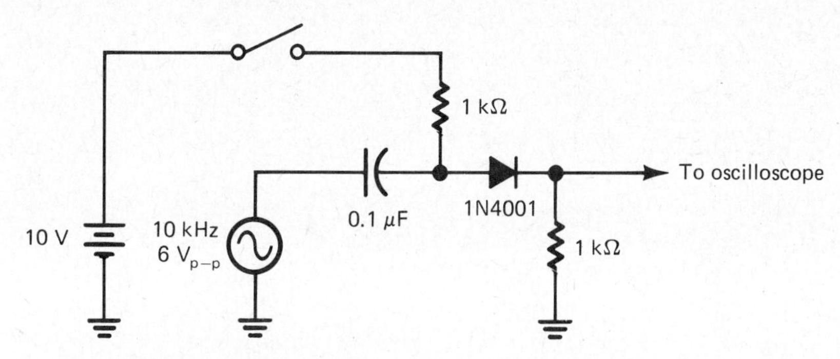

Fig. 3-9 Diode switching circuit.

2. Build the circuit shown in Fig. 3-9. Set your oscilloscope for ac coupling. Close the SPST switch and adjust the oscilloscope for a useful display of the 10-kHz signal. Now, open the switch and verify that the ac signal does not reach the oscilloscope.

DISCUSSION TOPICS

1. Refer to your copy of Table 3-1. The resistance of the resistor was measured as nearly constant on all three ohmmeter ranges. Why is the forward resistance of the diode so different on the three ranges?
2. What is the function of the 47-Ω resistor in Fig. 3-2 and the 270-Ω resistor in Fig. 3-3?
3. In Fig. 3-4 what is the purpose of the two 0.001-μF capacitors?
4. In Fig. 3-4 what is the purpose of the 100-Ω resistor?
5. Does your data in Table 3-4 show a linear voltage-versus-frequency tuning characteristic? Why?
6. Refer to your copy of Table 3-5. Is the voltage across the zener diode constant over the entire power-supply voltage range? Why?
7. What could happen to the circuit shown in Fig. 3-5 if the power-supply voltage became very high?
8. What determines the brightness of an LED?
9. Can LEDs be used under conditions of reverse bias?
10. What is the function of the 10-kΩ resistor in Fig. 3-7?
11. What is the function of the 1-μF capacitor in Fig. 3-8?

ACTIVITY 3.3
PROBLEM: DIODE MATRIX

THEORY AND BACKGROUND

Diodes can be used to isolate points in control circuits. They block reverse current, making isolation from circuit to circuit possible. A *matrix* is the symmetrical arrangement of parts (such as diodes) to accomplish memory, encoding, or decoding. These terms are related to digital electronics and will not be covered here, but the usefulness of the diode matrix will be clear.

Figure 3-10(*a*) shows an LED numeric display. The seven segments of the display are labeled *a* to *g*. To show the desired number, the correct segments must be turned on. Figure 3-10(*b*) shows one way of controlling the numeric display. The seven diodes are connected, with all the anodes tied together. This is a common-anode display. Common-cathode displays are also available. The resistors provide current limiting, and the switches provide control.

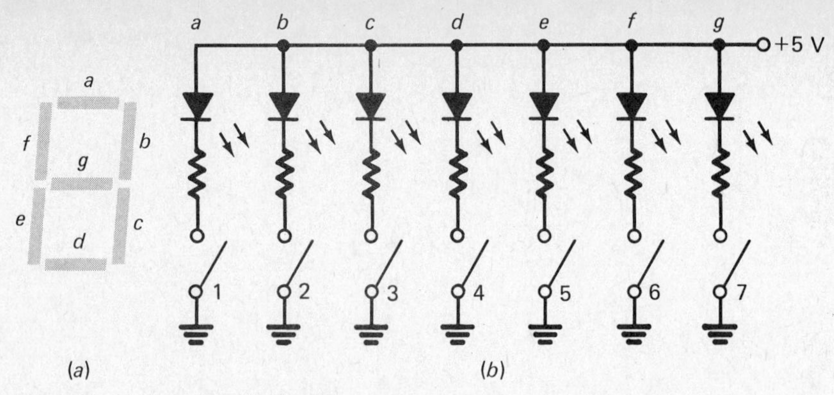

Fig. 3-10 LED numeric display.

Suppose that the LED numeric display is to be used to indicate which channel is selected in a four-channel police radio. A switch could be designed to turn on the correct segments for each of four positions, but a little thought will show this to be a complicated and expensive switch. A single-pole four-position switch is all that is needed if some diodes are added for isolation purposes.

The circuit of Fig. 3-11 is used to light the correct segments for each position of the rotary switch. To show the number 1 segments *b* and *c* must be turned on. Note that with the rotary switch in position 1, current can flow from ground up through the two isolation diodes, through the current-limiting resistors, through LED segments *b* and *c,* and finally to the + 5-V power supply. When position 2 is selected, segments *a, b, d, e,* and *g* are grounded. Because segment *b* must be on to show a 1 and a 2, the diodes are necessary to keep these two switch positions isolated. Without diodes, the display would show a letter "d" instead of 1 or 2 because segments *a, b, c, d, e,* and *g* would be tied together with no isolation. They would be tied together by segment *b,*

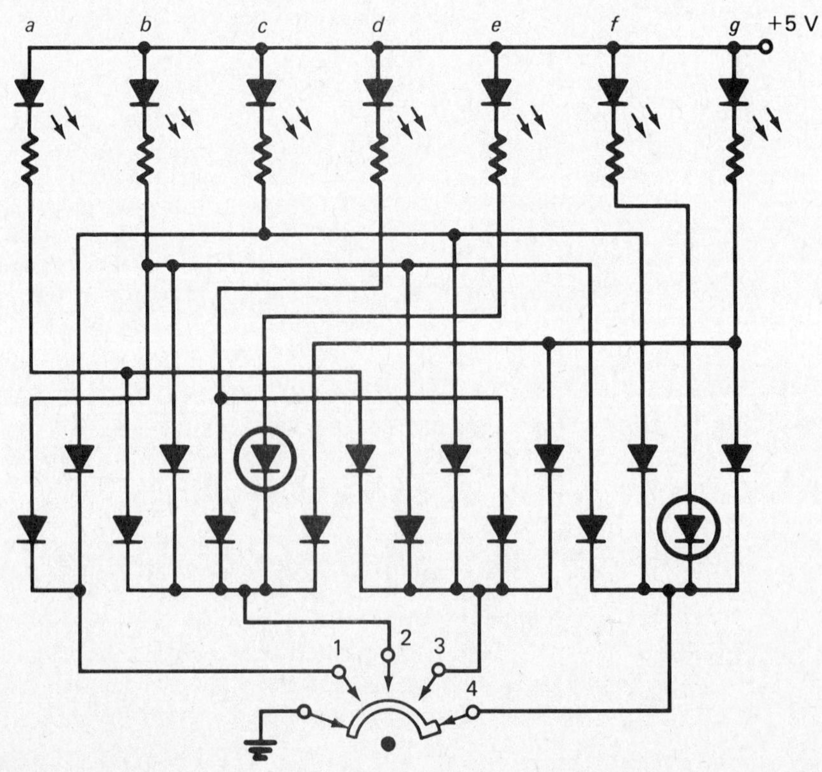

Fig. 3-11 Diode matrix.

which must be connected for indicating a 1 and a 2. Figure 3-12 is a simplified schematic with no isolation diodes. The short circuit between switch positions 1 and 2 is obvious.

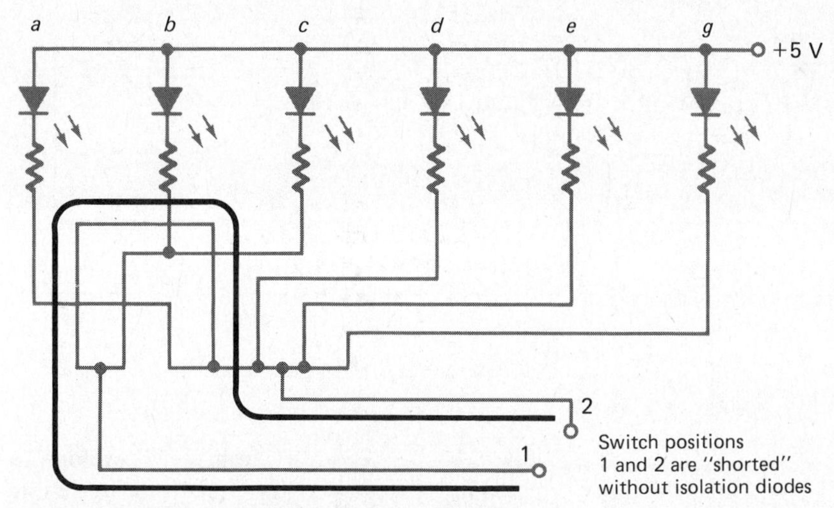

Fig. 3-12 Circuit shorts without isolation diodes.

The two diodes in Fig. 3-11 not needed for showing numbers 1 to 4 are circled. Since segment *e* is used only in the number 2, that diode could be eliminated. Segment *f* is used only in number 4.

PROBLEM

Expand the schematic to enable the display to indicate the number 0. You will need another switch position and some diodes for isolation.

ACTIVITY 3-4 CONSTRUCTION PROJECT: THE MYSTERY CIRCUIT

THE MYSTERY

Figure 3-13 shows an unusual circuit that can be quite a puzzle for those who do not know its secret. It consists of a hardboard or plastic base with two switches and two lamps. With both switches in the off position both lamps are off. When switch 1 is flipped to the on position lamp 2 lights. When switch 2 is flipped to the on position, lamp 1 lights. Since the circuit appears to be a simple series arrangement, this behavior is strange.

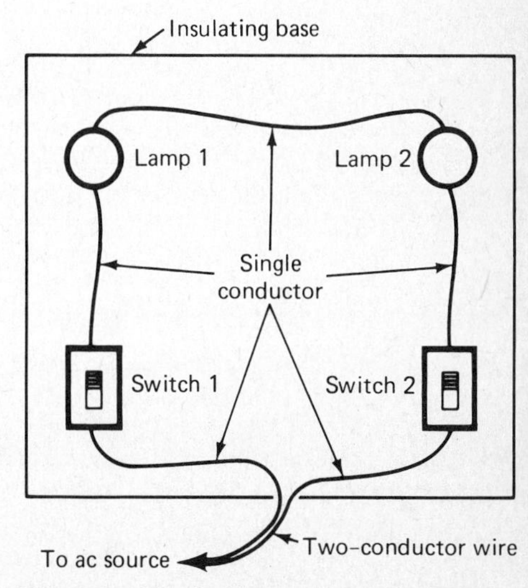

Fig. 3-13 Physical layout for the mystery circuit.

HOW IT WORKS

Figure 3-14 on the next page is the diagram for the mystery circuit. Four diodes produce the strange behavior. The diodes are mounted under the lamps and switches so they cannot be seen. With both S_1 and S_2 open, no current can flow because it is blocked in both directions by D_1 and D_2. If S_1 is closed, D_4 sets the current direction for the circuit: *clockwise.* With the current moving clockwise through the

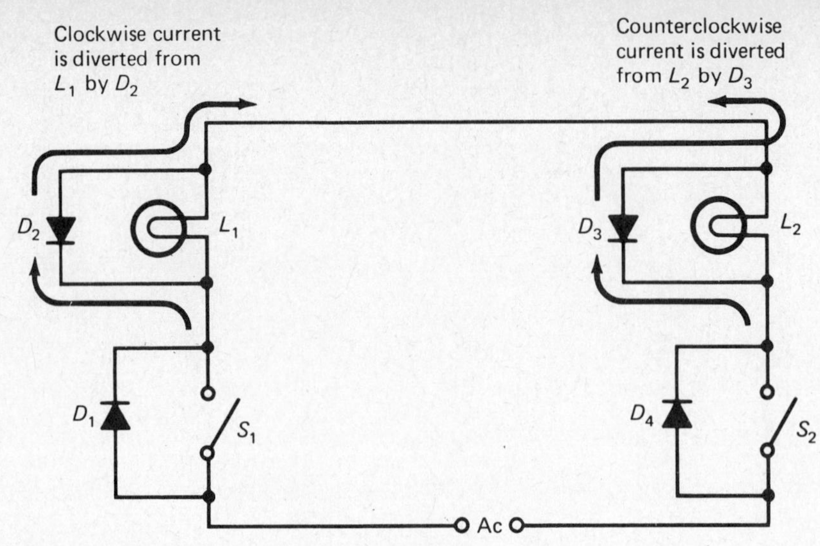

Fig. 3-14 Schematic for the mystery circuit.

circuit, D_2 is on and diverts most of the current from L_1. Therefore, L_1 does not light. Lamp 2 does light because D_3 is off for clockwise current flow. With only S_2 closed, the current flow is counterclockwise, so D_3 will bypass the current around L_2 and it will be off. Lamp 1 is on because D_2 does not conduct when the current flow is counterclockwise. With both switches on, both lamps will light since current will alternately flow in both directions.

If you decide to build the mystery circuit, good safety practices must be followed. Do not connect the circuit directly to the 115-V ac line. The best and safest way is to use a small step-down transformer with a secondary rated at 12.6 V ac. The lamps can be type 53 or a similar low-voltage type. The diodes can be general-purpose rectifier types rated at 1 A and at least 50 peak reverse volts (PRV).

CHAPTER 4

Power Supplies

ACTIVITY 4-1
TEST: POWER SUPPLIES

Choose the letter that best completes each statement.

1. In rectifier circuits, the positive end of the load is the one that contacts
   a. Ground
   b. The anode of the rectifier
   c. The center tap of the transformer
   d. The cathode of the rectifier
2. Sometimes manufacturers mark the cathode end of a rectifier with
   a. A band
   b. A plus (+) sign
   c. A bevel
   d. Any of the above
3. An isolation transformer is used in troubleshooting to
   a. Prevent damage in case there is a short
   b. Remove line noise
   c. Prevent ground loops
   d. Provide a chassis ground
4. If the diode in a half-wave-rectifier circuit is reversed, the voltage across the load will
   a. Remain the same
   b. Reverse in polarity
   c. Increase
   d. Decrease

Questions 5 to 12 refer to Figs. 4-1 and 4-2 on the next page. Assume plus to be up and minus to be down on the waveforms.

5. Waveform 1 can be found across
   a. A
   b. B
   c. C
   d. D

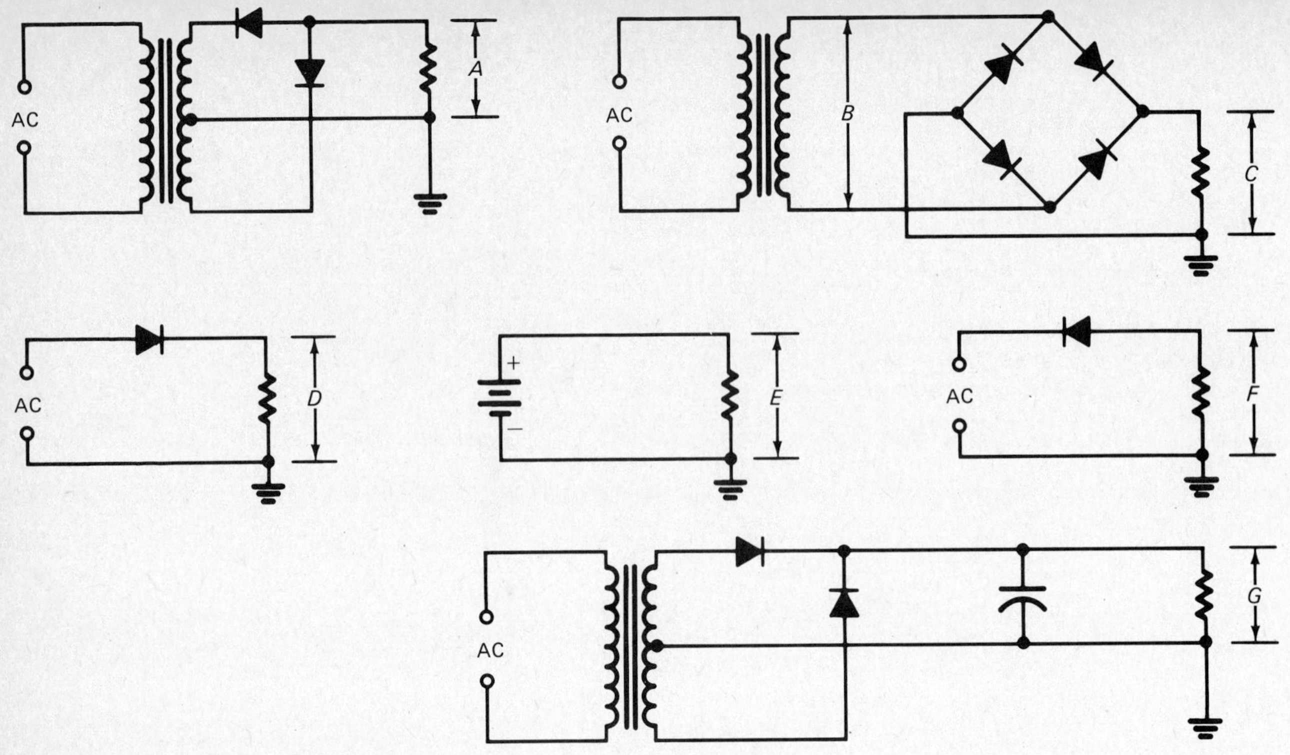

Fig. 4-1 Circuits for Questions 5 to 12.

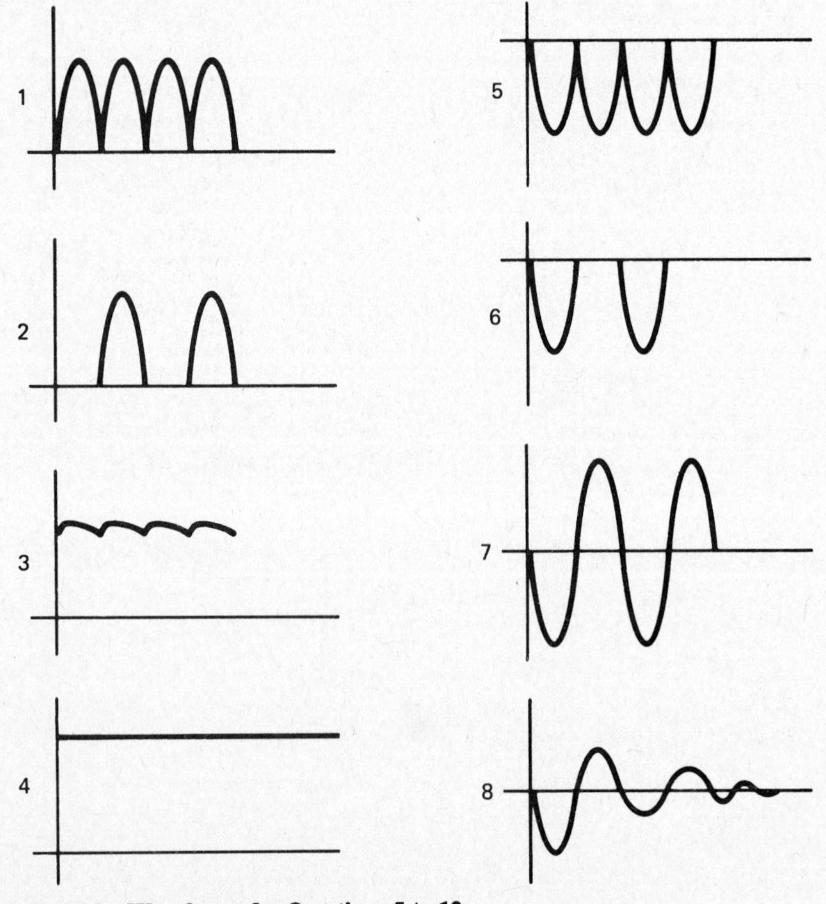

Fig. 4-2 Waveforms for Questions 5 to 12.

6. Waveform 2 can be found across
   a. *D*
   b. *E*
   c. *F*
   d. *G*
7. Waveform 3 can be found across
   a. *A*
   b. *B*
   c. *F*
   d. *G*
8. Waveform 4 can be found across
   a. *C*
   b. *D*
   c. *E*
   d. *F*
9. Waveform 5 can be found across
   a. *A*
   b. *C*
   c. *E*
   d. *G*
10. Waveform 6 can be found across
   a. *C*
   b. *D*
   c. *E*
   d. *F*
11. Waveform 7 can be found across
   a. *B*
   b. *C*
   c. *D*
   d. *E*
12. Waveform 8 can be found across
   a. *B*
   b. *D*
   c. *F*
   d. None of the above
13. The effectiveness of a capacitive filter is determined by
   a. The size of the capacitor
   b. The amount of load current
   c. The ripple frequency
   d. All of the above
14. Full-wave rectifiers are often preferred over half-wave rectifiers because
   a. They can deliver twice the power
   b. They are easier to filter
   c. Both of the above
   d. They use fewer parts

Questions 15 to 18 refer to Fig. 4-3 on the next page. In making your calculations, assume that

a. The ac source voltage is 120 V rms
b. The transformer has half as many secondary turns as primary turns
c. There is no loss for the diodes
d. R_L is large (only a small load current will flow)

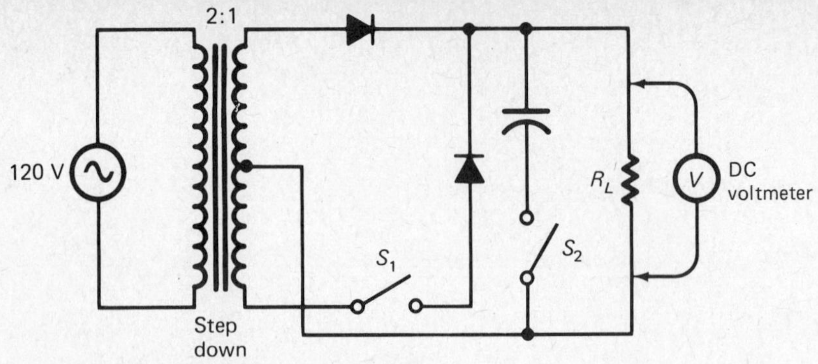

Fig. 4-3 Circuit for Questions 15 to 18.

15. With both S_1 and S_2 open the voltmeter will read
a. 0
b. 13.5 V
c. 27.0 V
d. 60.0 V

16. With both S_1 and S_2 closed the voltmeter will read
a. 27.0 V
b. 42.4 V
c. 54.0 V
d. 84.8 V

17. With S_1 open and S_2 closed the voltmeter will read
a. 0
b. 27.0 V
c. 42.4 V
d. 84.8 V

18. With S_1 closed and S_2 open the voltmeter will read
a. 0
b. 27.0 V
c. 60.0 V
d. 84.8 V

Questions 19 to 21 refer to Fig. 4-4. The assumptions are the same as those for Fig. 4-3.

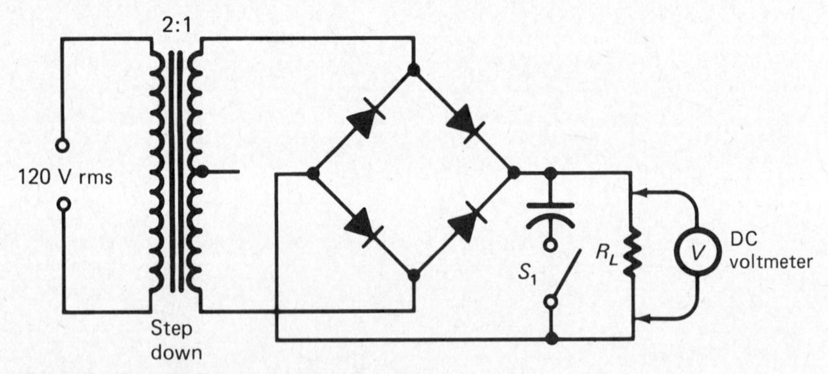

Fig. 4-4 Circuit for Questions 19 to 21.

19. With S_1 open the voltmeter will read
a. 0
b. 27.0 V
c. 54.0 V
d. 84.8 V

20. With S_1 closed the voltmeter will read
    a. 27.0 V
    b. 54.0 V
    c. 84.8 V
    d. 99.9 V
21. If a 60-Hz ac input is assumed, the ripple frequency across R_L will be
    a. 0 Hz
    b. 30 Hz
    c. 60 Hz
    d. 120 Hz
22. A polarized ac power plug can be used to
    a. Prevent a power supply from producing a reverse polarity
    b. Keep the chassis neutral
    c. Prevent overloads
    d. All of the above

Questions 23 to 31 refer to Fig. 4-5.

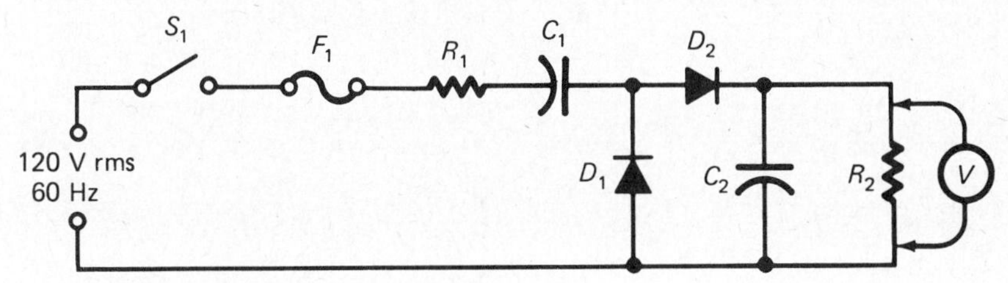

Fig. 4-5 Circuit for Questions 23 to 31.

23. This circuit is
    a. A bridge rectifier
    b. A half-wave doubler
    c. A full-wave doubler
    d. None of the above
24. The voltage rating of C_2 compared with the rating of C_1 should be
    a. Half
    b. The same
    c. Double
    d. Four times
25. If the load current is low, the voltmeter across R_2 may read as high as
    a. 120 V
    b. 170 V
    c. 220 V
    d. 339 V
26. The ripple frequency across R_2 would be
    a. 0 Hz
    b. 30 Hz
    c. 60 Hz
    d. 120 Hz
27. You are troubleshooting this power supply. You find the fuse blown and replace it. The new fuse blows as soon as you turn the power on. The trouble could be
    a. That R_1 is open
    b. That R_1 is shorted
    c. That D_1 is shorted
    d. Any of the above

28. You are troubleshooting this power supply. The output voltage is too low. The trouble could be that
  a. F_1 is blown
  b. R_1 is shorted
  c. C_1 has lost much of its capacity
  d. R_2 is open
29. You are troubleshooting this power supply. The output is zero. The fuse checks good. The trouble could be
  a. That S_1 is defective
  b. That R_1 is open
  c. That C_1 is open
  d. Any of the above
30. You are troubleshooting this power supply. The output is too high. The trouble could be that
  a. There is not enough load current
  b. D_2 is shorted
  c. D_2 is open
  d. C_2 is open
31. R_1 is a
  a. Bleeder resistor
  b. Half-wave rectifier
  c. Panel lamp
  d. Surge resistor

Questions 32 and 33 refer to a power supply with the following characteristics:

No-load output voltage = 14.2 V dc
No-load ripple = 0.01 V ac
Full-load output voltage = 12.6 V dc
Full-load ripple = 0.9 V ac

32. The voltage regulation of the power supply is
  a. 1.4 percent
  b. 3.6 percent
  c. 7.9 percent
  d. 12.7 percent
33. The ac ripple of the power supply is
  a. 0.08 percent
  b. 2.21 percent
  c. 6.34 percent
  d. 7.14 percent
34. Bleeder resistors
  a. Can improve the voltage regulation of a power supply
  b. Discharge the capacitors after the power supply is switched off
  c. Both of the above
  d. None of the above

Questions 35 to 40 refer to Fig. 4-6. Assume that the load requires 15 V at 100 mA and the zener current is to be 30 mA.

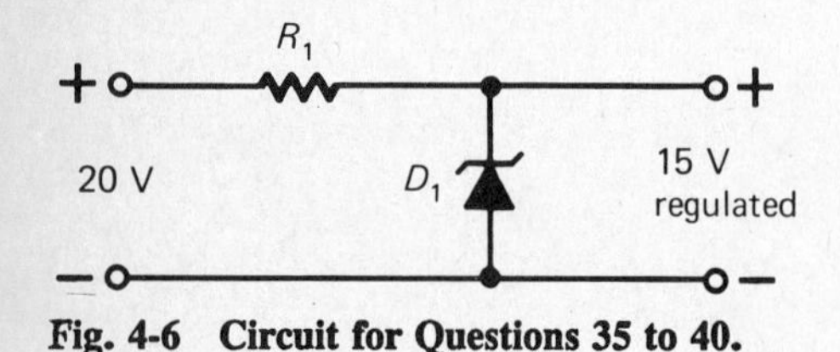

Fig. 4-6 Circuit for Questions 35 to 40.

35. The value of R_1 should be
  a. 38.5 Ω
  b. 50.0 Ω
  c. 167 Ω
  d. 667 Ω

36. The power dissipation of R_1 will be
   a. 0.15 W
   b. 0.65 W
   c. 1.95 W
   d. 2.60 W
37. The power dissipation in D_1 will be
   a. 0 W
   b. 0.45 W
   c. 1.50 W
   d. 2.00 W
38. If the load should be disconnected from the regulator, the power dissipation in R_1 will
   a. Drop to zero
   b. Remain the same
   c. Increase
   d. Decrease
39. If the load should be disconnected from the regulator, the power dissipation in D_1 will
   a. Drop to zero
   b. Remain the same
   c. Increase
   d. Decrease
40. If the voltage has to be changed from 15 V to some new value,
   a. The new voltage cannot approach 20 V if regulation is to be maintained
   b. D_1 will have to be changed
   c. R_1 may have to be changed
   d. All of the above

Questions 41 to 46 on the next page refer to Fig. 4-7.

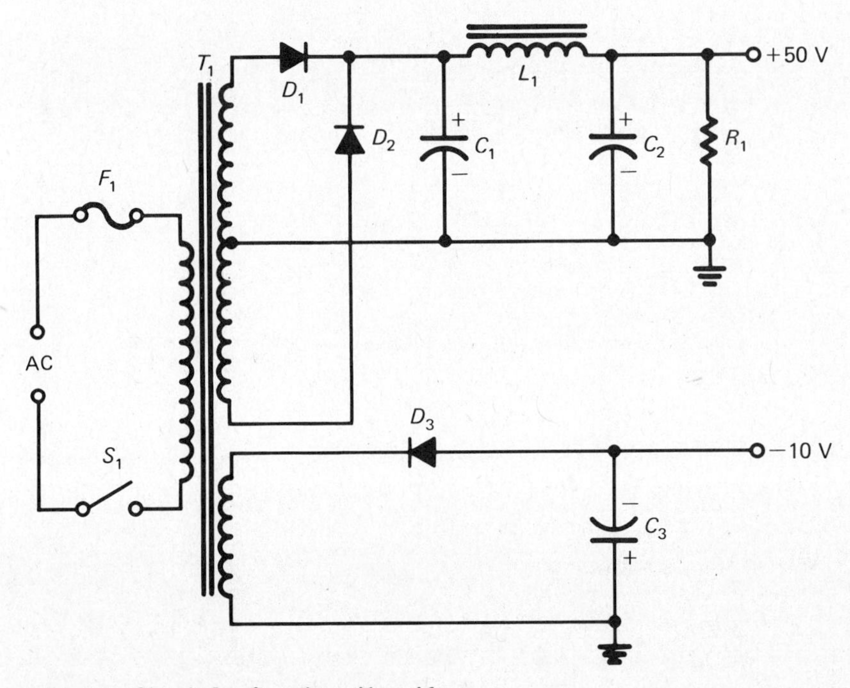

Fig. 4-7 Circuit for Questions 41 to 46.

41. D_3 is
   a. A half-wave rectifier
   b. A full-wave rectifier
   c. A voltage doubler
   d. Connected improperly
42. L_1 is
   a. An RF choke
   b. A filter choke
   c. A step-up transformer
   d. A step-down transformer
43. The −10-V output is zero, and the +50-V output is normal. The trouble could be that
   a. F_1 is blown
   b. S_1 is defective
   c. R_1 is open
   d. T_1 has a defective secondary winding
44. F_1 keeps blowing. The trouble could be
   a. That D_1 or D_2 is shorted
   b. That C_1 or C_2 is shorted
   c. That load current is excessive
   d. Any of the above
45. The −10-V output is normal, and the +50-V output is zero. The trouble could be that
   a. R_1 is open
   b. C_1 is open
   c. C_2 is open
   d. L_1 is open
46. The +50-V output is low, and there is excessive ripple on it. The trouble could be
   a. That C_1 is open
   b. That L_1 is open
   c. That R_1 is open
   d. Any of the above

ACTIVITY 4-2 LAB EXPERIMENT: POWER SUPPLIES

PURPOSE

To investigate various power-supply circuits and their performance and to measure their characteristics.

MATERIALS

Qty.		*Qty.*	
1	VOM or DMM	2	500 μF 25-V dc electrolytic capacitors
1	12.6-V center-tapped ac source (a separate transformer can be used; the Stancor P-8130, or equivalent, works well)	1	47-Ω 2-W resistor
4	rectifier diodes	1	1-kΩ 2-W resistor
		1	2.7-Ω ½-W resistor
		1	single-pole single-throw (SPST) switch

INTRODUCTION

There are some important safety precautions for this experiment. The transformer steps the line voltage down to a safe value, but the primary circuit can be dangerous. Be very careful with the primary circuit.

The second important safety precaution involves polarity. Errors in polarity may cause component damage or injury to you. This experiment uses electrolytic capacitors. When these capacitors are connected backward, or when the diodes are backward, they break down and produce large amounts of gas. This gas can cause the capacitors to explode.

This experiment has been divided into four parts. Be sure to record all data before moving on to the next part. If your time runs out, begin again where you left off. The experiment should be performed in sequence.

PROCEDURE

Part 1

1. Study the circuit shown in Fig. 4-8, which is convenient for comparing the characteristics of half-wave and full-wave rectifers. When S_1 is open, the circuit is a half-wave rectifier, and when S_2 is closed, the circuit is a full-wave rectifer. The first portion of this experiment will be for nonfiltered power-supply performance. For this reason, construct the circuit shown in Fig. 4-8 without C_1.

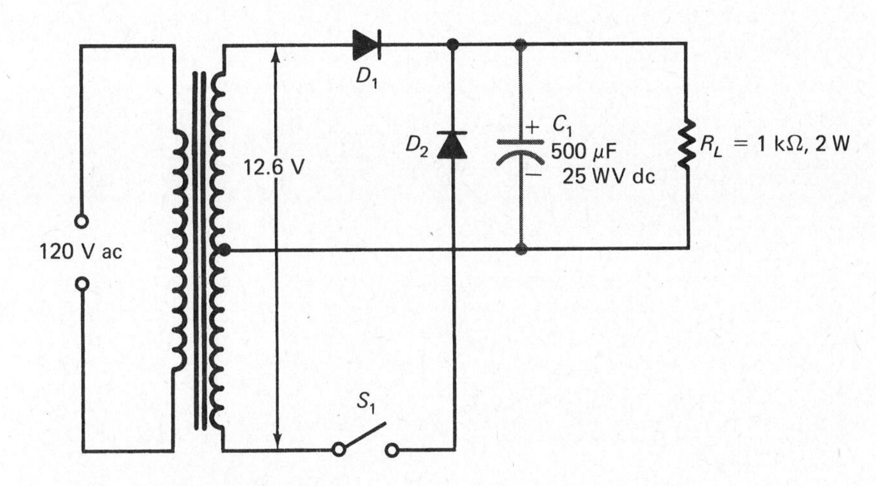

Fig. 4-8 Power-supply circuit.

CAUTION! ***Do not apply power until you are sure the circuit is properly wired and insulated from your person, the equipment, and the other parts of the circuit.***

2. Copy Table 4-1 onto a separate sheet of paper. Open S_1 and apply the ac power. Set your multimeter for dc volts. Measure the voltage across R_L, and record this reading in the table.

Table 4-1

Step	Half Wave (S_1 Open)	Step	Full Wave (S_1 Closed)
2	V_{R_L} =	6	V_{R_L} =
8	V_{R_L} =	9	V_{R_L} =
10	V_{R_L} =	11	V_{R_L} =
12	ac ripple =	12	ac ripple =
13	% voltage regulation =	13	% voltage regulation =
14	% ac ripple =	14	% ac ripple =

3. Check this reading with the calculated value for half-wave-rectified voltage.

$$dc_{av} = 0.45 \times ac_{rms}$$

How close does this check with your measurement? Some possible causes for error can be eliminated. First, switch your meter to ac and measure the actual secondary voltage. It could be a little more than 12.6 V. Second, did you remember to divide by 2 because of the center tap? Third, subtract 0.6 V for the diode loss. There should be close agreement between the measured and calculated dc voltages. If in doubt, check with your teacher.

4. Set up the oscilloscope as follows:

Horizontal sweep at 5 ms/div

Vertical input on alternating current

Vertical sensitivity at 0.2 V/div (this makes the actual sensitivity 2 V/div with the ÷10 probe)

Connect the probe across R_L. Adjust the brightness, focus, and triggering for a stable and sharp display. Record the waveform. Be sure to indicate the peak amplitude.

5. Close S_1, which changes the power supply to full-wave. Readjust the trigger if necessary. Record the waveform and indicate the peak amplitude.
6. Measure the dc voltage across the load resistor. Record this voltage in Table 4-1. Check this reading with the calculated value for full-wave-rectified voltage

$$dc_{av} = 0.90 \times ac_{rms}$$

7. Add C_1 to the circuit as shown in Fig. 4-8. Record the waveform.

CAUTION! ***Do not apply power until you are sure the circuit is connected correctly and that the diodes and capacitors are as shown on the schematic. If there is any doubt, check with your instructor first.***

8. Open S_1. Measure the dc voltage across the load resistor. Record this in Table 4-1.
9. Close S_1 and record the voltage across R_L. Check this reading with the calculated value. For half-wave or full-wave circuits.

$$V_P = 1.414 \times V_{rms}$$

10. Turn off the power. Remove R_L and replace it with a 47-Ω 2-W resistor. Open S_1. Turn on the power. Record the voltage across the load resistor in Table 4-1. Record the waveform.
11. Close S_1. Record the voltage across the load in Table 4-1. Record the waveform.
12. The meter must now be set up to measure the ac ripple across the load. Most VTVMs and DMMs automatically block the dc content when switched to an ac function. If you are using a VOM, the output jack or function must be used. If in doubt, check with your instructor. Record the ac ripple for both half-wave and full-wave rectifiers in Table 4-1. This is not the true rms value of the ripple unless your meter is capable of reading true rms for nonsinusoidal alternating current.
13. Calculate the voltage regulation for both rectifier circuits. The no-load voltage will be the reading from step 8, and the full-load voltage will be the reading from step 10. Record the regulation percentages in Table 4-1.
14. Calculate the percentage of ripple for both rectifier circuits. The ac and dc readings are in Table 4-1. Record your calculated values for the ripple percentages in Table 4-1.
15. Turn off the power. Refer to Fig. 4-8. Break the circuit between the top of the transformer secondary and D_1. Insert a 2.7-Ω ½-W resistor. Open S_1. Turn on the power. Connect the oscilloscope probe across the 2.7-Ω resistor. This allows you to see the waveform of the current through the diode. It would be better to use a current probe with the oscilloscope. The technique in this step is very useful when a current probe is not available. Record the waveform and be sure to indicate the peak amplitude. The oscilloscope is calibrated in volts. Ohm's law can be used to convert the voltage waveform into a current waveform

$$I_P = \frac{V_P}{R} = \frac{V_P}{2.7}$$

The capacitive filter causes the peak rectifier current to be much greater than the load current. Measure the load current with your multimeter and record the value.

PROCEDURE

Part 2

1. This part of the experiment will use the schematic diagram of Fig. 4-9. Construct the circuit exactly as shown. Measure and record the dc voltage across the load resistor.

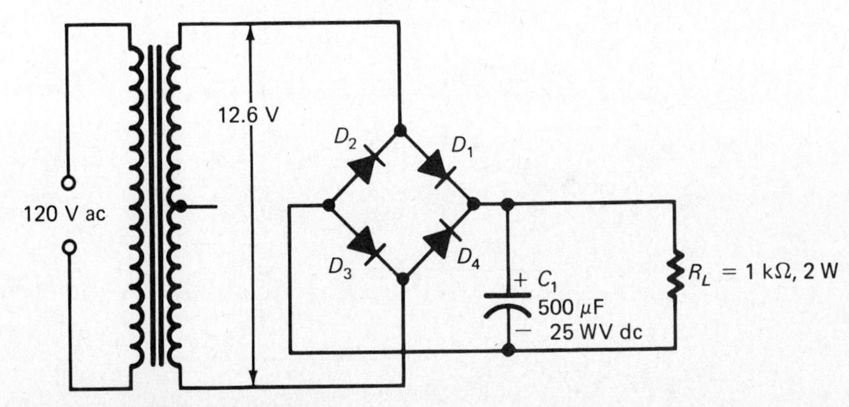

Fig. 4-9 Bridge-rectifier circuit.

2. Calculate the voltage that should be across the load resistor. The filter capacitor should charge to the peak value of the alternating current

$$V_P \times 1.414 \ V_{rms}$$

How closely do the two voltages above agree? Some of the causes for error can be eliminated. The transformer tends to develop more than 12.6 V when lightly loaded, as it is in this circuit. Make an ac measurement across the secondary. In a bridge rectifier, the current is flowing through two diodes at anygiven time. Since each silicon diode will drop about 0.6 V, you can compensate for this loss by subtracting about 1.2 V from the actual ac secondary voltage. Now, multiply again by 1.414 to find the peak voltage. There should be close agreement between the calculated peak voltage and the measured dc voltage. If not, check with your instructor.
3. Turn off the power. Remove C_1 from the circuit. Turn the power back on. Measure and record the dc voltage across the load resistor.
4. Calculate the voltage that should be across the load resistor. With no filter, the meter will read the average value of the waveform. Do not forget to subtract 1.2 V from the rms voltage first to compensate for the diode drops

$$dc_{av} = 0.90 \times ac_{rms}$$

There should be close agreement between the above two dc voltages.

5. Set up the oscilloscope as it was for part 1. Decrease the vertical sensitivity to 0.5 V/div. Connect the probe across the load resistor. Record the waveform and indicate the peak amplitude.
6. Turn off the power. Reconnect C_1 and turn the power back on. What waveform is shown on the oscilloscope now?

PROCEDURE

Part 3

1. Construct the circuit shown in Fig. 4-10. Measure and record the dc voltage across the load resistor, across C_1, and across C_2.

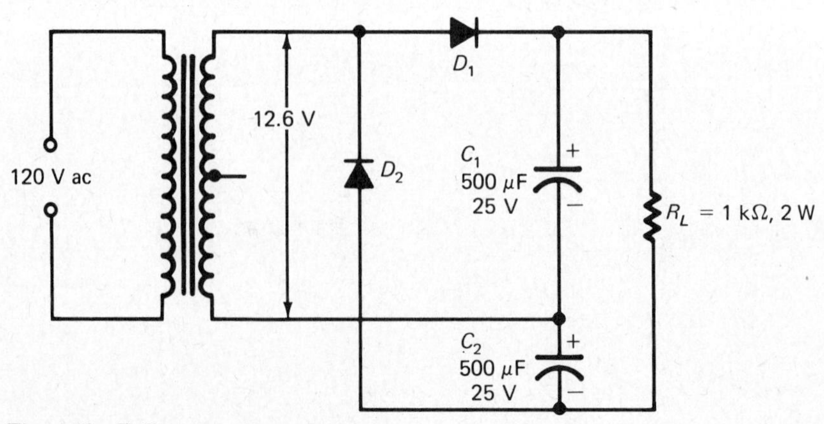

Fig. 4-10 Full-wave voltage doubler.

2. Add the voltage across C_1, and C_2. This sum should be equal to the voltage across the load resistor. Each capacitor should charge to the peak value of the ac input. Subtract 0.6 V from the ac input for good accuracy.

$$V_P = 1.414 \times V_{rms}$$

This calculated peak value should agree closely with the voltage measured across C_1 or C_2.

3. Connect the oscilloscope probe across the load resistor. Adjust the vertical gain and trigger until a stable waveform is obtained. In a full-wave doubler, the ripple frequency should be 120 Hz with a 60-Hz line frequency. The period will be

$$T = \frac{1}{f} = \frac{1}{120} = 8.33 \text{ ms}$$

What is the ripple frequency of this power-supply circuit?

PROCEDURE

Part 4

1. Refer to Fig. 4-11. Note that only half of the transformer secondary is used. Construct this circuit and be sure not to apply the full 12.6 V of the entire transformer secondary. Measure and record the dc voltage across R_L, across C_1, and across C_2. Are the voltages across the capacitors equal?

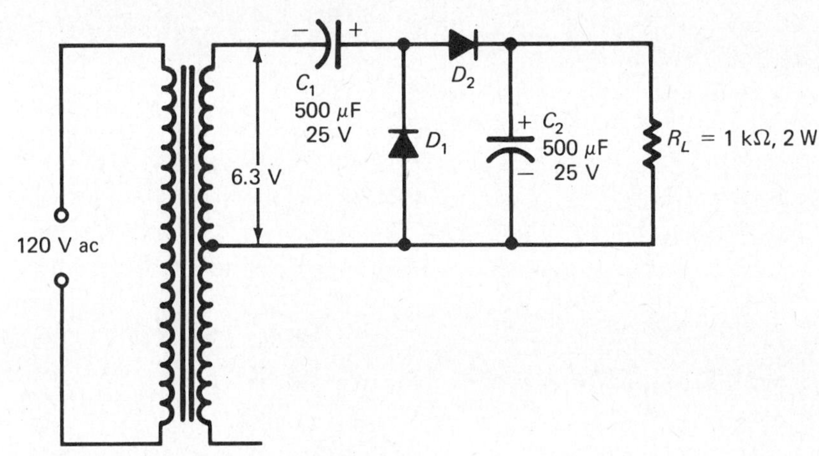

Fig. 4-11 Half-wave voltage doubler.

2. Connect the oscilloscope probe across the load resistor. Adjust the vertical gain and trigger for a stable waveform. In a half-wave doubler, the ripple frequency should be 60 Hz. The period will be

$$T = \frac{1}{f} = \frac{1}{60} = 16.67 \text{ ms}$$

What is the ripple frequency of this power-supply circuit?

3. Turn off the power. Insert a 2.7-Ω ½-W resistor between the top of the secondary and C_1. Connect the oscilloscope across this resistor. Turn on the power. Record the waveform and its peak amplitude.
4. Use Ohm's law to calculate the peak rectifier current in the half-wave-doubler circuit

$$I_P = \frac{V_P}{R} = \frac{V_P}{2.7}$$

Measure the load current with your multimeter and record the valve.

DISCUSSION TOPICS

1. Refer to Table 4-1. Which of the two rectifier circuits is better in terms of voltage regulation and ripple?
2. Refer to the waveform from step 15 of part 1. How does the rectifier peak current compare with the load current? How would they compare if the filter were removed from the circuit?
3. How do the dc output voltages for the bridge circuit (Fig. 4-9) compare with the dc output voltages for the full-wave circuit (Fig. 4-8)? Why?
4. Refer to Fig. 4-10. How should the voltage ratings of the two capacitors compare?
5. Refer to Fig. 4-11. How should the voltage ratings of the two capacitors compare?
6. In Fig. 4-11, why must the ac input to the half-wave doubler be limited to 6.3 V ac?
7. Refer to the waveform from step 3, part 4. Why is this waveform different from the waveform of step 15, part 1?

ACTIVITY 4-3 ADVANCED PROBLEM: COMBINATION POWER SUPPLY

THEORY AND BACKGROUND

Electronic equipment may require several voltages for proper operation. This can be accomplished in several ways. A voltage divider can be made up of series connected resistors to provide several voltage outputs. This approach shows poor voltage regulation and is usually limited to low-power applications. Another approach uses a transformer with several secondaries, each connected to a separate rectifier and filter circuit. Still another approach is shown in Fig. 4-12. This circuit provides two dc output voltages from one secondary winding and does not use a resistive divider. The voltages shown are based on no-load current. The diode drops are not taken into account.

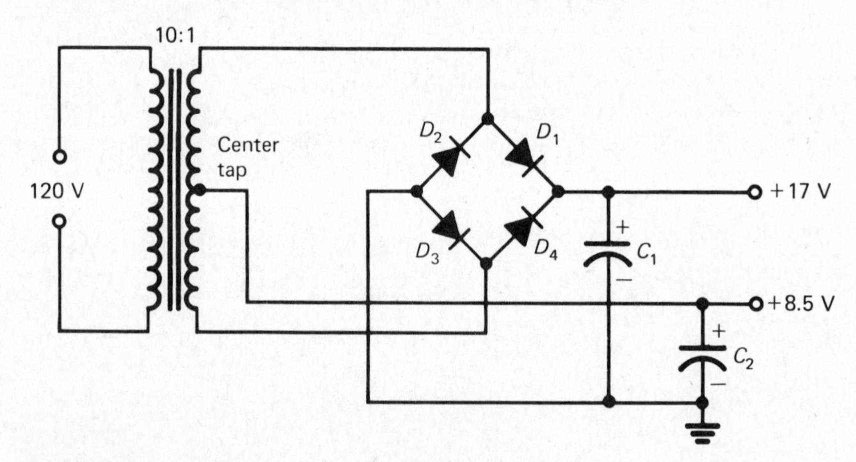

Fig. 4-12 Combination power-supply problem.

PROBLEM

Explain the two output voltages.

ACTIVITY 4-4
ADVANCED PROBLEM: COMBINATION BRIDGE-DOUBLER

THEORY AND BACKGROUND

Figure 4-13 shows the schematic diagram for a power supply that uses a combination of a bridge rectifier and two voltage doublers to provide three dc output voltages. Two of the voltages are positive with respect to ground, and one is negative. The voltages shown could be expected at no-load current. The diode drops are not taken into account.

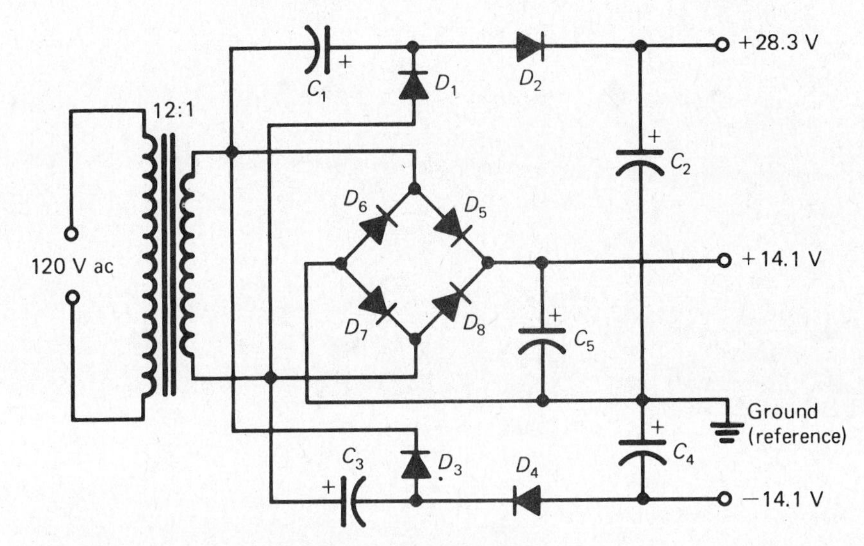

Fig. 4-13 Combination bridge-doubler problem.

PROBLEM

Explain all three output voltages.

CHAPTER 5

Junction Transistors

ACTIVITY 5-1
TEST: JUNCTION TRANSISTORS

Choose the letter that best completes each statement or answers the question.

1. If an amplifier has a voltage gain of 5 and a current gain of 3, its power gain is
   a. 3
   b. 5
   c. 8
   d. 15
2. If an amplifier has a voltage gain of 50, what input signal will be required to drive its output to 2 V peak-to-peak?
   a. 25 mV peak-to-peak
   b. 40 mV peak-to-peak
   c. 50 mV peak-to-peak
   d. 400 mV peak-to-peak
3. To qualify as an amplifier, a device or circuit must provide
   a. Voltage gain
   b. Power gain
   c. Current gain
   d. All of the above
4. The term "voltage amplifier" is often used to describe
   a. Large-signal amplifiers
   b. Small-signal amplifiers
   c. DC amplifiers
   d. AC amplifiers
5. The term "power amplifier" is often used to describe
   a. Large-signal amplifiers
   b. Small-signal amplifiers
   c. DC amplifiers
   d. AC amplifiers
6. The function of the base in a bipolar junction transistor (BJT) is to
   a. Emit the carriers
   b. Collect the carriers
   c. Control current flow
   d. Ground the transistor

7. The term "bipolar" as applied to a transistor indicates
   a. A north and south magnetic pole
   b. Two polarities of current carriers
   c. That the device can be biased two different ways
   d. All of the above

Questions 8 to 12 refer to Fig. 5-1.

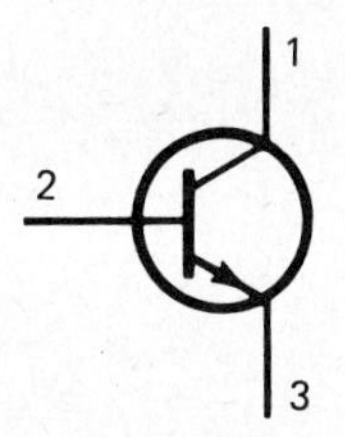

Fig. 5-1 Questions 8 to 12.

8. The symbol shows a(n)
   a. FET
   b. BJT
   c. UJT
   d. VMOS transistor
9. The device has
   a. One junction
   b. Two junctions
   c. Three junctions
   d. Four junctions
10. Terminal 3 is the
    a. Collector
    b. Base
    c. Gate
    d. Emitter
11. What is the normal bias for terminals 1 and 2?
    a. 10 mA
    b. 10 μA
    c. 1 should be more positive than 2
    d. 2 should be more positive than 1
12. Where does the largest electron current normally flow?
    a. From 2 to 3
    b. From 1 to 3
    c. From 1 to 2
    d. From 3 to 1

Questions 13 and 14 refer to Fig. 5-2.

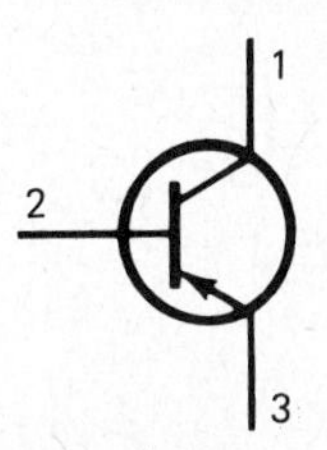

Fig. 5-2 Questions 13 and 14.

13. The device is
    a. An N-channel JFET
    b. An NPN BJT
    c. A UJT
    d. None of the above
14. The emitter lead is
    a. 1
    b. 2
    c. 3
    d. This device has no emitter
15. In order to turn on a BJT
    a. The emitter-base junction must be forward-biased
    b. The emitter-base junction must be reverse-biased
    c. The emitter-base junction must be zero-biased
    d. None of the above
16. Compared with NPN transistors, PNP transistors are
    a. Capable of higher power dissipation
    b. More easily damaged
    c. Electrical opposites as far as polarity is concerned
    d. Directly interchangeable in any given circuit

17. Why is the collector-base resistance of a BJT greater than its emitter-base resistance?
a. The collector is lightly doped
b. The base is lightly doped
c. The emitter is physically larger than the base
d. One is forward-biased and the other is reverse-biased

18. How much emitter current will be found in a BJT with a β of 100 if its collector current is 1 A?
a. 10 mA
b. 490 mA
c. 990 mA
d. 1.01 A

19. Why is the collector current in a BJT almost equal to the emitter current?
a. The collector is biased to attract the emitter carriers
b. The base is very thin, which makes the collector field strong
c. Carrier combination is unlikely in the lightly doped base
d. All of the above

Questions 20 to 25 refer to Fig. 5-3.

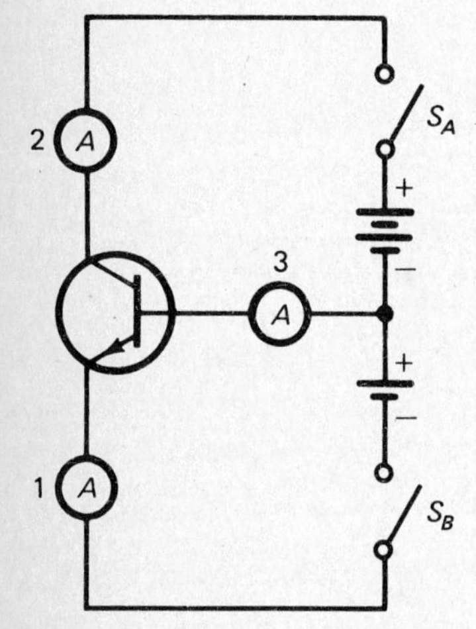

Fig. 5-3 Circuit for Questions 20 to 25.

20. Assume that both switches are closed. Which meter will show the most current flow?
a. 1
b. 2
c. 3
d. 1 and 3 will read the same and be greater than 2

21. If both switches are closed, which meter will show the smallest current flow?
a. 1
b. 2
c. 3
d. 1 and 3 will read the same and be smaller than 2

22. S_B is closed, and S_A is open. The conditions are
a. Meter 2 shows current flow
b. Meter 1 shows no current
c. Meter 3 shows no flow
d. Meters 1 and 3 show identical current flow

23. S_A is closed and S_B is open. The conditions are
a. Meter 1 shows no current
b. Meter 2 shows no current
c. Meter 3 shows no current
d. All of the above

24. Both switches are closed, meter 2 reads 10 mA, and meter 3 reads 0.1 mA. Meter 1 should read
a. 0.1 mA
b. 5.9 mA
c. 10.1 mA
d. 11.9 mA

25. Use the data from question 24 and calculate β
a. 10
b. 50
c. 100
d. 190

26. Transistors with the same part number will usually show β values that
   a. Vary considerably
   b. Are the same
   c. Vary only a very small amount
   d. Are the same as the last three digits of the part number

27. Why are NPN transistors more widely applied than PNP devices?
   a. There is a better selection of NPN devices
   b. NPN devices tend to have better high-frequency gain
   c. Negative-ground systems are common
   d. All of the above

28. BJT characteristic curves that show V_{CE} versus I_C for various values of I_B are called
   a. Collector families of curves
   b. Base families of curves
   c. Constant-power-transfer curves
   d. All of the above

Questions 29 to 35 refer to Fig. 5-4.

29. Refer to the curves in Fig. 5-4(*a*). What is the collector current when V_{CE} = 15 V and I_B = 60 μA?
   a. 0.5 mA
   b. 5.1 mA
   c. 15 mA
   d. 20 mA

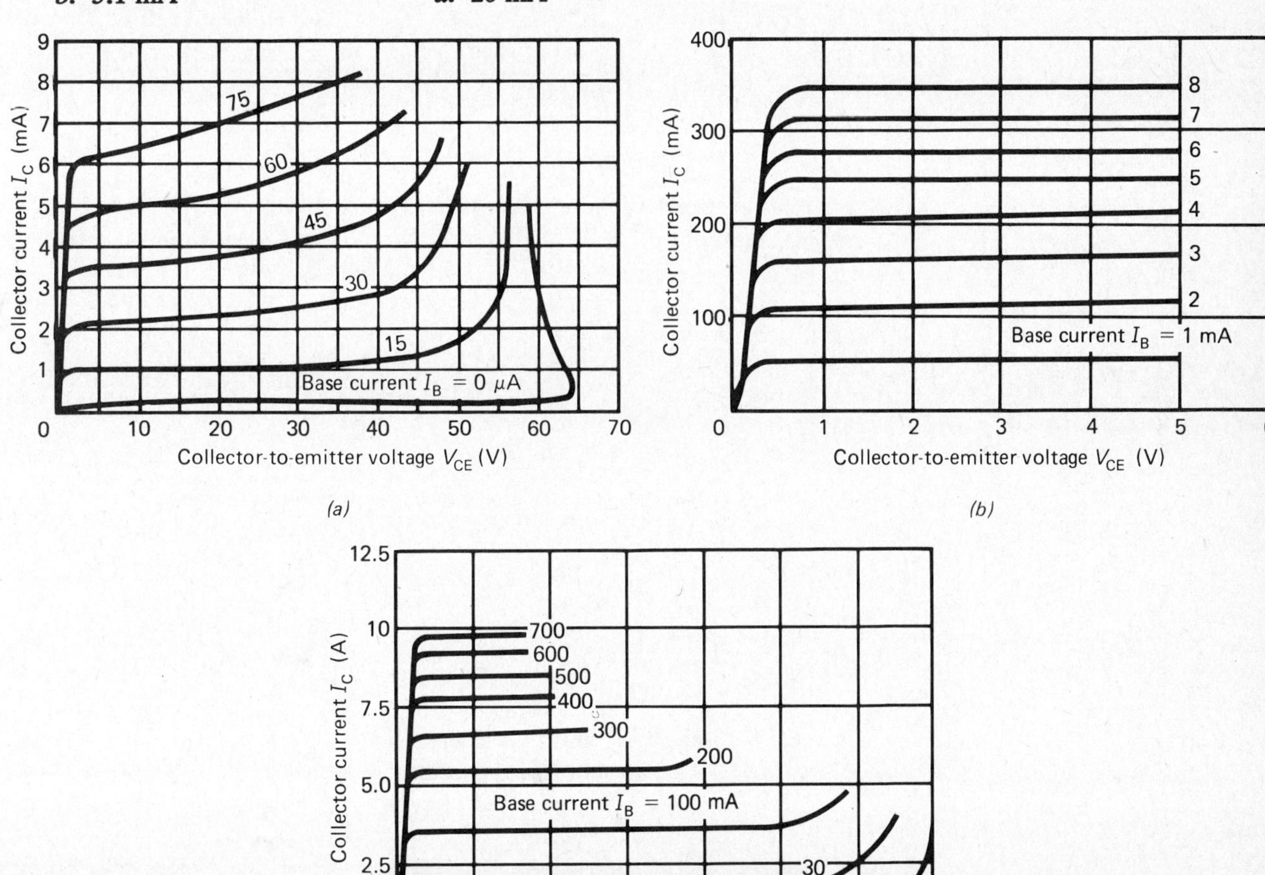

Fig. 5-4 Curves for Questions 29 to 35.

30. Refer to Fig. 5-4(*a*) on page 41. What is β when V_{CE} = 30 V and I_B = 30 μA?
a. 25
b. 38
c. 67
d. 83

31. Refer to Fig. 5-4(*a*). What is the value of I_B when V_{CE} = 20 V and I_C = 6 mA?
a. 35 μA
b. 60 μA
c. 67 μA
d. 75 μA

32. Refer to Fig. 5-4(*a*). I_B = 15 μA, and V_{CE} is greater than 55 V. What does the graph show?
a. Collector breakdown
b. A base-emitter failure
c. Thermal runaway
d. All of the above

33. Refer to Fig. 5-4(*b*). V_{CE} = 3 V, and I_B = 5 mA. What is the collector dissipation?
a. 0.15 W
b. 0.25 W
c. 0.45 W
d. 0.75 W

34. Refer to Fig. 5-4(*b*). If V_{CE} is constant at 3 V, where is β greatest?
a. At low values of I_B (near 1 mA)
b. At high values of I_B (near 8 mA)
c. β is constant
d. None of the above

35. Refer to Fig. 5-4(*c*). If a constant power curve would intersect at a point where V_{CE} = 10 V and I_C = 10 A, where would it intersect when I_C = 2.5 A?
a. At V_{CE} = 80 V
b. At V_{CE} = 60 V
c. At V_{CE} = 40 V
d. At V_{CE} = 20 V

36. Refer to Fig. 5-4(*c*). Find the collector dissipation for V_{CE} = 40 V and I_B = 100 mA.
a. 0.125 W
b. 12.5 W
c. 150 W
d. 455 W

37. A technician is checking a normal BJT with an ohmmeter and finds two leads with very high resistance. When the ohmmeter polarity is reversed, the resistance is still very high. The technician has
a. Found the emitter and base leads
b. Found the base and collector leads
c. Found the emitter and collector leads
d. None of the above

38. The positive lead of an ohmmeter is connected to the base lead of a BJT, and a low resistance is indicated when the negative ohmmeter lead is connected to either of the two transistor leads. The transistor is
a. Open
b. An NPN device
c. A PNP device
d. A special high-power type

39. When testing normal BJTs with an ohmmeter, the emitter-base and collector-base junctions should check as
 a. Diodes
 b. Opens
 c. Shorts
 d. One junction should show high resistance and the other low

40. BJT leakage current I_{CBO} is
 a. Measured in the collector-base circuit
 b. Measured in the collector-emitter circuit
 c. Measured in the emitter-base circuit
 d. $\beta \times I_{CEO}$

41. BJT leakage current I_{CEO} is
 a. Measured in the collector-base circuit
 b. Measured in the emitter-base circuit
 c. Less than I_{CBO}
 d. $\beta \times I_{CBO}$

42. In-circuit transistor testing with the power turned on can be accomplished with
 a. Ohmmeters
 b. Leakage meters
 c. Curve tracers
 d. Voltmeters, by signal tracing, or by signal injection

43. Compared with BJTs, FETs are
 a. Less expensive
 b. Voltage-controlled devices
 c. Larger
 d. Available in only one polarity

Questions 44 to 47 refer to Fig. 5-5.

44. Terminal *A* of symbol 1 represents a
 a. Gate lead
 b. Source lead
 c. Drain lead
 d. Emitter lead

45. The N-channel JFET is represented by symbol
 a. 1
 b. 2
 c. 3
 d. 5

46. The N-channel MOSFET is represented by symbol
 a. 1
 b. 2
 c. 3
 d. 5

47. The N-channel enhancement mode MOSFET is represented by symbol
 a. 1
 b. 2
 c. 3
 d. 4

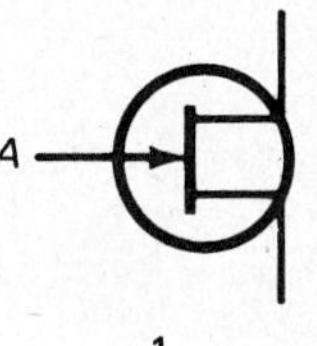

1

2

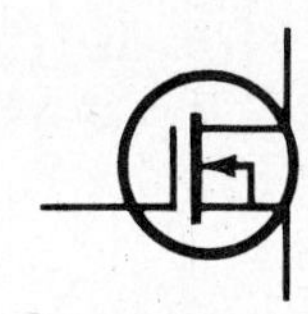

3

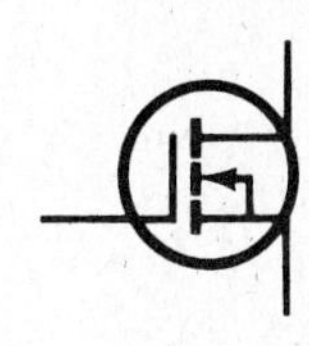

4

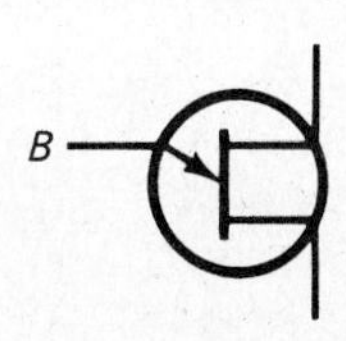

5

Fig. 5-5 Symbols for Questions 44 to 51.

Questions 48 to 51 refer to Fig. 5-5 on page 43.

48. Terminal *B* of symbol 5 represents
   a. A gate lead
   b. A source lead
   c. A drain lead
   d. An emitter lead

49. Which symbol represents a device that is not used as an amplifier?
   a. 1
   b. 3
   c. 4
   d. 5

50. Which symbol represents a device that exhibits negative resistance?
   a. 2
   b. 3
   c. 4
   d. 5

51. Which symbol would represent a VMOS transistor?
   a. 1
   b. 2
   c. 3
   d. 4

52. VMOS transistors are
   a. Power devices
   b. Small-signal devices
   c. Negative-resistance devices
   d. Three-junction devices

53. VMOS transistors may be preferred over BJTs in some applications because
   a. They do not suffer from thermal runaway
   b. They do not require an input current for control
   c. They can be turned off rapidly
   d. All of the above

ACTIVITY 5-2
LAB EXPERIMENT: TRANSISTORS

PURPOSE

To verify some important electrical characteristics of bipolar, field-effect, and unijunction transistors.

MATERIALS REQUIRED

Qty.	
2	multimeters
1	oscilloscope
1	0- to 20-V dc power supply
1	0- to 10-V dc power supply (or a battery as shown)
1	12.6-V Stancor P-8130 ac source or equivalent
1	100-kΩ ½-W carbon resistor
1	270-kΩ ½-W carbon resistor
1	10-kΩ linear-taper potentiometer
1	1-kΩ 2-W carbon resistor
1	1N4001 rectifier diode or equivalent
1	2N4220 FET or equivalent
1	2N2646 UJT or equivalent
1	2N4401 transistor or equivalent

INTRODUCTION

This experiment has been designed to be safe. Be careful when setting the dc power supply. Many power supplies are capable of high voltages. The transistors can be severely damaged by excess voltage. Check your circuits carefully before turning on the power. Be sure that the polarities are all correct and that the meters are on the proper range. If in doubt, check with your instructor.

The experiment has been divided into three parts. Record all data before moving on to the next part. The parts can be completed in any order.

PROCEDURE

Part 1

1. This part of the experiment involves working with a BJT. Test the transistor with the ohmmeter. Use the 2N4401 transistor or equivalent. Answer the following questions.
   a. Are both junctions good?
   b. Can you identify all three leads?
   c. What is the polarity of the transistor?
   d. Does the transistor show gain?
   e. Is there any leakage current? If any of the above questions cannot be answered, or if a check shows that the transistor is bad, consult with your instructor. You must have a good transistor to proceed with the experiment.
2. Figure 5-6 shows the circuit to be used for collecting data for the BJT. Note that it requires three meters. If three meters are not available, the experiment can still be accomplished by moving the base-current meter to the collector circuit after the base current is set. Of course, the range will have to be changed. If this is the case, remember to set the base current with a few volts across the transistor from collector to emitter. If the base current is set with V_{CE} = 0 V, it will change as V_{CE} is increased.

   If two dc power supplies are not available, the base power supply can be replaced with a battery power supply, shown in Fig. 5-7.
3. Build the circuit as shown in Fig. 5-6. Use a VOM to measure current. The voltmeter range should be low for the best accuracy. As

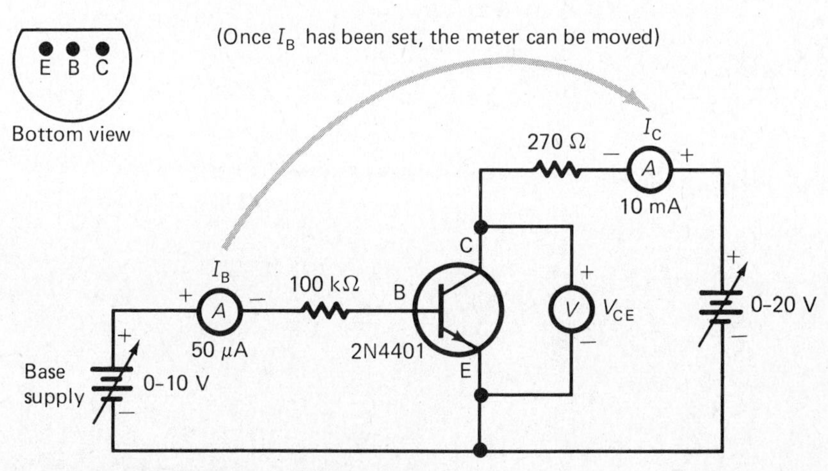

Fig. 5-6 Transistor characteristic circuit.

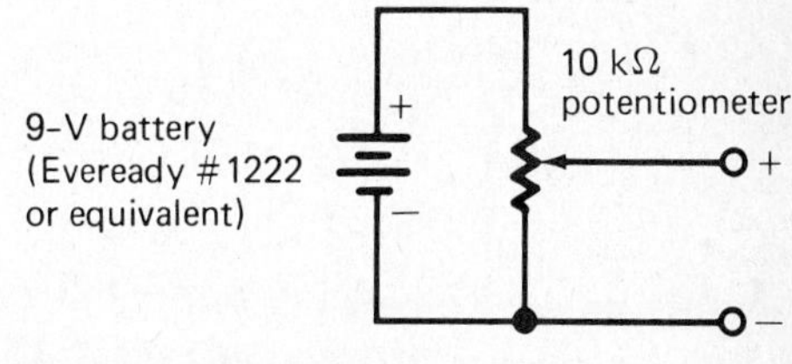

Fig. 5-7 Battery supply.

V_{CE} increases, switch to a higher range. Set I_B to 0. Set V_{CE} to 0. Copy Table 5-1 onto a separate sheet of paper and record I_C. Now increase V_{CE} to 0.5 V. Again, record I_C. Complete the I_C column of your table for $I_B = 0$.

4. Complete the next I_C column of your table by first setting I_B to 25 μA. If you are moving the meter from the base circuit to the collector circuit, be sure there are a few volts across the collector and emitter when setting I_B.
5. Complete the last I_C column in your table for $I_B = 50$ μA.

Table 5-1

$I_B = 0$		$I_B = 25$ μA		$I_B = 50$ μA	
V_{CE} (V)	I_C (mA)	V_{CE} (V)	I_C (mA)	V_{CE} (V)	I_C (mA)
0		0		0	
0.5		0.5		0.5	
1.0		1.0		1.0	
1.5		1.5		1.5	
3		3		3	
6		6		6	
9		9		9	
12		12		12	
15		15		15	
18		18		18	

6. Refer to Fig. 5-8. Draw a family of three curves for the transistor on similar graph paper. The curves should be labeled $I_B = 0$, $I_B = 25$ μA, and $I_B = 50$ μA.

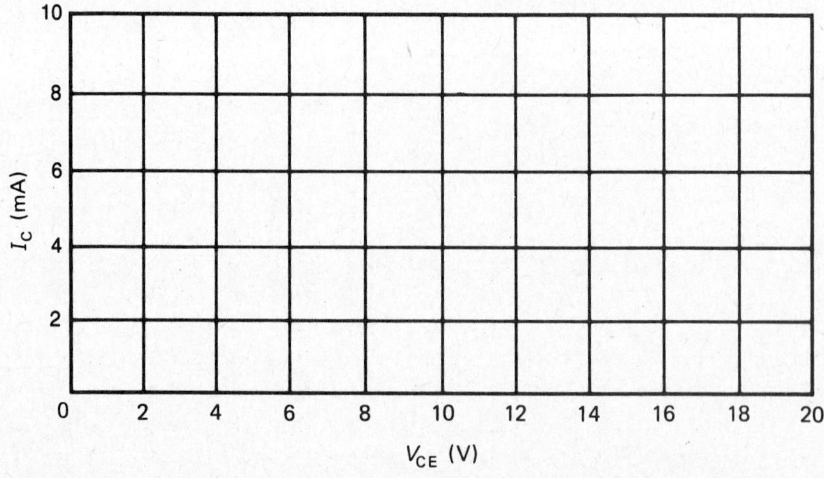

Fig. 5-8 Example of graph paper used for plotting transistor characteristic curves.

7. The curves can also be observed on an oscilloscope. The circuit to accomplish this is shown in Fig. 5-9. Set up the oscilloscope for external horizontal input. Connect the circuit to the oscilloscope as shown in Fig. 5-9. Set the dc power supply for $I_B = 0$. Adjust the oscilloscope brightness, focus, positioning, and horizontal-gain controls for a sharp horizontal line that almost fills the screen. Set the vertical sensitivity to 0.2 V/div. If a ÷10 probe is in use, set the sensitivity at 0.02 V/div.

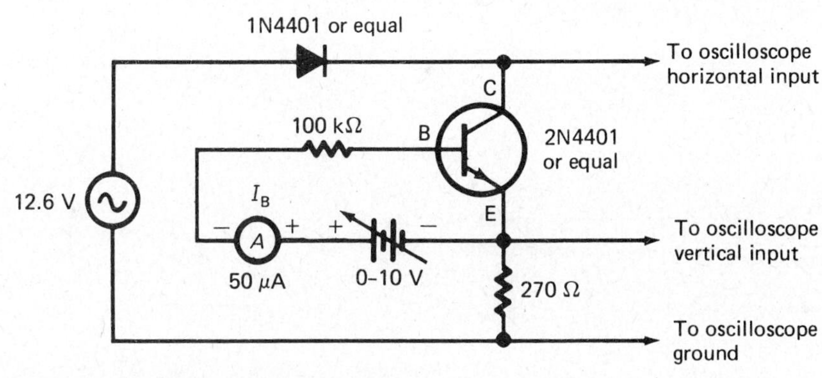

Fig. 5-9 Transistor curve tracer circuit.

8. Adjust the dc supply for I_B = 25 μA. The curve shown on the oscilloscope should change and appear like the one you plotted in step 6. In fact, the values should agree. The vertical deflection is caused by the transistor current flowing through the 270-Ω resistor. This resistor is in the emitter circuit. The emitter current is very close to being equal to the collector current. Therefore, only a slight error is caused. If the oscilloscope vertical input is calibrated, the current can be found by Ohm's law. If the oscilloscope vertical sensitivity is 0.2 V/div, a 270-Ω resistor will produce a current-per-division factor of

$$I = \frac{V}{R} = \frac{0.2\ \text{V}}{270\ \Omega} = 0.74\ \text{mA/div}$$

This makes it possible for you to compare the curve on the oscilloscope with the plotted curve of step 6. How well do they agree? Finally, increase I_B to 50 μA. The oscilloscope should show a new characteristic curve. How well does this curve agree with your curves from step 6?

PROCEDURE

Part 2

1. This part of the experiment deals with the characteristics of an N-channel junction field-effect transistor. Place your ohmmeter on the $R \times 100$ range and check the field-effect transistor. The source and drain leads should show no diode behavior. A diode check can be made from the gate lead to either the source or drain leads. Figure 5-10, on the next page, shows the lead locations for the transistor.
2. With the ohmmeter across the drain and source leads, touch the gate lead only with your finger. Do this without holding the ohmmeter probes by the metal portion. This allows your body to place a small (or large, depending on conditions) charge on the gate. The ohm-

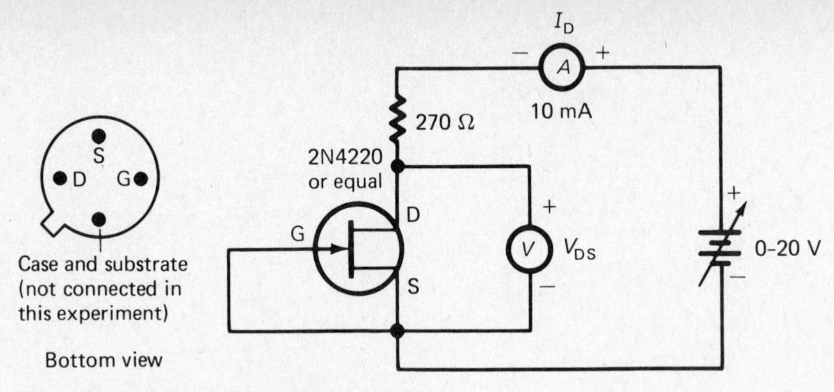

Fig. 5-10 FET characteristic circuit.

meter should respond and show a change in conduction. Answer the following questions:

a. Does the channel show conduction?
b. Does the gate diode check good?
c. Is the gate lead sensitive? You should have answered yes to all three questions. If not, the transistor may be bad. Check with your instructor. You will need a good transistor to proceed.

3. Build the circuit shown in Fig. 5-10. Use a VTVM or DMM to measure the drain to source voltage V_{DS}. Set the power supply for zero output. Copy Table 5-2 onto a separate sheet of paper and record the drain current I_D. Increase the power-supply output until V_{DS} = 0.5 V. Again, record I_D. Complete Table 5-2.

Table 5-2

V_{DS} (V)	I_D (mA)
0	
0.5	
1.0	
1.5	
2.0	
2.5	
3.0	
3.5	
4.0	
5.0	
6.0	
7.0	
8.0	
9.0	
10.0	
15.0	

4. Use graph paper similar to that in Fig. 5-11 to plot the characteristic curve for the FET.

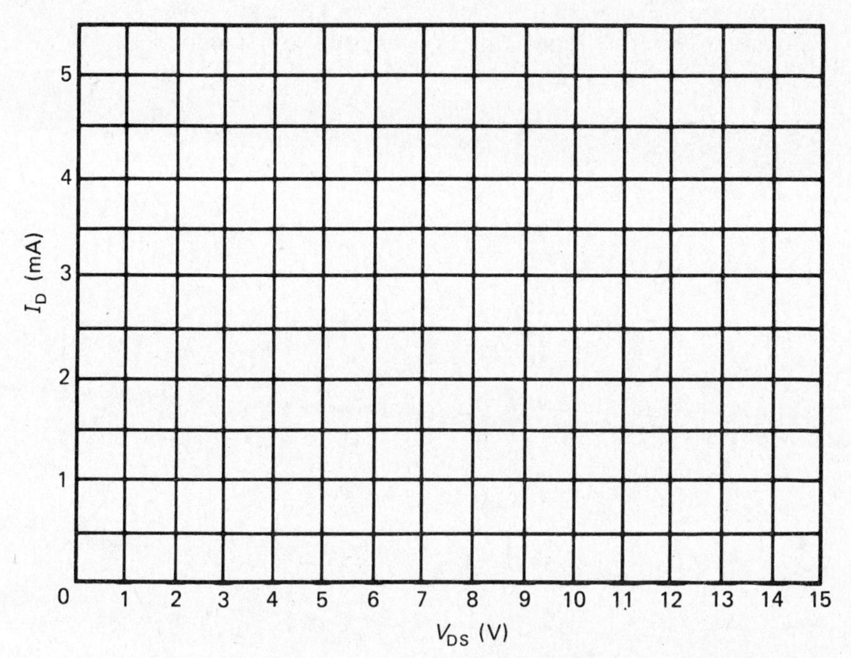

Fig. 5-11 Example of graph paper used for plotting FET charecteristic curves.

5. An oscilloscope can be used to observe characteristic curves. Figure 5-12 shows a circuit that can be used to accomplish this. Set the oscilloscope for external horizontal input. Adjust the brightness, focus, positioning, and gain controls until the trace is similar to the characteristic curve you have drawn in step 4. The curves should be similar. The current axis (vertical) can be calculated with Ohm's law. Assuming that the vertical sensitivity is set at 0.2 V/div, a 270-Ω resistor will produce a current-per-division factor of

$$I = \frac{V}{R} = \frac{0.2\ \text{V}}{270\ \Omega} = 0.74\ \text{mA/div}$$

This makes it possible for you to compare the curve on the oscilloscope with the plotted curve of step 4. How well do they agree?

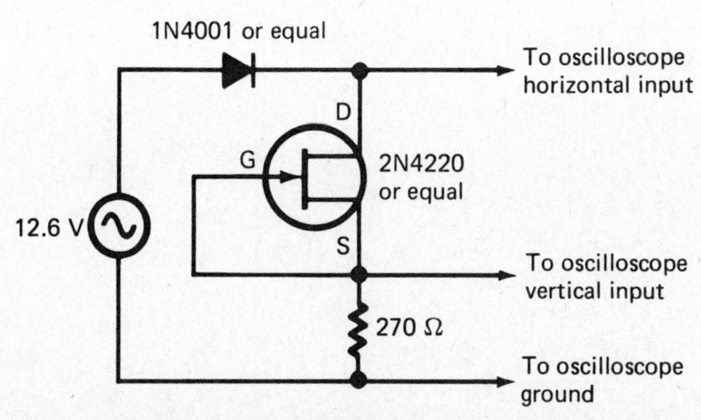

Fig. 5-12 FET curve tracer circuit.

6. Turn off the power and change the circuit to that shown in Fig. 5-13. This will allow you to see how the characteristic curve changes with various values of V_{GS}. Turn on the power. Adjust the dc supply for zero output. The trace should be just as it was before. Gradually increase the dc voltage. Eventually, the trace should become a horizontal line. This shows that the transistor is not conducting any current. The channel has been cut off by the gate voltage.

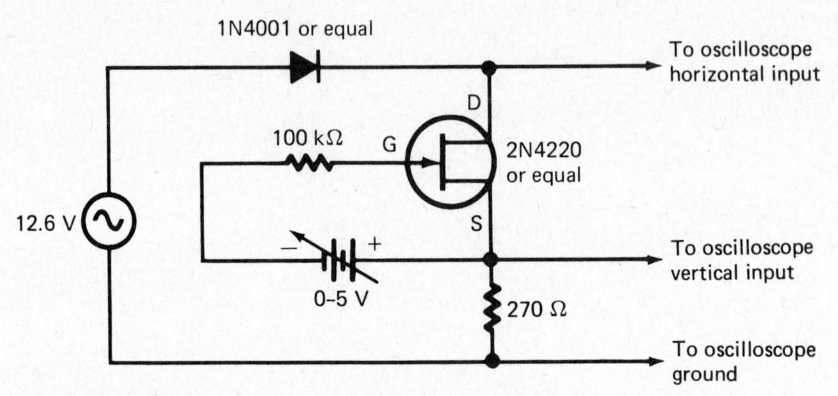

Fig. 5-13 FET curve tracer circuit with gate supply.

PROCEDURE

Part 3

1. This part of the experiment will give you some of the characteristics of a UJT. Test the UJT with your ohmmeter. Use the $R \times 1000$ range. Measure the resistance from B_1 to B_2. Figure 5-14 shows the lead locations. The resistance should be between 4 and 9 kΩ.
2. Check the emitter diode with the ohmmeter. This can be done from the emitter to either base lead. Answer the following questions:
   a. Is the interbase resistance in the correct range?
   b. Is the emitter diode good? You should have answered yes to both questions. If a check shows that the transistor is not good, consult your instructor. You must have a good transistor to complete the rest of the experiment.
3. Build the circuit shown in Fig. 5-14. Set the dc power supply to 10 V. Use a VTVM or DMM to measure the emitter voltage V_E. Adjust the 10-kΩ potentiometer for $V_E = 0$. Slowly adjust the potentiometer. The voltmeter should show V_E gradually increasing. A point will be reached where the voltmeter shows a sudden drop

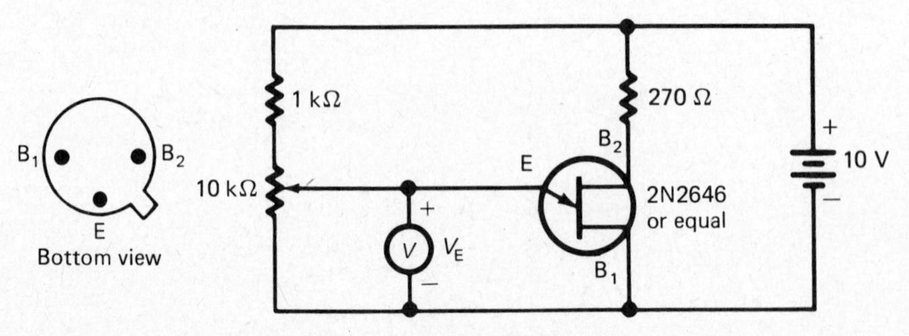

Fig. 5-14 Unijunction-transistor characteristic circuit.

caused by the UJT transistor turning on. The sudden decrease in resistance within the transistor makes the voltage drop.
4. Repeat the procedure several times. Carefully note the exact voltage required to fire, or turn on, the UJT. Record this voltage.

DISCUSSION TOPICS

1. Refer to Fig. 5-6. What component ensures that the base current will be very low?
2. Refer to the curves you plotted in step 6 of part 1. Does V_{CE} or I_B have the greatest effect on I_C?
3. From the curves you plotted in step 6 of part 1, calculate β for V_{CE} = 10 V and I_B = 50 μA. How does your answer compare with other answers in your class?
4. Refer to Fig. 5-9. Ignore the voltage dropped across the diode and the 270-Ω resistor. What is the *peak* voltage across the transistor? Could this information be useful? Why?
5. Refer to Fig. 5-13. Why is there no gate current?
6. Refer to Fig. 5-9. Why is there base current?
7. What are the two greatest differences between the way the bipolar and field-effect transistors are controlled in this experiment?
8. When using an oscilloscope as a curve tracer as in this experiment, what are some sources of error?
9. Refer to the curves you plotted in step 4 of part 2. With the gate shorted to the source, the flat part of the curve shows a current called I_{DSS}. What value did you obtain for I_{DSS}, and how does your value compare with results obtained by other members in the class?
10. Refer to Fig. 5-14. Explain why V_E drops when the UJT fires.

ACTIVITY 5-3
ADVANCED PROBLEM:
TRANSISTOR-DIODE SPECIFICATIONS

THEORY AND BACKGROUND

One of the important jobs for an electronics technician is to gather data on semiconductor devices, data which is important over the entire range of occupations in the electronic field. The sources for such data include

1. Data sheets
2. Data volumes
3. Substitution guides
4. Catalogs

The first two sources listed will give the most complete data. Many ratings, characteristic curves, and circuits are generally listed. Some manufacturers also publish application notes for the devices they make. These show typical circuits using their devices and the performance that can be expected. Application notes are very helpful for those involved in the design and development phase of electronics.

The second two sources listed will provide limited data. You may expect to find the general description of the device, the polarity, the case style, the material, and a few of the ratings. In many cases, this is all the information that is needed.

Table 5-3 lists some of the information that would be required when replacing transistors and diodes. It is not complete enough for design work but will give sufficient information for making device substitutions. The table has been completed for the first three devices listed to show you how it is to be used. Data not applicable or not available is marked N.A.

You will become aware of some of the traps in device substitution when looking up data. For example, in Table 5-3 on page 53 the base diagram is shown for a GE-20 transistor. The original transistor is in a different style case and has a different lead arrangement. The replacement transistor can work, but the leads will have to be arranged properly. Obviously, this kind of information is good to have.

PROBLEM

Consult the materials available to you and complete Table 5-3 for those devices listed. Your instructor may wish to add a few device numbers to the table.

ACTIVITY 5-4 CONSTRUCTION PROJECT: TRANSISTOR-DIODE CURVE TRACER

INTRODUCTION

A few electronic technicians have access to a curve tracer. Such equipment is usually found where much of the work is in the design and development area. Curve tracers for this purpose tend to be expensive; they are complex instruments because high accuracy and good flexibility are required for design and development work.

Curve tracers can be very simple devices. Figure 5-15 on page 54 shows the schematic diagram for a curve tracer that will work with most oscilloscopes and will allow the average technician to view transistor and diode volt-ampere characteristic curves. Although it is not as complex as an industrial curve tracer, it can provide very useful results.

A curve tracer is useful for testing transistors and diodes. Most junction transistors and diodes fail because of

1. Open junctions
2. Shorted junctions
3. Excess leakage

The curve tracer of Fig. 5-15 is capable of locating such faults.

CONSTRUCTION

The best cabinet for this device would be a plastic utility cabinet, available in many electronic supply stores.

Use good construction practices. Insulated terminal strips should be used to support the resistors. Be sure that a metal screw does not come in contact with any part of the circuit. Have your instructor check your completed curve tracer before plugging it in.

Table 5-3

Device Number	Description	Polarity	Case	Material	Function	Maximum Dissipation	Maximum Voltage	Maximum Current	β	Replaced by	Base Diagram
1N3022	Zener diode	N.A.	D0-13	Silicon	Regulator	1W	N.A.	N.A.	N.A.	GE ZD-12	N.A.
1N34A	Small-signal diode	N.A.	D0-7	Germanium	General purpose	0.130 W	75 V PRV	N.A.	N.A.	1N34AS	N.A.
2N2714	Transistor	NPN	T0-18	Silicon	General audio	0.200 W	C-B 18 V	200 mA	75-225	GE-20	E C B
1N2862											
2N4416											
40673											
2N6476											
2N2646											

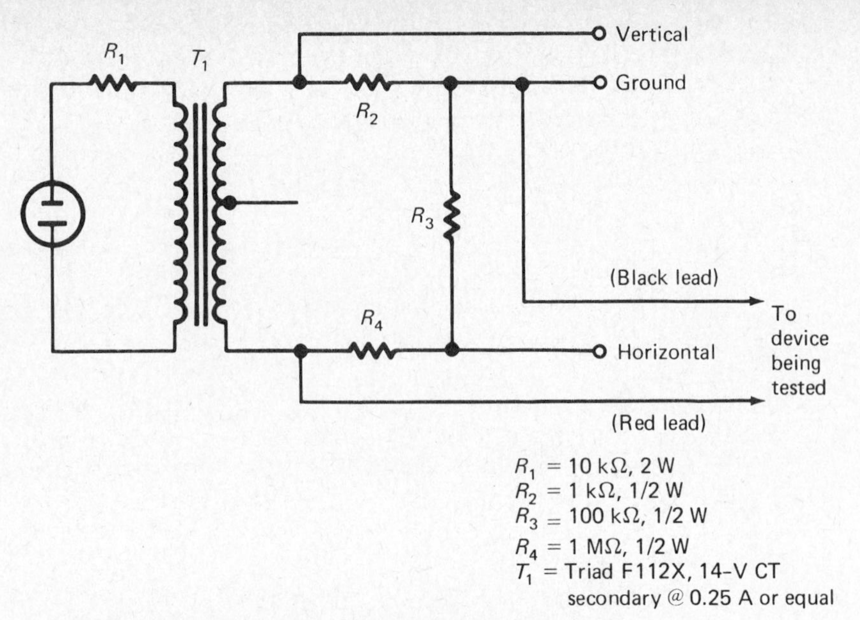

Fig. 5-15 Schematic diagram for the curve-tracer project.

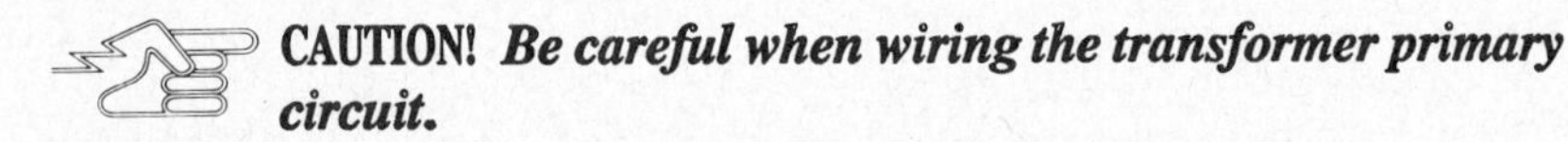

CAUTION! ***Be careful when wiring the transformer primary circuit.***

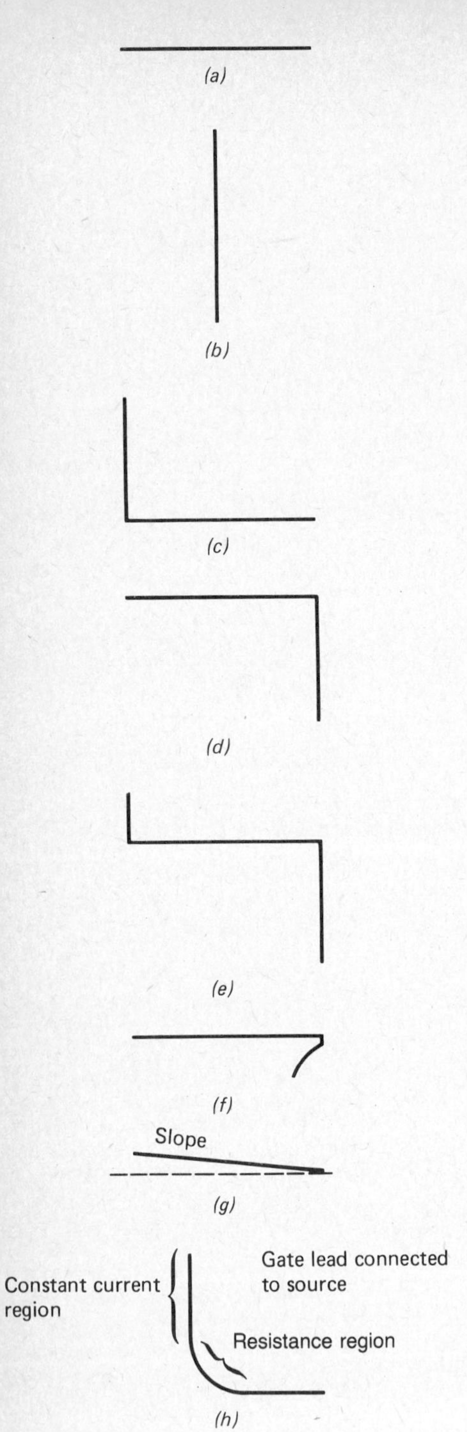

Fig. 5-16 Using the curve tracer.

OPERATION

To use the curve tracer, it must first be connected to an oscilloscope. The oscilloscope must have an external horizontal input. Switch the oscilloscope to external horizontal and connect the terminal marked "horizontal" on Fig. 5-15 to the external horizontal input jack on the oscilloscope. Connect the oscilloscope ground to the ground terminal and the vertical input to the vertical terminal. This completes the connections.

Plug in the curve tracer. A horizontal line should appear on the screen of the oscilloscope. Adjust the focus, brightness, positioning, and horizontal gain controls for a sharp trace in the center of the screen. The gain control should be set so that the trace fills a little over half the screen. Next, short the red and black test leads together. This should produce a vertical line on the screen. Adjust the vertical gain so that the trace fills about two-thirds of the screen. If these adjustments can be made, the curve tracer is ready for use.

Using the curve tracer is very easy. If a transistor or diode junction is open, the trace will show a flat line, as shown in Fig. 5-16(*a*). If the junction is shorted, the trace will appear as a vertical line, as shown in Fig. 5-16(*b*). A good diode or transistor junction will show a trace like that in Fig. 5-16(*c*) or (*d*). If the black test lead contacts the anode of the junction, the trace should appear as in Fig. 5-16(*c*). If the black test lead contacts the cathode, the trace appears as in Fig. 5-16(*d*). This depends on the oscilloscope. Most oscilloscopes deflect up for a positive voltage applied to the vertical input and to the right for a positive voltage applied to the horizontal input. If your oscilloscope is different, the patterns may be different.

Figure 5-16(*e*) shows the trace produced by connecting the test leads across the emitter-base junction of a silicon transistor. This is the same trace that will be shown for a low-voltage zener diode. Silicon junction transistors do have a zener characteristic in their emitter-base junction. The curve tracer will show the zener characteristic only if the breakover point occurs low enough on the voltage axis. For safety reasons and to avoid damaging parts the curve-tracer voltage is limited. Remember that the trace of Fig. 5-16(*e*) will be seen on low-voltage zener diodes and on some silicon emitter-base junctions. It will not be seen on germanium transistors and high-voltage zener diodes.

Figure 5-16(*f*) shows a trace obtained with the test leads connected across the emitter and collector leads of a silicon transistor. Note that collector breakover is indicated by the small downward portion of the trace to the right. This will occur on transistors that have a low collector-breakdown-voltage rating.

Figure 5-16(*g*) shows a trace that was obtained with the test leads connected across B_1 and B_2 of a unijunction transistor. Note that the trace slopes downward from left to right. This indicates the resistance of the silicon material between the two base leads. An ordinary 1-kΩ resistor across the test leads produces a straight line with about a 45° slope. This means that the base-to-base resistance of the UJT transistor is greater than 1 kΩ. With experience, approximate resistance readings can be obtained with the curve tracer. When one of the test leads is moved to the emitter lead of the UJT, a diode characteristic curve appears on the screen. This is to be expected since the emitter lead does contact one end of a PN junction.

Figure 5-16(*h*) shows a trace obtained with the test leads connected across the source and drain leads of an N-channel junction field-effect transistor (JFET). The slope indicates the resistance of the N-type channel, and the constant current behavior of the device produces the vertical portion of the trace. The curve tracer can provide much information to someone with experience and a knowledge of devices.

This curve tracer is not recommended for in-circuit checking of devices. It can be used in this way, but the results will depend on the other components connected to the device being tested. Shunt resistances will produce the characteristic slope. Capacitance will cause a phase shift, which will show up as a looping effect in the trace. With experience, in-circuit checking may be useful, but it is easy to be confused by the results.

The curve tracer is not recommended for checking MOS devices, which have a delicate gate structure that is easy to damage. Diode-protected MOS devices are more rugged. If in doubt, be very careful.

The curve tracer is not recommended for checking UHF diodes, which are very easy to damage. Such diodes may be found in the UHF tuner of a television receiver. If in doubt, be careful.

Some oscilloscope horizontal amplifiers may be overdriven by the curve tracer. This will show up as distortion on the trace. If you suspect this problem, try changing R_4 of Fig. 5-15 to 2.7 MΩ.

CHAPTER 6

Introduction to Small-Signal Amplifiers

ACTIVITY 6-1
TEST: SMALL-SIGNAL AMPLIFIERS

Choose the letter that best completes each statement.

1. The input signal to an amplifier is 45 mV, and the output signal is 3.6 V. The voltage gain of the amplifier is
   a. 20
   b. 80
   c. 100
   d. 164
2. The sensitivity of human hearing for loudness is
   a. Logarithmic
   b. Linear
   c. Based on voltage gain
   d. Capable of detecting change as small as 0.1 dB
3. A 1-W audio signal drives an amplifier with a gain of 20 dB. The power output of the amplifier will be
   a. 0.1 W
   b. 10 W
   c. 10υ W
   d. 1 kW
4. An amplifier with a voltage gain of 15 drives a second amplifier with a voltage gain of 40. The overall voltage gain is
   a. 15
   b. 25
   c. 55
   d. 600
5. A two-stage amplifier has a first-stage gain of +28 dB and a second-stage gain of +12 dB. The overall gain is
   a. +40 dB
   b. +68 dB
   c. +336 dB
   d. None of the above

6. A low-pass filter is designed to attenuate 20 kHz by 20 dB. If a 20-kHz signal has an amplitude of 10 V across the filter input, the amplitude across the filter output will be
   a. 0 V
   b. 10 mV
   c. 100 mV
   d. 1 V
7. An amplifier develops an output signal of 10 V when it is driven with an input signal of 1 V. The *power* gain of this amplifier is 20 dB only if
   a. Its input impedance is very high
   b. Its output impedance is very high
   c. Its input impedance and output impedance are equal
   d. It operates in the emitter-follower configuration

Questions 8 to 14 refer to Fig. 6-1.

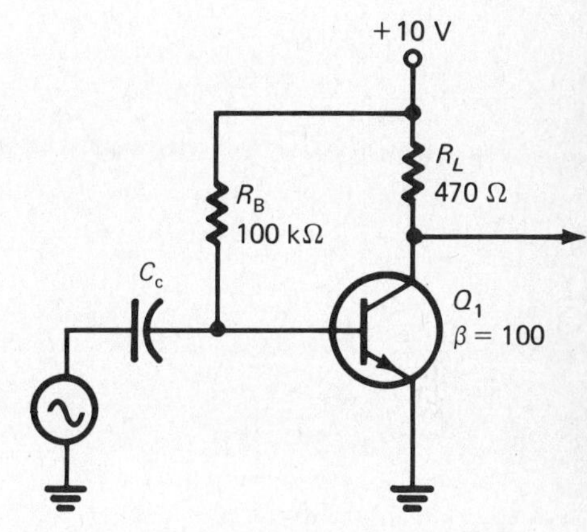

Fig. 6-1 Circuit for Questions 8 to 14

8. What is the configuration of the amplifier?
   a. Common-base
   b. Common-collector
   c. Common-emitter
   d. Emitter-follower
9. What is the value of I_B?
   a. 10 μA
   b. 100 μA
   c. 1 mA
   d. 10 mA
10. What is the value of I_C?
    a. 10 μA
    b. 100 μA
    c. 1 mA
    d. 10 mA
11. What is the value of V_{CE}?
    a. 10 V
    b. 5.3 V
    c. 5.0 V
    d. 4.7 V
12. Where is the operating point of the amplifier?
    a. Near saturation
    b. Near cutoff
    c. Near the center of the load line
    d. None of the above
13. What is the major shortcoming of the amplifier?
    a. Too expensive
    b. Not enough gain
    c. Too many parts
    d. Sensitive to β
14. Which component prevents the signal source from shorting the base-emitter junction?
    a. R_B
    b. C_C
    c. R_L
    d. Q_1

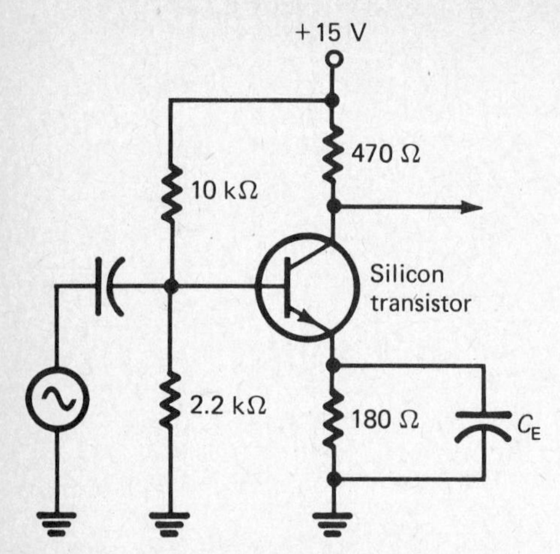

Fig. 6-2 Circuit for Questions 15 to 21.

Questions 15 to 21 refer to Fig. 6-2.

15. What is the value of V_{BE}?
    a. 2.70 V
    b. 2.00 V
    c. 1.30 V
    d. 0.70 V
16. What is the value of V_{CE}?
    a. 5.24 V
    b. 7.76 V
    c. 9.81 V
    d. 12 V
17. Where is the amplifier operating?
    a. Near saturation
    b. Near cutoff
    c. Near the center of the load line
    d. None of the above
18. What is the configuration of the amplifier?
    a. Common-base
    b. Common-collector
    c. Common-emitter
    d. Emitter-follower
19. What is the function of C_E?
    a. To increase the voltage gain
    b. To decrease the disortion
    c. To increase the bandwidth
    d. To move the operating point to the center of the load line
20. What is the range of A_V for the amplifier?
    a. 105 to 209 *c.* 38 to 64
    b. 75 to 125 *d.* 2.58 to 2.61
21. How do the input and output signals compare according to phase?
    a. 90° out of phase (input leading)
    b. 90° out of phase (input lagging)
    c. In phase
    d. 180° out of phase
22. A signal source has a characteristic impedance of 50 Ω. It will transfer the most power to an amplifier with an input impedance
    a. In excess of 50 Ω
    b. Less than 50 Ω
    c. Equal to 50 Ω
    d. None of the above

Questions 23 to 29 refer to Fig. 6-3.

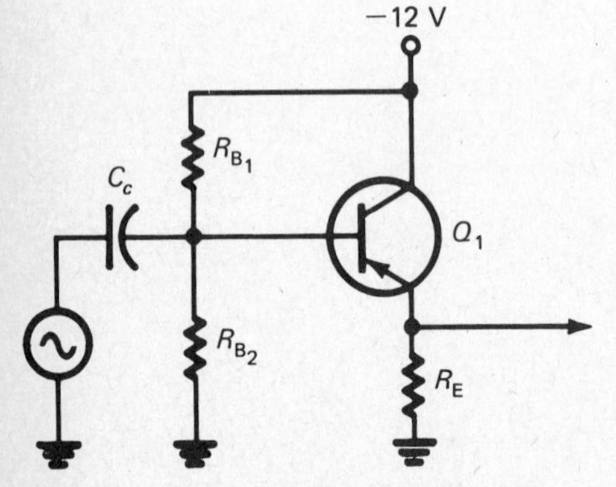

Fig. 6-3 Circuit for Questions 23 to 29.

23. What is the configuration of the amplifier?
    a. Common-base
    b. Common-collector
    c. Common-emitter
    d. None of the above
24. How do the input and output signals compare according to phase?
    a. 90° out of phase (input leading)
    b. 90° out of phase (input lagging)
    c. 180° out of phase
    d. None of the above
25. Assume that R_{B_1} and R_{B_2} are equal. V_{CE} should be
    a. Near 6 V *c.* Near 0 V
    b. Near 12 V *d.* Impossible to determine

26. The input impedance of the amplifier should be
  a. 0 Ω
  b. Low
  c. High
  d. Infinite

27. An NPN transistor could be used in this circuit by
  a. Reversing the signal source
  b. Reversing C_C
  c. Reversing both of the above
  d. Reversing the supply polarity

28. The output impedance of the amplifier should be
  a. 0 Ω
  b. Low
  c. High
  d. Infinite

29. The voltage gain of the amplifier should be
  a. 0.05
  b. A little less than 1
  c. 20
  d. 40

Questions 30 to 32 refer to Fig. 6-4.

30. What is the configuration of the amplifier?
  a. Common-base
  b. Common-collector
  c. Common-emitter
  d. None of the above

31. The input impedance of the amplifier should be
  a. 0 Ω
  b. Low
  c. High
  d. Infinite

32. How do the input and output signals compare according to phase?
  a. 90° out of phase (input leading)
  b. 90° out of phase (input lagging)
  c. 180° out of phase
  d. In phase

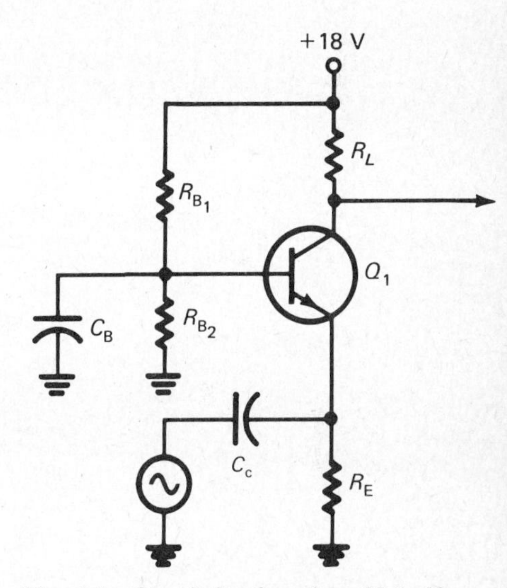

Fig. 6-4 Circuit for Questions 30 to 32.

ACTIVITY 6-2 LAB EXPERIMENT: SMALL-SIGNAL AMPLIFIERS

PURPOSE

To learn the basic concepts of small-signal amplifiers.

MATERIALS REQUIRED

Qty.		*Qty.*	
2	multimeters	1	audio-signal generator
1	oscilloscope with ÷10 probe	1	digital frequency counter (optional)
1	0- to 20-V dc power supply	3	100-kΩ resistors

Materials list continued on the next page

Qty.		*Qty.*	
2	22-kΩ resistors	1	0.5-μF paper or Mylar capacitor
1	10-kΩ resistor	1	0.1-μF paper or Mylar capacitor
1	3.3-kΩ resistor	1	2N4401 transistor, or equivalent
1	1-kΩ resistor	1	2N4403 transistor, or equivalent
1	500-kΩ linear potentiometer		
1	30-mH choke		
2	500-μF 25-V electrolytic capacitors		

INTRODUCTION

Be careful when setting the dc power supply and be sure that all polarities are correct. Check your work before turning on the power. If in doubt, ask your instructor.

The experiment has been divided into four parts. Record all data before moving on to the next part. The parts can be completed in any order.

PROCEDURE

Part 1

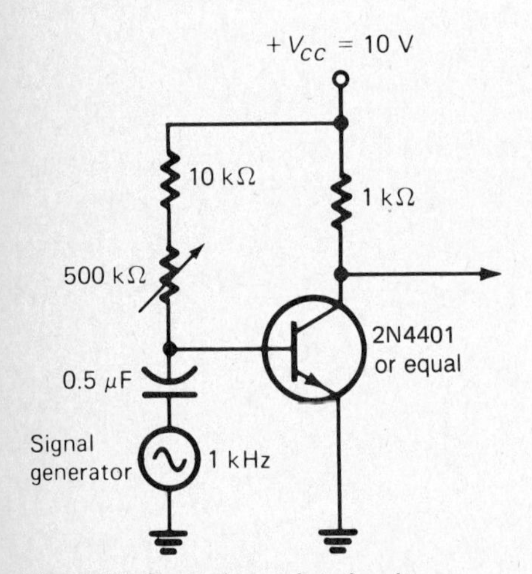

Fig. 6-5 Operating-point circuit.

1. This part of the experiment deals with operating a small-signal amplifier at various points along the dc load line. Build the circuit shown in Fig. 6-5. Adjust the signal generator output to zero. Use a voltmeter and measure the drop across the 1-kΩ load resistor. Set the 500-kΩ potentiometer so that exactly 5 V drops across the 1-kΩ load resistor. Answer the following questions:
   a. Where does the other 5-V drop appear (V_{CC} = 10 V)?
   b. Where is the amplifier now operating along the dc load line?
2. Connect your oscilloscope across ground and the collector terminal of the transistor. This will allow you to view the signal developed by the amplifier.
3. Check to see that your audio generator is adjusted for a 1-kHz sine-wave output. Slowly increase the output amplitude of the generator while watching the oscilloscope. Adjust the oscilloscope for a good stable display. Continue to increase the amplitude until the waveform shows signs of clipping. Answer these questions:
   a. Is the level of clipping about the same for the positive and negative signal peaks?
   b. What is the maximum peak-to-peak output for this amplifier?
4. Study Fig. 6-6 on the next page which shows the dc load line for your amplifier. Do your results agree with this graph?
5. Set up your oscilloscope to measure phase between the base and collector of the transistor amplifier. If your oscilloscope has dual-trace operation, this mode will be good. If not, you will have to set the oscilloscope for external triggering. Consult your oscilloscope manual for information.
6. Decrease the signal-generator amplitude until the oscilloscope shows a collector signal of 4 V peak-to-peak. Now move the oscilloscope to the base of the transistor. The signal here will be low in amplitude. Note the amplitude and the phase of the base signal compared with the collector signal. Answer these questions:

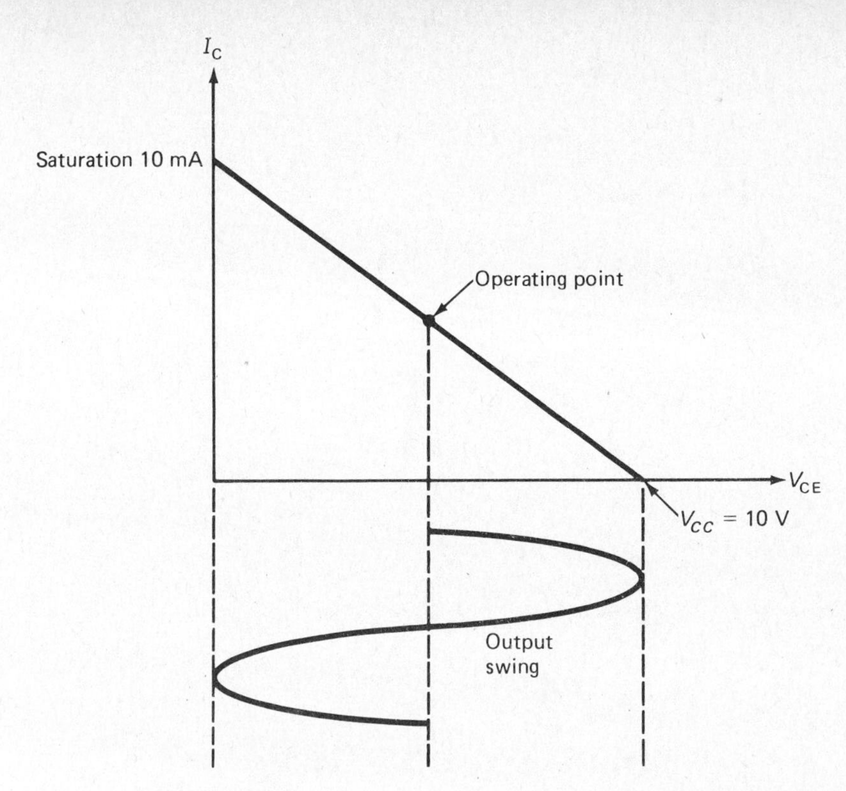

Fig. 6-6 Amplifier load line.

a. What is the configuration of the amplifier?
b. What is the phase relationship between the base signal and the collector signal?
c. What is the voltage gain of the amplifier?

$$A_V = \frac{V_{out}}{V_{in}}$$

The voltage gain for this amplifier should be 100 or more; that is, a base signal will cause a collector signal to appear 100 times greater in amplitude. This assumes that the amplifier is not clipping.

7. Adjust the power supply to 20 V. Draw the new load line. Adjust the 500-kΩ potentiometer for the center of the new load line. The maximum output swing should now be 20 V peak-to-peak. The voltage gain will increase a little.
8. Turn off the power. Reverse the power-supply polarity. Now V_{CC} will be negative with respect to ground. Substitute the PNP transistor for the NPN unit. Turn on the power supply and repeat enough of the procedure to verify that the major difference is simply the power-supply polarity.
9. You may complete this part of the experiment using either the NPN or the PNP transistor since the results will be the same. Just be sure to use the correct polarity for V_{CC}.

   Set V_{CC} to 10 V. Reduce the amplitude of the signal generator to 0. Adjust the 500-kΩ potentiometer until V_{CE} = 0.5 V. The drop across the load resistor should be 9.5 V at this operating point. This is an operating point *very near saturation.*

10. Increase the amplitude of the generator so that the oscilloscope shows a collector signal of 10 V peak-to-peak. Answer these questions:
    a. Is the output a good replica of the input?
    b. Would this circuit be considered linear?
    c. Why is an operating point near saturation not a good choice for linear amplification? Study Fig. 6-7, the dc load line, which shows the new operating point. Does this graph help explain your results?

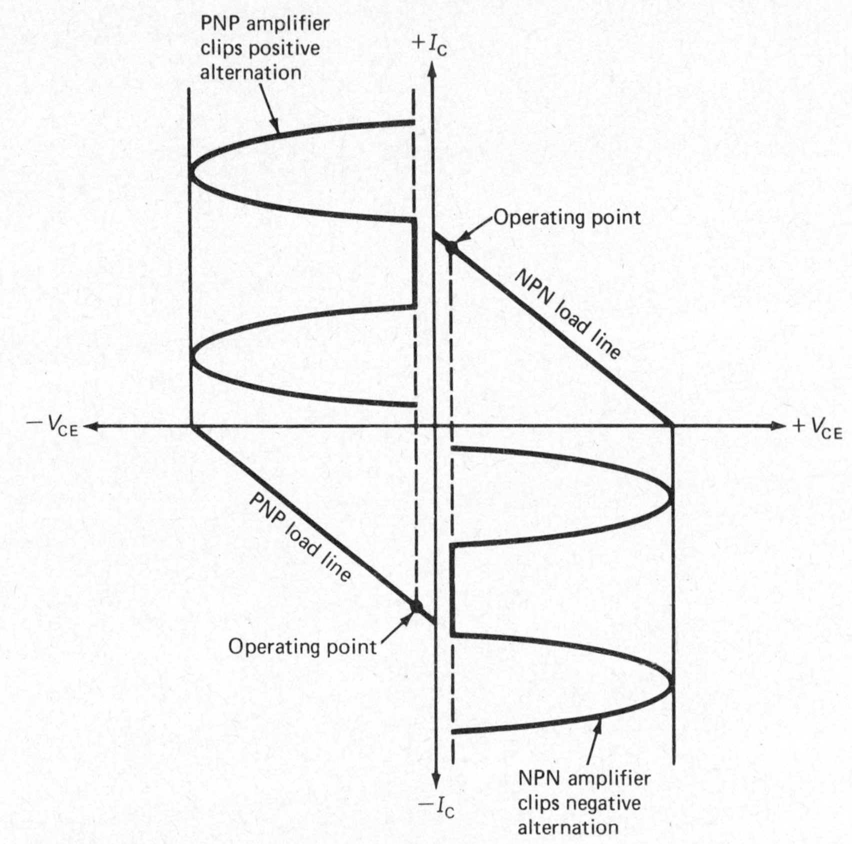

Fig. 6-7 Operating point near saturation.

11. Set the amplitude of the signal generator to 0. Open the connection between the 500-kΩ potentiometer and the 10-kΩ resistor. This will reduce the base current to 0. Answer these questions:
    a. What should the collector current be?
    b. What will the operating point be?
    c. What should V_{CE} be? (Verify your answer with the meter.)
12. Increase the amplitude of the signal generator until the oscilloscope shows a collector signal of 10 V peak-to-peak. Answer these questions:
    a. Is the output a good replica of the input?
    b. Is the amplifier operating in a linear fashion? Draw a load line and the operating point for this amplifier with no base current. Can you verify your results with the graph?

PROCEDURE

Part 2

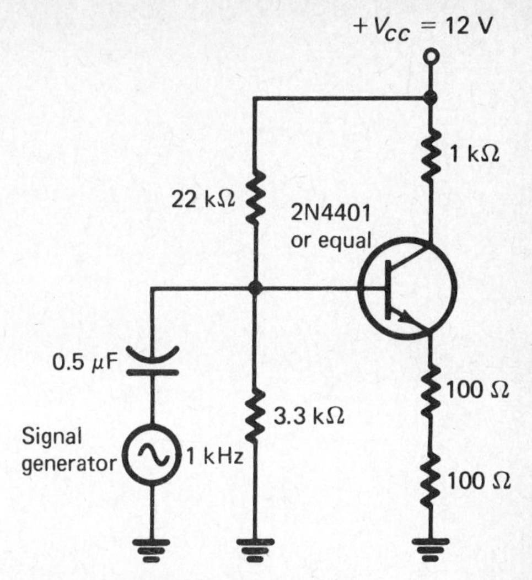

Fig. 6-8 β-independent circuit.

1. This part of the experiment concerns a small-signal amplifier designed to be relatively independent of β and temperature variations. Build the circuit shown in Fig. 6-8. Decrease the amplitude of the signal generator to zero.
2. Copy Table 6-1 onto a separate sheet of paper. Calculate and record all the values shown in the table. Use your multimeters to measure the values. Record them in Table 6-1. Any large error from a calculated value to a measured value should be investigated. Due to resistor tolerance, a 20 percent error is not considered large. Error of 40 percent may indicate a defective component. Refer to Table 6-1. Answer the following questions:
   a. Was β needed to solve this circuit for the dc conditions?
   b. Is the amplifier properly designed for linear operation?
   c. If V_{CE} had been near 0 V, where would the amplifier be operating?
   d. If V_{CE} had been near 12 V, where would the amplifier be operating?
3. Now measure voltage gain for the amplifier. Increase the amplitude of the signal generator until your oscilloscope shows a collector signal of 4 V peak-to-peak. The output signal should not be distorted. Measure the input signal on the base of the transistor. Answer the following questions:
   a. What is the voltage gain of the amplifier?

$$A_V = \frac{V_{out}}{V_{in}}$$

   b. Why is the voltage gain so low for this circuit?
4. Add an emitter bypass capacitor to the amplifier, as shown in Fig. 6-9. Adjust the signal-generator amplitude until the oscilloscope shows a collector signal of 4 V peak-to-peak. Measure the input signal on the base. Answer the following questions:
   a. What is the voltage gain of the amplifier?
   b. Why did the gain increase with the addition of C_E?
5. Change the emitter-bypass-capacitor connection, as shown in Fig. 6-10 on the next page. Adjust the signal-generator amplitude for a collector output of 4 V peak-to-peak. Measure the input signal on the base of the transistor. Answer the following questions:
   a. What is the voltage gain of the amplifier?
   b. Why did the gain increase when C_E was changed, as shown in Fig. 6-10?
6. Set up your oscilloscope to measure phase between the base and collector of the amplifier. If your oscilloscope has dual-trace operation, this mode will be good. If not, use the external-triggering input on the oscilloscope. Consult the oscilloscope manual for information.
7. Remove the emitter bypass capacitor from the circuit. Adjust the generator until the oscilloscope shows a collector signal of 4 V peak-to-peak. Note the phase of the base signal compared with the collector signal. Answer these questions:
   a. What is the configuration of this amplifier?
   b. What is the phase relationship from the base terminal to the collector terminal of the amplifier?

Table 6-1

	Calculated	Measured
V_B		
V_E		
I_E		
V_{RL}		
V_{CE}		

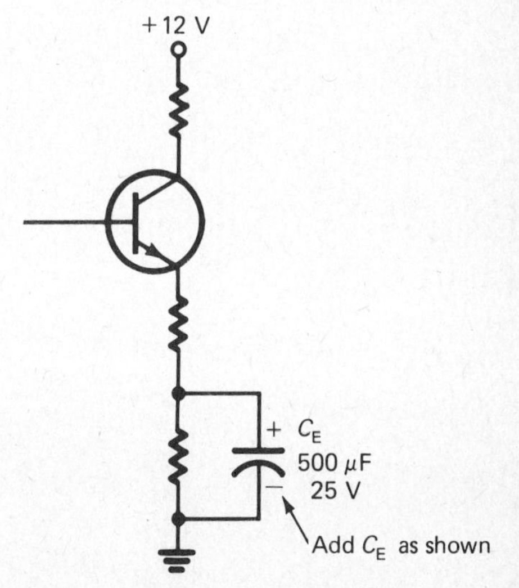

Fig. 6-9 Adding the emitter bypass capacitor.

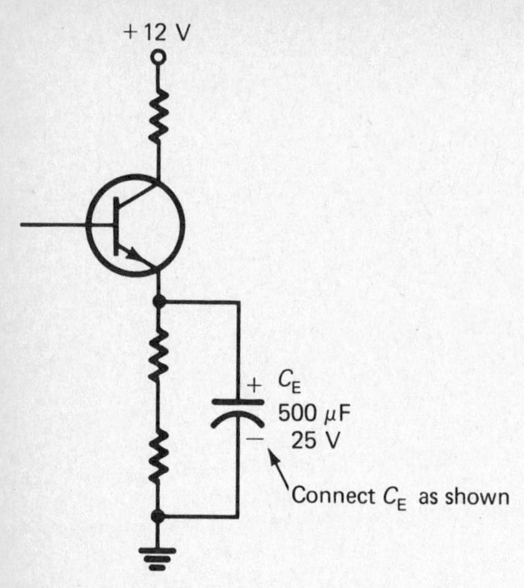

Fig. 6-10 Bypassing both emitter resistors.

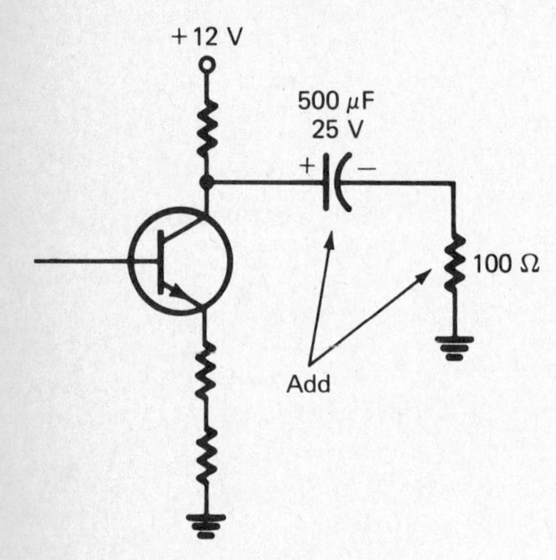

Fig. 6-11 Loading the amplifier.

c. What would have to be done to the amplifier to use a PNP transistor? You may set up a PNP circuit if time permits, using the 2N4403 transistor or equivalent.

8. This step of the experiment investigates loading effect on the common-emitter amplifier. Adjust the generator for a collector output of 4 V peak-to-peak. Add a 100-Ω load to the amplifier output and change the connection of the 500-μF capacitor, as shown in Fig. 6-11. Note that the collector signal drops to about 0.4 V peak-to-peak. The output impedance of a common-emitter amplifier is about equal to R_L (1 kΩ in this case). The 100-Ω resistor will cause a considerable loading effect on a signal source with an output impedance of 1 kΩ.

PROCEDURE

Part 3

1. This part of the experiment investigates the common-base and common-collector amplifier configurations. Build the circuit shown in Fig. 6-12. Answer the following questions:
   a. What is the configuration of this amplifier?
   b. What dc voltage drop can be expected across the emitter load resistor? (Measure it with your multimeter (or meter) and confirm your answer.)
2. Connect your oscilloscope across ground and the emitter terminal of the transistor. Adjust the output amplitude of the signal generator for a signal of 4 V peak-to-peak. Set up your oscilloscope to measure phase between the base of the transistor and the emitter. If your oscilloscope has dual-trace operation, this mode will work. If not, use the external-triggering input on the oscilloscope. Consult the oscilloscope manual for information.
3. Make careful measurements of the signal present at the emitter and base terminals of the amplifier. Note the amplitude and the phase. Answer the following questions:
   a. What is the voltage gain of the amplifier?
   b. What is the phase relationship from the base terminal to the emitter terminal of the amplifier?
   c. Could a PNP transistor be used in this circuit by making a change? (You may wish to verify this by substituting the 2N4403 transistor or equivalent.)

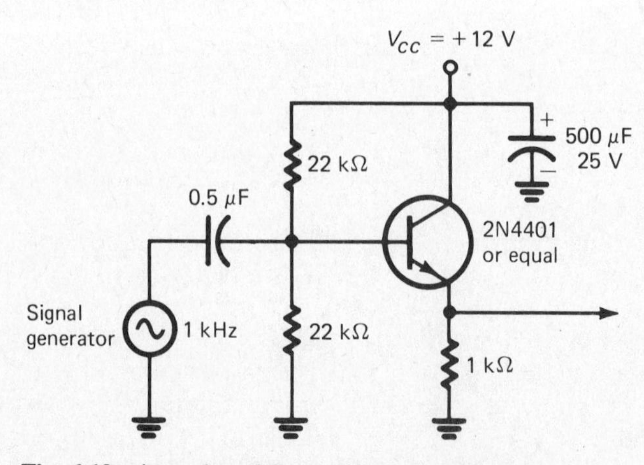

Fig. 6-12 An emitter follower (common collector).

4. Adjust the signal generator for an output signal of 500 mV peak-to-peak. Add a 100-Ω load and a 500-μF capacitor to the amplifier, as shown in Fig. 6-13. Note that the emitter signal changes very little. The output impedance of a common-collector amplifier can be much lower in value than the emitter load resistor. In this case, the amplifier output impedance is around 25 Ω. A 100-Ω resistor will cause only a slight loading effect on a signal source with an impedance of 25 Ω.
5. Construct the circuit shown in Fig. 6-14. Answer the following questions:
   a. What is the configuration of this amplifier?
   b. How will the dc voltage drops of this circuit compare with the amplifier shown in Fig. 6-8?
   c. How could a PNP transistor be used in this circuit?

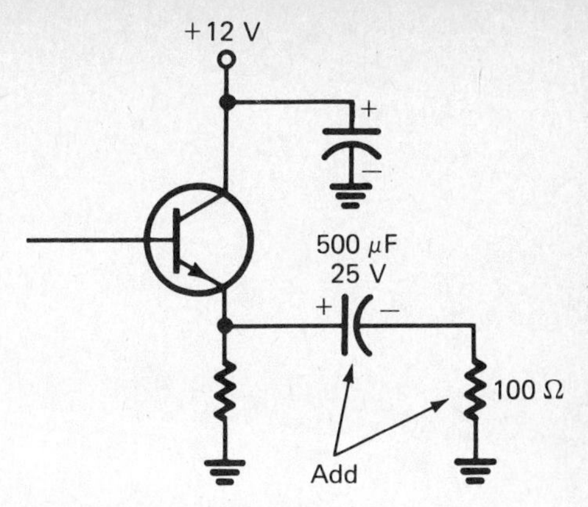

Fig. 6-13 Loading the emitter follower.

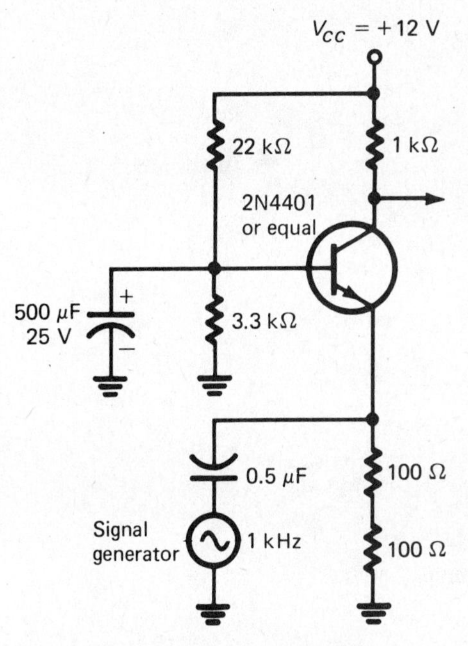

Fig. 6-14 A common-base amplifier.

6. Connect your oscilloscope across ground and the collector of the transistor. Adjust the amplitude of the signal generator for a collector signal of 4 V peak-to-peak. Make careful measurements of the signal at the emitter. Note the amplitude and the phase. Answer the following questions:
   a. What is the voltage gain of the amplifier?
   b. What is the phase relationship from the emitter to the collector of the transistor?
7. Check to see that the collector signal is still 4 V peak-to-peak. Load the amplifier as shown in Fig. 6-15 on the next page. Measure the collector signal again. Answer the following questions:
   a. What happens to the collector signal when the 100-Ω load is added to the amplifier?
   b. The output impedance of a common-base amplifier is roughly equal to the collector load (1 kΩ in this case). How does this help explain the loading effect of the 100-Ω resistor?

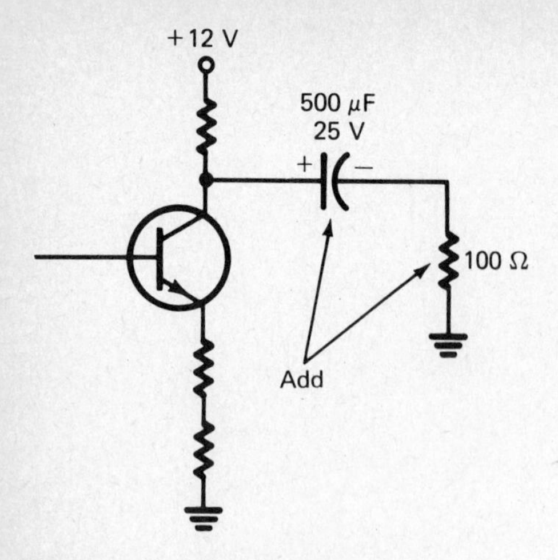

Fig. 6-15 Loading the common-base amplifier.

PROCEDURE

Part 4

1. An amplifier can be *tuned* to give maximum gain for one band of frequencies. Figure 6-16 shows a common-base amplifier that uses a parallel *LC* circuit as its collector load. The gain of this amplifier will be greatest at the frequency where the coil and the capacitor are resonant. Find this frequency:

$$f_r = \frac{1}{6.28\sqrt{LC}}$$

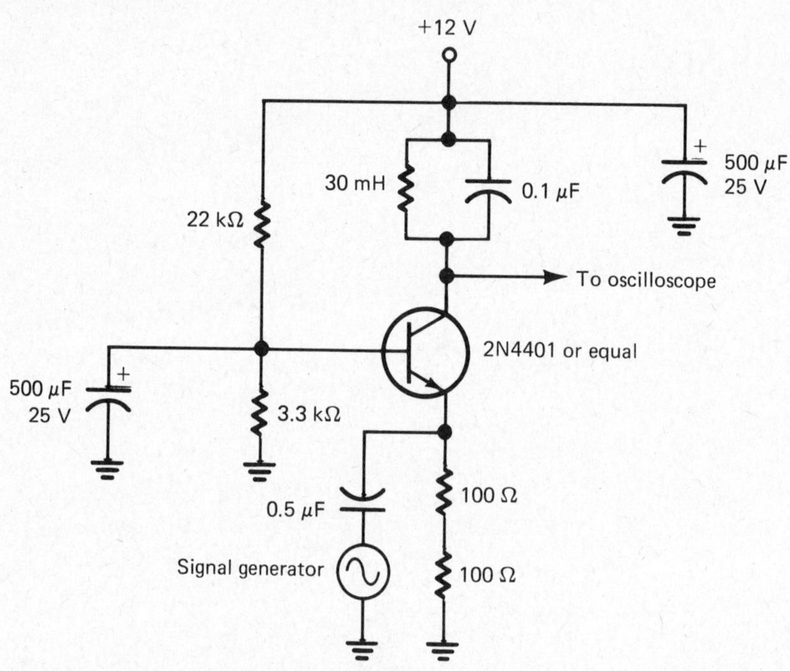

Fig. 6-16 Tuned common-base amplifier.

2. Build the circuit shown in Fig. 6-16, using the shortest leads possible. Amplifiers of this type have a tendency to become unstable, and short leads are less likely to cause problems. Connect the oscilloscope to the collector using a ÷10 probe. Set the generator to f_r and adjust its amplitude for an oscilloscope display of 6 V peak-to-peak. If you have a digital counter, connect it across the output of the generator for an accurate display of frequency. Now, rock the generator frequency dial back and forth until the amplifier output is maximum. The amplifier will show a definite peak in output at one frequency. Leave the frequency at the maximum point and reset the generator amplitude, if necessary, for a maximum output of 6 V peak-to-peak. Measure the *bandwidth* of the amplifier. This is the difference between the upper and lower cutoff frequencies. A cutoff frequency is where the output drops 3 dB from its maximum value. The oscilloscope will display 4.24 V peak-to-peak at the −3-dB (cutoff) points:

$$A_V = 20 \times \log\frac{4.24}{6} = -3\text{dB}$$

Find the two cutoff frequencies by adjusting generator frequency and watching the oscilloscope. The bandwidth is found by subtracting the lower frequency from the upper frequency.

$$BW = f_{high} - f_{low}$$

3. Figure 6-17 shows an example of a graph for plotting the gain of the tuned amplifier versus frequency. Make a copy of this graph. Note that the vertical axis is calibrated in decibels. You will have to measure both the base and collector ac signal voltages with your oscilloscope and use this formula:

$$A_{V(dB)} = 20 \times \log \frac{V_C}{V_B}$$

Be sure to measure the base voltage and not the generator voltage. This amplifier has a low input impedance, and the input coupling capacitor causes a substantial voltage drop. Complete the graph by changing the generator frequency and finding the decibel voltage gain for each point.

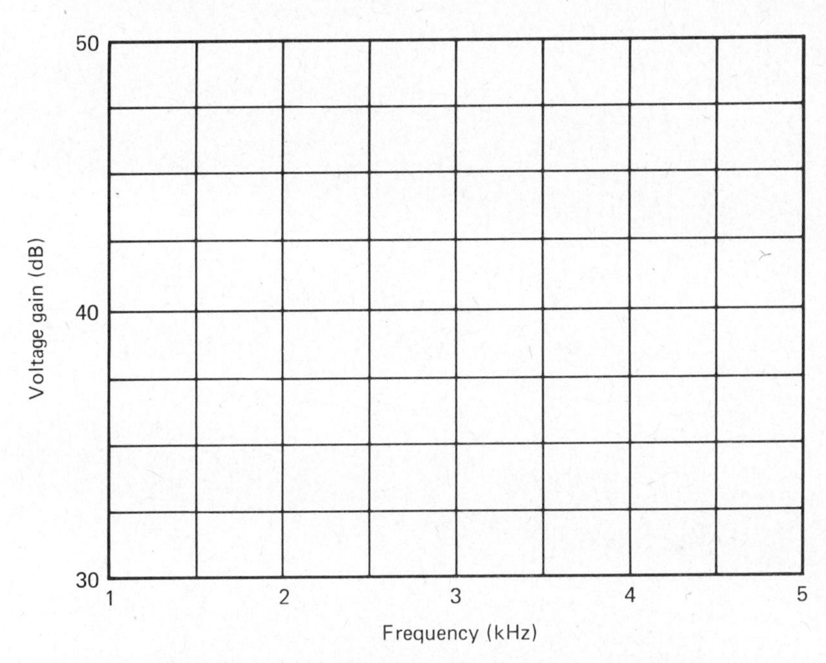

Fig. 6-17 Example of graph for plotting frequency response curve.

DISCUSSION TOPICS

1. Refer to Fig. 6-1. Suppose that C_C is shorted. The amplifier could be driven into saturation or cutoff, depending on the signal source. Why?
2. Refer to Fig. 6-2. Suppose that a germanium transistor were substituted. The amplifier is now going to operate closer to saturation. Why?
3. Refer to Fig. 6-4. Suppose that C_B is shorted. Where will the amplifier operate?
4. Refer to Fig. 6-8. Suppose that one of the 100-Ω resistors opens; V_C will measure 12 V. Why?
5. Refer to Fig. 6-12. In some cases the 500-μF capacitor in this circuit can be eliminated without affecting circuit operation. *It depends on the power supply.* Explain.

CHAPTER 7

More About Small-Signal Amplifiers

ACTIVITY 7-1
TEST: COUPLING, FETS, AND NEGATIVE FEEDBACK

Choose the letter that best completes the statement or answers the question.

Questions 1 to 7 refer to Fig. 7-1.

1. What type of coupling does the amplifier use?
   a. Direct
   b. Capacitive
   c. Transformer
   d. Resistance
2. The amplifier will provide gain for
   a. Both dc and ac signals
   b. Only dc signals
   c. Only ac signals
   d. None of the above
3. Which of the following is not a coupling capacitor?
   a. C_1
   b. C_2
   c. C_3
   d. C_4
4. The voltage across C_3 is
   a. 14 V
   b. 9 V
   c. 5 V
   d. 0 V
5. The C_3 is an electrolytic capacitor. The schematic shows it connected
   a. In the correct position and with correct polarity
   b. In the wrong position
   c. In the correct position but with reverse polarity
   d. None of the above
6. How will the amplifier perform if C_1 malfunctions and provides only a portion of its rated capacity?
   a. Poor high-frequency response
   b. Poor low-frequency response
   c. All signals will be distorted due to clipping
   d. There will be a large dc error in the second stage (Q_2)

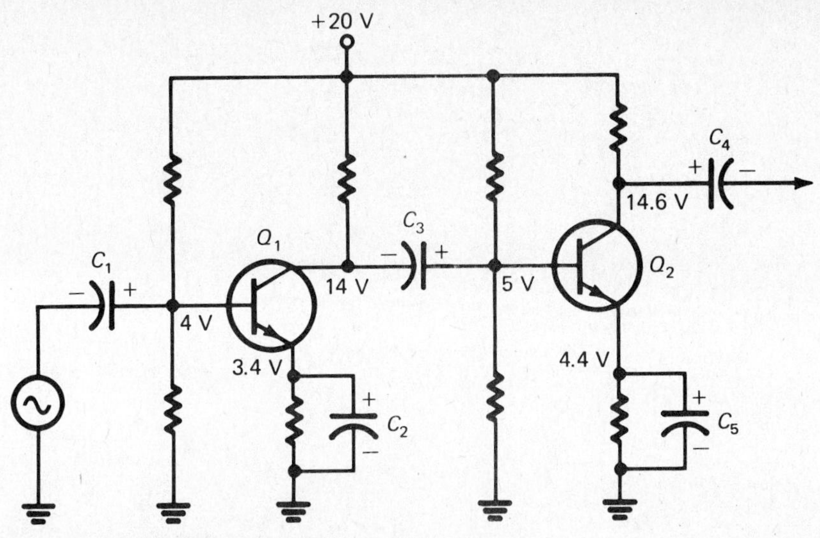

Fig. 7-1 Circuit for Questions 1 to 7.

7. What is the major function of C_5?
   a. Eliminates distortion
   b. Increases dc gain
   c. Increases ac gain
   d. All of the above
8. The Darlington connection is an example of
   a. Direct coupling
   b. Capacitive coupling
   c. Transformer coupling
   d. Resistive coupling
9. A direct-coupled amplifier will provide gain for
   a. Both dc and ac signals
   b. Only dc signals
   c. Only ac signals
   d. None of the above
10. Two transistors are Darlington-connected. The first one has a β of 50 and the second has a β of 100. What is their combined current gain?
   a. 50
   b. 150
   c. 500
   d. 5000

Questions 11 to 14 refer to Fig. 7-2 on the next page.

11. What type of coupling does the amplifier use?
   a. Direct
   b. Capacitive
   c. Transformer
   d. Resistive
12. The amplifier will provide gain for
   a. Both dc and ac signals
   b. Only dc signals
   c. Only ac signals
   d. None of the above

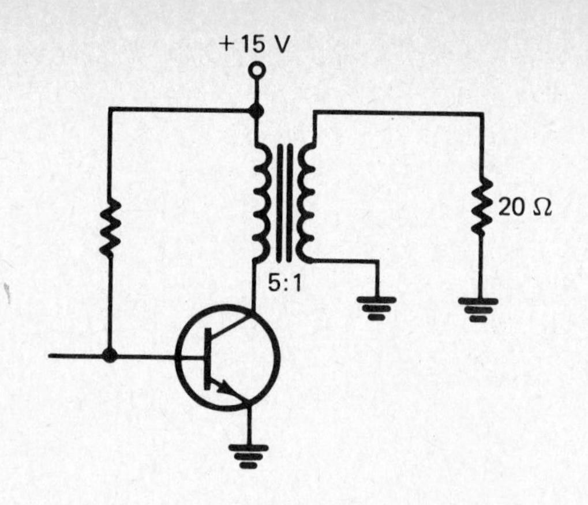

Fig. 7-2 Circuit for Questions 11 to 14.

13. The load seen by the collector of the transistor will be
    a. 0 Ω
    b. 20 Ω
    c. 100 Ω
    d. 500 Ω
14. Assume that the signal at the collector of the transistor is 30 V peak-to-peak. What will the signal across the 20-Ω load be?
    a. 150 V peak-to-peak
    b. 30 V peak-to-peak
    c. 6 V peak-to-peak
    d. 2.3 V peak-to-peak

Questions 15 to 17 refer to Fig. 7-3.

15. What is the input impedance of the amplifier?
    a. 100 Ω
    b. 2.9 kΩ
    c. 3.9 kΩ
    d. 27 kΩ

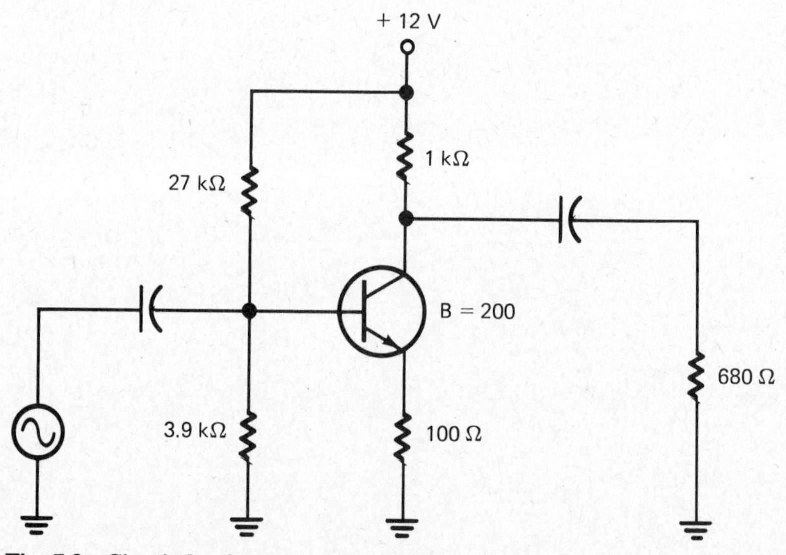

Fig. 7-3 Circuit for Questions 15 to 17.

16. The signal source has an internal impedence of 1 kΩ. If it develops 500 mV peak-to-peak open circuit (not loaded), what signal amplitude will it produce at the base of the transistor?
    a. 150 mV peak-to-peak
    b. 250 mV peak-to-peak
    c. 370 mV peak-to-peak
    d. 500 mV peak-to-peak
17. What is the voltage gain of the amplifier?
    a. 3.9
    b. 26
    c. 59
    d. 100

Questions 18 to 20 refer to Fig. 7-4.

18. What is the configuration of the amplifier?
    a. Common-source
    b. Common-drain
    c. Common-gate
    d. Source-follower
19. What is the function of the source bypass capacitor?
    a. To produce source bias
    b. To increase the bandwidth of the amplifier
    c. Both of the above
    d. None of the above
20. The V_S is
    a. 0.98 V
    b. 1.68 V
    c. 9.90 V
    d. 20.0 V
21. The V_{DS} is
    a. 0 V
    b. 5.00 V
    c. 8.42 V
    d. 10.0 V

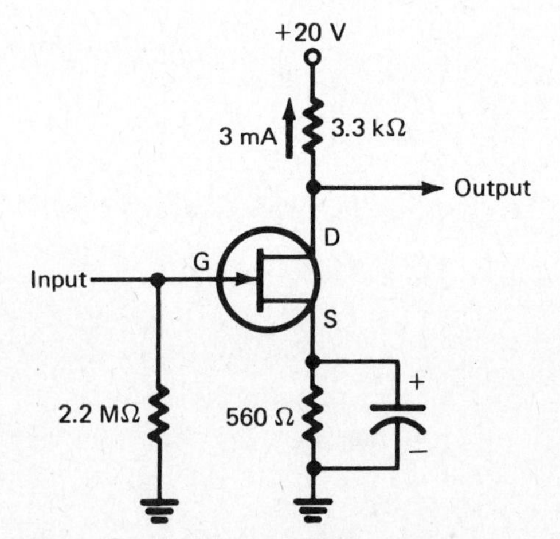

Fig. 7-4 Circuit for Questions 18 to 24.

Questions 22 to 24 refer to Fig. 7-4 on page 71.

22. The V_{GS} is
   a. 0 V
   b. −0.2 V
   c. −0.68 V
   d. −1.68 V

23. What is the polarity of the gate with respect to the source?
   a. Positive
   b. Negative
   c. Alternating
   d. No polarity (zero bias)

24. The transistor has a forward transfer admittance of 2 mS. What is the voltage gain of the amplifier?
   a. 6.6
   b. 12.9
   c. 33.0
   d. 100

25. Field-effect transistors are noted for
   a. High input impedance
   b. Low noise
   c. Good linearity
   d. All of the above

26. A transistor amplifier has some of its output signal fed back to its input. If the feedback acts to cancel a part of the input signal, it is considered
   a. Out-of-phase feedback
   b. Negative feedback
   c. Both of the above
   d. None of the above

27. A transistor common-emitter amplifier has signal feedback from its collector to its base. This feedback will
   a. Lower the voltage gain of the amplifier
   b. Increase the input impedance of the amplifier
   c. Increase the current gain of the amplifier
   d. Decrease the current gain of the amplifier

28. A transistor common-emitter amplifier has an unbypassed emitter resistor. The resulting feedback will
   a. Lower the voltage gain of the amplifier
   b. Increase the bandwidth of the amplifier
   c. Increase the input impedance of the amplifier
   d. All of the above

29. A feedback path in an amplifier uses two series resistors, and the junction of the resistors is bypassed to ground with a capacitor. The capacitor will
   a. Eliminate ac feedback
   b. Eliminate dc feedback
   c. Both of the above
   d. None of the above

30. The use of "dc only" feedback in an amplifier is generally used to
   a. Increase bandwidth
   b. Decrease noise and distortion
   c. Increase input impedance
   d. Stabilize the operating point

ACTIVITY 7-2
LAB EXPERIMENT: AMPLIFIER COUPLING, LOADING, AND FEEDBACK

PURPOSE

To analyze several coupling methods, loading, a common-source FET amplifier, and a negative-feedback amplifier.

MATERIALS

Qty.		*Qty.*	
1	multimeter	1	1-MΩ ½-W resistor
1	oscilloscope with ÷10 probe	1	100-kΩ 2-W linear potentiometer
1	audio-signal generator	2	0.1-μF paper or Mylar capacitors
1	0- to 15-V dc power supply	3	25-μF 15-V electrolytic capacitors
2	100-Ω ½-W resistors	2	2N4401 transistors or equivalent
3	1-kΩ ½-W resistors	1	2N4403 transistor or equivalent
1	1.2-kΩ ½-W resistor	1	2N4220 transistor or equivalent
1	2.7-kΩ ½-W resistor		
1	5.1-kΩ ½-W resistor		
1	10-kΩ ½-W resistor		
1	27-kΩ ½-W resistor		
1	47-kΩ ½-W resistor		

INTRODUCTION

This experiment demonstrates some important amplifier characteristics. Work carefully to obtain the best results. Double-check components and wiring before applying power to the circuits. Mistakes can cause damage. Consult your instructor before turning on the power if you are uncertain.

The work has been divided into four parts. Be sure to record all data and answer all questions before moving on to the next part. The parts may be performed out of sequence.

PROCEDURE

Part 1

NOTE: ***This part will give best results when the resistors are close to their nominal values. It is recommended that you measure the resistors with an accurate ohmmeter before building the circuit. Use the most accurate ones you can find.***

1. Figure 7-5 on the next page shows a two-stage capacitor-coupled amplifier. The input stage is at the left, and the output stage is at the right. Copy Table 7-1 onto a separate sheet of paper. Begin this part of the experiment by calculating the dc voltages listed in the table (V_B through V_C). Now, compare V_C for the input stage with V_B for the output stage.
   a. Which of the two is more positive?
   b. Calculate the value of the dc voltage drop across the coupling capacitor between the two stages.
   c. Is the polarity of the capacitor correct as shown in Fig. 7-5?

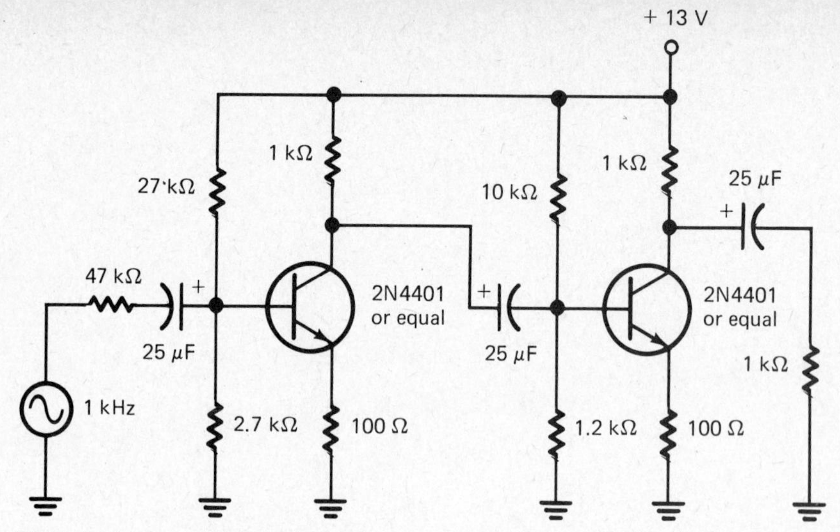

Fig. 7-5 Two-stage amplifier.

Table 7-1

	Input Stage		Output Stage	
	Calculated	Measured	Calculated	Measured
V_B				
V_E				
V_{R_L}				
V_{CE}				
V_C				
r_E		N.A.		N.A.
Z_{in}		N.A.		N.A.
A_V				

2. Build the circuit shown in Fig. 7-5 but don't connect the signal generator. Turn on the dc supply and adjust it for 13 V. Measure all the dc voltages and record them in your copy of Table 7-1. The calculated values and the measured values should agree within ±20 percent. Large errors may be due to improper wiring or component tolerance and must be investigated.

3. You may assume a β value of 200 for your transistors. Calculate and record the remaining values shown in Table 7-1 (r_E through A_V). Connect your oscilloscope to the amplifier output (the right-hand 1-kΩ resistor in Fig. 7-5). Set your signal generator for a 1-kHz sine-wave output and connect it to the input of the amplifier. Adjust the generator amplitude until the oscilloscope shows 6 V peak-to-peak. Note: The waveform should not be clipped. If it is, the dc conditions are out of tolerance. Measure and record the

voltage gain for both stages. Again, your calculated values should agree with your measured values. The overall gain in a multistage amplifier is the *product* of the individual gains.
a. Find the overall gain by multiplying the calculated gains.
b. Measure the overall gain by dividing the signal at the base of the input stage into 6 V peak-to-peak.

4. Set up your oscilloscope to compare the phase of the signals at the input and output of the second (output) stage. If your oscilloscope has dual-trace operation, this will work well. If not, set up for external triggering. Consult your oscilloscope manual for information.
a. What is the configuration of the output stage?
b. What is the phase relationship between input and output?
5. Repeat step 4 for the first (input) stage of your amplifier.
a. What is the configuration of the input stage?
b. What is the phase relationship between input and output?
6. If a signal is phase-inverted, it can be inverted a second time to put it back in phase (180° + 180° = 360° = 0°). Use your oscilloscope to compare the phase at the base of the input stage to the collector of the output stage.
a. What is the overall phase response of the amplifier?
7. The supply voltage for the experimental amplifier is 13 V. However, the maximum swing at the output stage will be less than 13 V peak-to-peak. This is due to the 1 k-Ω resistor that loads the output stage and the signal loss across the 100-Ω emitter resistor. Connect your oscilloscope to the collector of the output stage. Increase the generator amplitude until the signal is clipped on both positive and negative peaks.
a. What is the maximum peak-to-peak output swing?
8. A properly designed linear amplifier will start clipping at about the same time on positive and negative peaks. Vary the generator amplitude while watching the oscilloscope.
a. Is the clipping nearly symmetrical?
9. The oscilloscope should still be connected to the collector of the output transistor. Adjust the generator amplitude for a display of 6 V peak-to-peak. Now, disconnect the output coupling to the 1-kΩ resistor at the far right in Fig. 7-5. This unloads the amplifier.
a. What happens to the gain of the output stage?
b. Is the output signal distorted?
10. Restore the output coupling. The waveform should be back to normal. Now, short the capacitor that couples the input stage to the output stage by placing a jumper wire in parallel with it. This simulates a fault that sometimes occurs in capacitive-coupled amplifiers.
a. What happens to the output signal?
b. Why? (Hint: Measure V_{CE} of the the output stage.)

PROCEDURE

Part 2

1. Figure 7-6 on the next page shows a two-stage direct-coupled amplifier. The amplifier uses both an NPN and a PNP transistor to simplify biasing. Examine the circuit carefully and answer the following questions:
a. What is the configuration of transistor Q_1?
b. What is the configuration of transistor Q_2?
2. Build the circuit as shown in Fig. 7-6. The signal generator and coupling components will be connected later. Carefully set the 100-kΩ variable resistor for V_{CE} = 7.5 V measured at Q_2.

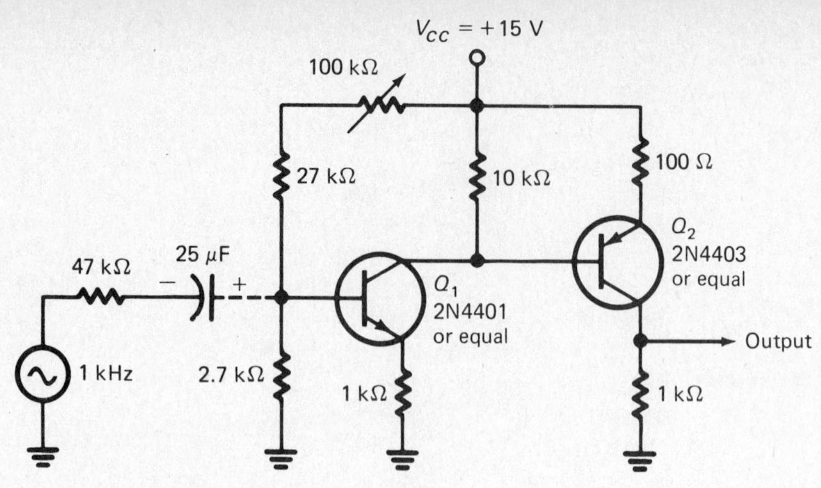

Fig. 7-6 Two-stage direct-coupled amplifier.

a. Does this operating point guarantee linear operation for the PNP transistor?
b. Why?
3. Measure all transistor terminal voltages. Copy Table 7-2 onto a separate sheet of paper and record all voltages. Refer to the voltages to answer the following questions:
a. Is the base-emitter bias of the NPN transistor near +0.6 V?
b. Is the base-emitter bias of the PNP transistor near −0.6 V?
c. Are both transistors biased properly for linear operation?
4. Use your voltmeter and monitor V_{CE} for Q_2. It should still be 7.5 V. Use a mild heat source to increase the temperature of Q_1 slightly. You may direct a stream of hot air from a vacuum desoldering tool onto the transistor or try touching the case of the transistor with your finger tip. This will raise the temperature a small amount if the room temperature is not too high. Another possibility is to cool the transistor a little using some freeze spray. Your instructor will tell you which method to try.
a. What happens to V_{CE} as the first transistor is heated or cooled?
b. What conclusion can you draw concerning the temperature stability of this circuit?
5. Refer to Fig. 7-6. Complete the signal-generator connection. Adjust the amplitude of the generator until the output of the direct-coupled amplifier is 8 V peak-to-peak as measured with your oscilloscope.
a. Is the output signal a good replica of the input?
b. What is the amplitude of the input signal to Q_1?
c. What is the overall voltage gain of the amplifier?
6. Set up your oscilloscope to compare the phase of the signal at various points in the amplifier. If your oscilloscope has dual-trace operation, this will work. If not, set up for external triggering. Consult your oscilloscope manual for information.
a. What is the phase relationship from the base of Q_1 to the collector of Q_2?
b. Why?
c. What is the voltage gain of the first stage?
d. What is the voltage gain of the second stage?
e. Is the overall gain equal to the product of the individual gains?
7. Increase the amplitude of the signal generator until the output signal just begins to show signs of clipping. This should be a signal level of just below 15 V peak-to-peak. Now, monitor the output sig-

Table 7-2

	Q_1 (V)	Q_2 (V)
V_B		
V_E		
V_C		

nal with the oscilloscope and raise the temperature of the NPN transistor slightly. What happens to the positive signal peaks as the temperature increases?

PROCEDURE

Part 3

1. Build the circuit shown in Fig. 7-7. The 25-μF source bypass capacitor will be added later. Decrease the amplitude of the signal generator to zero. Use your voltmeter and answer the following questions:
   a. What is the voltage drop across the source resistor?
   b. What is the voltage across the gate and source terminals?
   c. What is the polarity of the gate with respect to the source?
   d. What is this type of bias called?

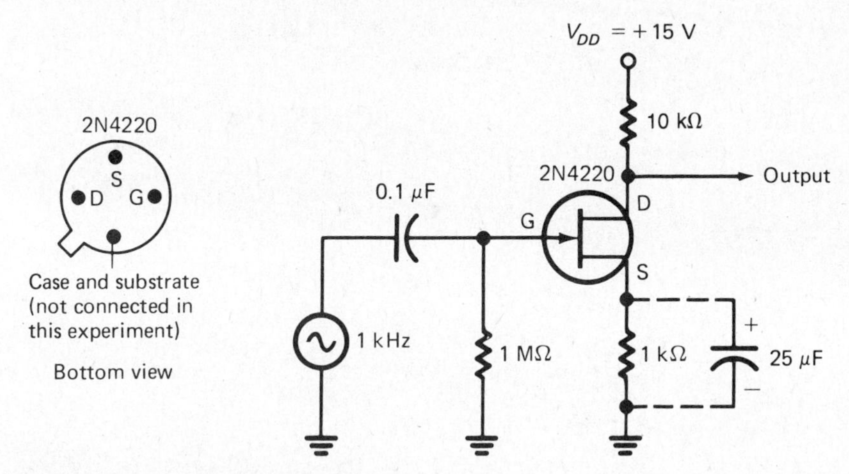

Fig. 7-7 Common-source amplifier.

2. Increase the amplitude of the signal generator until the amplifier output signal measures 8 V peak-to-peak on your oscilloscope. Set up the oscilloscope to compare phase at the input and output of the amplifier. Use dual-trace operation or external triggering. Consult your oscilloscope manual for information.
   a. With the amplifier output at 8 V peak-to-peak, what is the amplitude of the input signal?
   b. What is the voltage gain of the amplifier?
   c. What is the phase relationship of the input and output signals?
3. Add the source bypass capacitor as shown in Fig. 7-7. Adjust the amplitude of the signal generator so that the output signal from the amplifier is once again 8 V peak-to-peak.
   a. What is the amplitude of the input signal?
   b. What is the voltage gain of the amplifier?
   c. The voltage gain of a common-source FET amplifier is set by the transistor's forward transfer admittance and the load resistor. If Y_{fs} = 2.2 mS, calculate the voltage gain for the amplifier of Fig. 7-7

$$A_V = Y_{fs} \times R_L$$

   d. Does the voltage gain of step 3b agree reasonably well with the gain of step 3c?

4. Note the setting of the amplitude control on the signal generator. Disconnect one end of the gate resistor (the 1-MΩ resistor). Monitor the output signal of the amplifier with the oscilloscope. Turn the amplitude of the signal generator all the way up and then return it to its original setting.
   a. What happens to the output signal?
   b. Reconnect the gate resistor. Is the output signal restored?
   c. What has happened?

PROCEDURE

Part 4

1. Build the circuit shown in Fig. 7-8. Do not connect the feedback path until you are instructed to do so. Monitor the output signal from the amplifier with your oscilloscope. Adjust the amplitude of the signal generator for an output signal of 8 V peak-to-peak. The frequency of the signal generator should be 10 kHz.

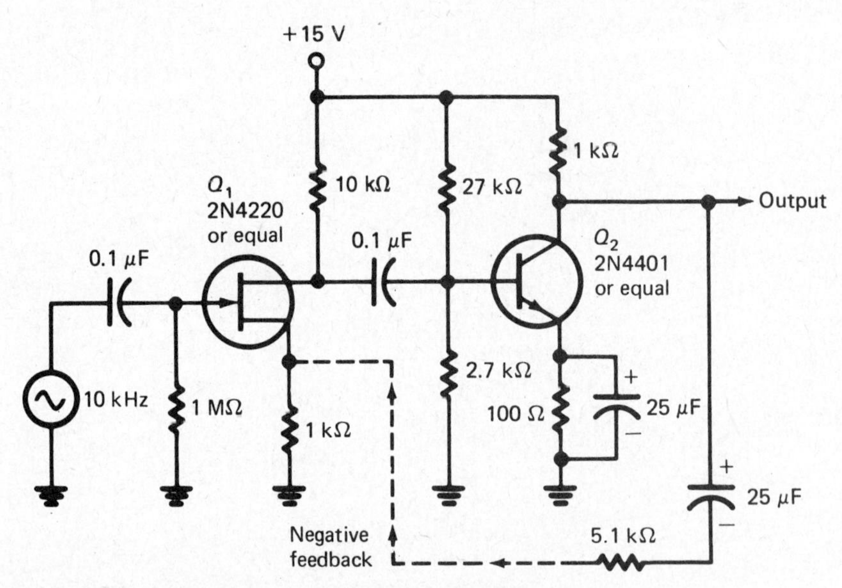

Fig. 7-8 Two-stage amplifier with negative feedback.

2. This amplifier is going to be tested for its frequency response. We want to know over what range the circuit gain is nearly constant. Generally, the bandpass of an amplifier is specified over the range where the gain does not drop more than 3 dB. A 3-dB loss of gain in this circuit will show up as a decrease in signal output from 8 to 5.6 V peak-to-peak. Keep increasing the frequency output of the signal generator until the oscilloscope shows that the output signal is down to 5.6 V peak-to-peak. This frequency is the high-frequency cutoff point of the amplifier f_{high}. Of course, the amplitude of the generator signal must be constant as this test is being made. Then, keep reducing the frequency output of the generator until the output signal is again down to 5.6 V peak-to-peak. This marks the low-frequency cutoff point of the amplifier f_{low}. Copy Table 7-3 onto a separate sheet of paper and record your results.

Table 7-3

	f_{high} (Hz)	f_{low} (Hz)
Without feedback		
With feedback		

3. Complete the feedback path as shown in Fig. 7-8. The signal-generator amplitude should be as it was, and the frequency should be 10 kHz.
   a. The output amplitude was 8 V peak-to-peak. What is it now?
   b. What does the negative feedback do to the amplifier gain?
4. Restore the amplifier output to 8 V peak-to-peak by increasing the generator amplitude. Now repeat the frequency-response test with negative feedback. The upper frequency f_{high} is going to be very high with feedback. If it is beyond the range of your signal generator, you will have to use a signal source capable of reaching several megahertz. Record the results in Table 7-3.
   a. What happens to f_{low} with negative feedback?
   b. What happens to f_{high} with negative feedback?
   c. What does negative feedback do to the bandwidth of an amplifier? Refer to Fig. 7-9. It shows graphically how the feedback affects the amplifier bandpass.

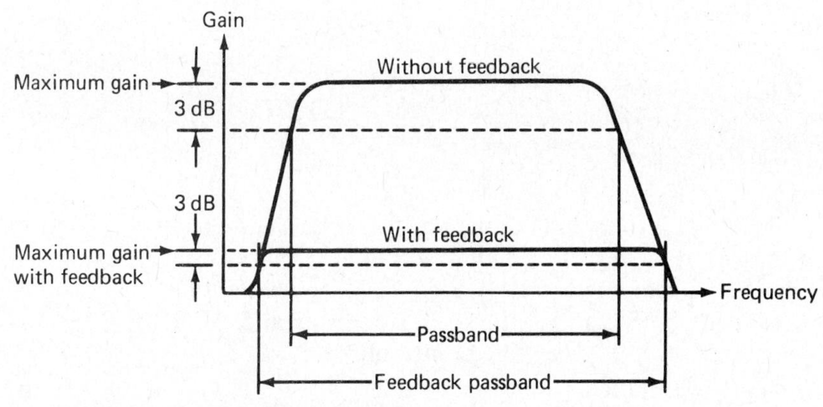

Fig. 7-9 How feedback affects bandpass.

5. You can investigate another important aspect of negative feedback by feeding a triangle wave into the amplifier. The straight sides of the triangle make it very easy to see amplifier distortion. If your generator is capable of generating triangle waveforms, examine the output of the amplifier carefully with and without negative feedback. In each case, adjust the amplitude for an output signal from the amplifier of 8 V peak-to-peak. Does the negative feedback reduce the distortion in the triangle wave?
6. If your signal generator is capable of square-wave output, you can make another test. Figure 7-10(*a*) shows that a square wave will tilt at the top and bottom if the amplifier has poor low-frequency

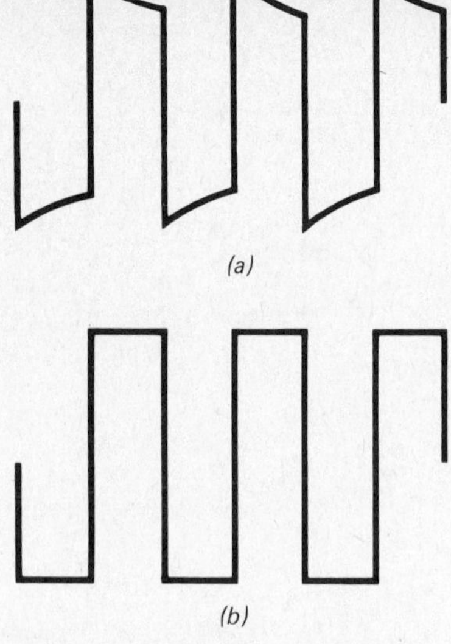

Fig. 7-10 Amplifier square-wave response.

response. Figure 7-10(*b*) shows a perfect square-wave response. Feed a 5-kHz square-wave signal into the amplifier and monitor the output with your oscilloscope. In each case (with and without feedback) adjust the amplitude for an output signal of 8 V peak-to-peak from the amplifier. Does the negative feedback improve the square-wave response of the amplifier?

ACTIVITY 7-3 CONSTRUCTION PROJECT: WIDEBAND VOLTMETER

INTRODUCTION

The wide-band voltmeter can be very valuable for high-frequency circuit analysis and troubleshooting. The performance of most ac voltmeters drops off rapidly at the higher frequencies. This instrument will allow relative measurements well into the RF spectrum.

The voltmeter is not intended for making absolute measurements of RF voltages. Such instruments are complex and expensive. This is a simple device, yet it is useful since often we need know only whether a signal is present or absent in a circuit. It is also very useful for circuit alignment.

Figure 7-11 shows the performance of the voltmeter. The 3-dB bandwidth ranges from 8 kHz to 10 MHz. The midband sensitivity is 10 mV peak-to-peak for full-scale meter deflection. Of course, the voltmeter is useful at frequencies beyond the −3-dB point at reduced sensitivity. For example, at 75 MHz the sensitivity is −30 dB. This means that a 75-MHz signal will have to be +30 dB over 10 mV to give a full-scale meter reading. This translates to a signal level of 300 mV peak-to-peak.

CAUTION! ***Be very careful around high-voltage circuits. They can be dangerous. High-power transmitters can also be dangerous. Consult with your instructor before attempting any measurements.***

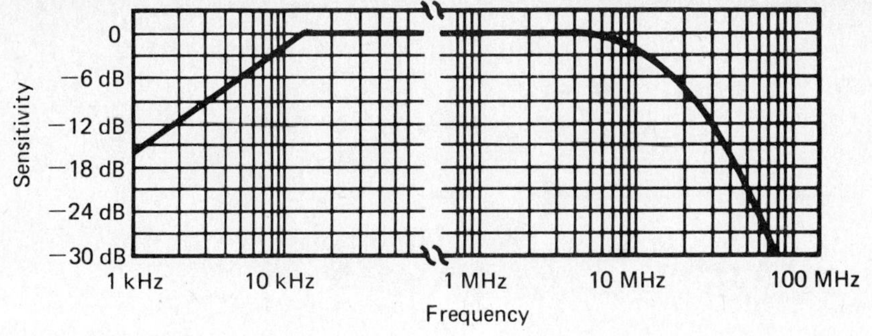

0 dB = 10 mV peak-to-peak

Fig. 7-11 Wideband-voltmeter performance.

Parts List

Part Numbers	Description
B_1	9-V Eveready 1222 battery or equivalent
C_1	0.02-μF 50-V ceramic capacitor
C_2–C_6	4.7-μF 15-V tantalum capacitor
C_3–C_5, C_7	0.1-μF 50-V ceramic capacitor
C_8	0.05-μF 50-V ceramic capacitor
D_1	IN914 (IN4148) diode
R_1	3.3-MΩ ¼-W 10% resistor
R_2	2.2-MΩ ¼-W 10% resistor
R_3	220-Ω ¼-W 10% resistor
R_4	1-kΩ ¼-W 10% resistor
R_5	120-Ω ¼-W 10% resistor
R_6, R_8	4.7-kΩ resistors
R_7, R_9	470-Ω resistors
R_{11}	680-Ω resistor
R_{10}	10-kΩ ½-W linear potentiometer
S_1	SPST switch (part of R_{10})
Q_1	MPF102 FET
Q_1, Q_2	2N5179 transistors
J_1	BNC connector
M_1	100-μA meter
Misc.	Cabinet, wire, hardware, battery clip, knob, circuit board

Figure 7-12 on the next page is the schematic diagram for the voltmeter. The first amplifier, Q_1, is a common-drain FET configuration. This gives the voltmeter a reasonably high input impedance. The voltmeter can be used in conjunction with a ÷10 oscilloscope probe to minimize circuit-loading effects. Most standard oscilloscope probes designed for an instrument impedance of 1 MΩ will work well. Do not forget that the probe will reduce the sensitivity of the voltmeter 10 times (20 dB).

Referring again to Fig. 7-12, we see that Q_2 and Q_3 are both common-emitter amplifiers. This is where the voltage gain is developed. Capacitor C_7 couples the output of Q_3 to a simple half-wave rectifying and metering circuit. Note that the sensitivity is adjustable with potentiometer R_{10}. This makes it possible to use the voltmeter when the signal level is greater than the fullscale sensitivity of the meter. In practice, R_{10} is set at *minimum* sensitivity and then advanced until a usable reading is obtained.

The wide-band voltmeter circuit draws about 34 mA from the bat-

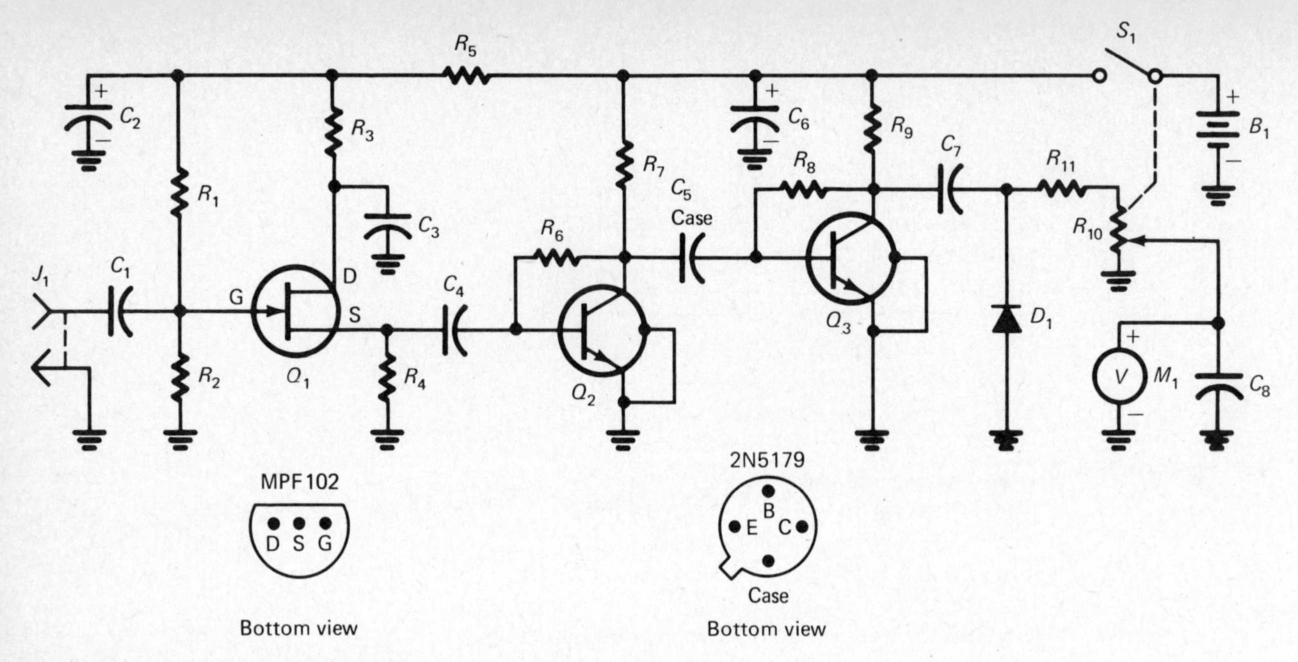

Fig. 7-12 Wideband-voltmeter schematic.

tery. An alkaline-type battery is suggested if the voltmeter is to be used often. Do not leave the voltmeter turned on between measurements, as this will shorten its life.

The usefulness of the voltmeter can be extended by building an RF coupling coil, as shown on the next page in Fig. 7-13. This will allow the voltmeter to operate as an RF *sniffer.* When the coupling coil is brought near an active RF coil, the meter will deflect. This will not work on toroid-type coils since they have very little external field to couple to the sniffer coil. Nor will it work on coils with low-level RF signals, found in some receiver circuits. It is mainly useful in transmitters, oscillators, or any circuit where strong signals are expected.

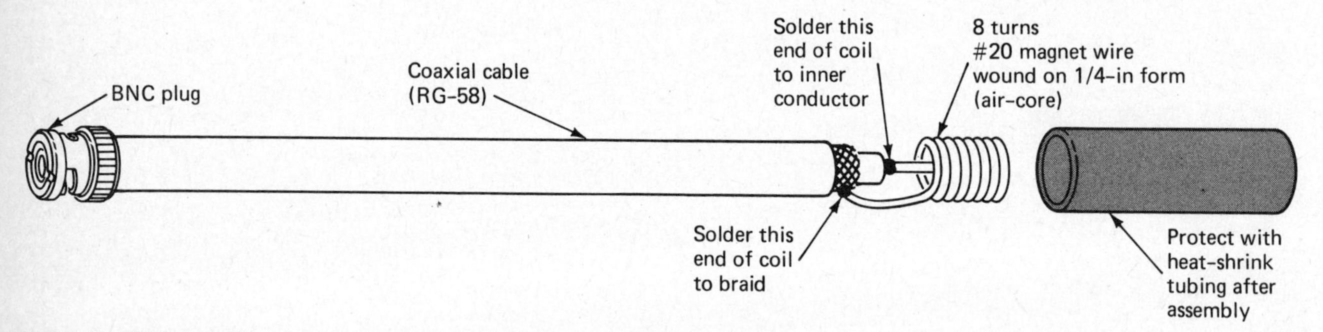

Fig. 7-13 Pick-up coil.

CONSTRUCTION DETAILS

Good layout and construction practices are required for building this project. The amplifier will become unstable and the voltmeter will be useless if the layout is not well designed. A circuit board is strongly recommended. It is not necessary to etch a circuit board. Pad-cutting tools (made by Vector and others) make it possible to fabricate good high-frequency circuits quickly. The important part of this technique is the ground-plane effect of the board, which helps ensure the stability of the amplifier.

If you do decide to design and etch your own board, remember the *ground plane.* Leave as much copper on the board as possible. Also make sure that the copper ground completely surrounds the other circuit traces.

Lay the circuit out *in a straight line.* Keep the input connector and the first amplifier as far away as possible from the final amplifier and the metering circuit. This reduces unwanted feedback to a minimum. It may be necessary to place a small grounded metal shield between the first and second amplifiers. Be very careful about using substitute transistors. Substitutions may produce inferior performance.

The cabinet suggested in the parts list will work only if miniature components and a compact layout are used. It may be best to buy the cabinet last. This will ensure easy assembly.

When the circuit is wired, measure the total current drain. It should be near 34 mA. Any large error here may mean a wiring error or a defective component. If the current is normal, advance the sensitivity control. There should be no reading on the meter. A reading with no input signal usually indicates that the amplifier is unstable.

As with any instrument, experience will make the meter readings more meaningful. Try injecting various signals into the voltmeter. Use it with various pieces of equipment to see where it is possible to detect high-frequency signals.

CHAPTER 8

Large-Signal Amplifiers

ACTIVITY 8-1
TEST: LARGE-SIGNAL AMPLIFIERS

Choose the letter that best completes the statement or answers the question.

1. A certain amplifier delivers 4 W of signal power while drawing 0.6 A from a 12-V power supply. What is the efficiency of the amplifier?
   a. 80 percent
   b. 76 percent
   c. 56 percent
   d. 33 percent
2. An amplifier is 25 percent efficient and is capable of delivering up to 100 W of output power. What is the most power it will take from its power supply?
   a. 400 W
   b. 300 W
   c. 200 W
   d. 100 W
3. Which amplifier class has a conduction angle of 360°?
   a. A
   b. B
   c. C
   d. AB
4. Which amplifier class has a conduction angle of 180°?
   a. A
   b. B
   c. C
   d. AB
5. The current a certain amplifier draws from its power supply varies as the signal level changes. This amplifier cannot be operating class
   a. A
   b. B
   c. C
   d. AB

6. What determines amplifier class?
   a. The output transformer
   b. The number of transistors used
   c. V_{CC}
   d. Base-emitter bias
7. An amplifier delivers a 40-V peak-to-peak sine wave across a 10-Ω load. What is the rms power delivered to the load?
   a. 100 W
   b. 60 W
   c. 20 W
   d. 5 W
8. What is the maximum theoretical efficiency for a transformer-coupled class A amplifier?
   a. 15 percent
   b. 25 percent
   c. 50 percent
   d. 65 percent
9. A class A amplifier is driven with a *very small* signal. The efficiency will be
   a. Very poor
   b. Moderate
   c. High
   d. Very high
10. A class A power amplifier has a transformer-coupled output. What is the maximum peak-to-peak swing across the load assuming a 12:1 step-down ratio and a 35-V power supply?
    a. 5.83 V
    b. 11.67 V
    c. 35.00 V
    d. 70.00 V
11. How much current will a class B push-pull amplifier take from the power supply when there is no input signal driving the amplifier?
    a. None
    b. About 10 percent of its maximum current drain
    c. Depends on V_{CC}
    d. Depends on V_{CC} *and* R_L
12. When are both transistors in a push-pull class B amplifier conducting at the same time?
    a. At the beginning of a positive-going input signal
    b. At the end of a positive-going input signal
    c. When the input signal goes negative
    d. Never
13. What is the biggest drawback for using class B push-pull in audio work?
    a. Crossover distortion
    b. Transistors must handle a large power dissipation
    c. Very large heat sinks are required
    d. A large power supply is required
14. Which class of amplifier has the least distortion?
    a. A
    b. B
    c. C
    d. AB

15. Crossover distortion is most noticeable at
   a. High volume levels
   b. Low volume levels
   c. Zero volume level
   d. None of the above

Questions 16 through 20 refer to Fig. 8-1.

16. An oscilloscope shows that the top of the secondary of T_1 is driven positive by the input signal. This will
   a. Increase conduction in Q_2
   b. Increase conduction in Q_1
   c. Increase conduction in Q_1 and Q_2
   d. Shut off both transistors

17. Transformer T_2 would be called
   a. A driver transformer
   b. An isolation transformer
   c. An output transformer
   d. A power transformer

18. Resistor R_1 opens (develops infinite resistance). The result will be
   a. That Q_1 will run hot
   b. That Q_2 will run hot
   c. Both of the above
   d. Crossover distortion

19. Capacitor C_1 shorts (develops zero resistance). The result will be
   a. That T_2 burns out from excessive current flow
   b. That the power-supply fuse will blow
   c. No audio output to the speaker
   d. Crossover distortion

20. The transistors are running very hot. The problem might be that
   a. Resistor R_2 is open
   b. The transistors are open
   c. The speaker is open
   d. Transformer T_2 has an open center tap

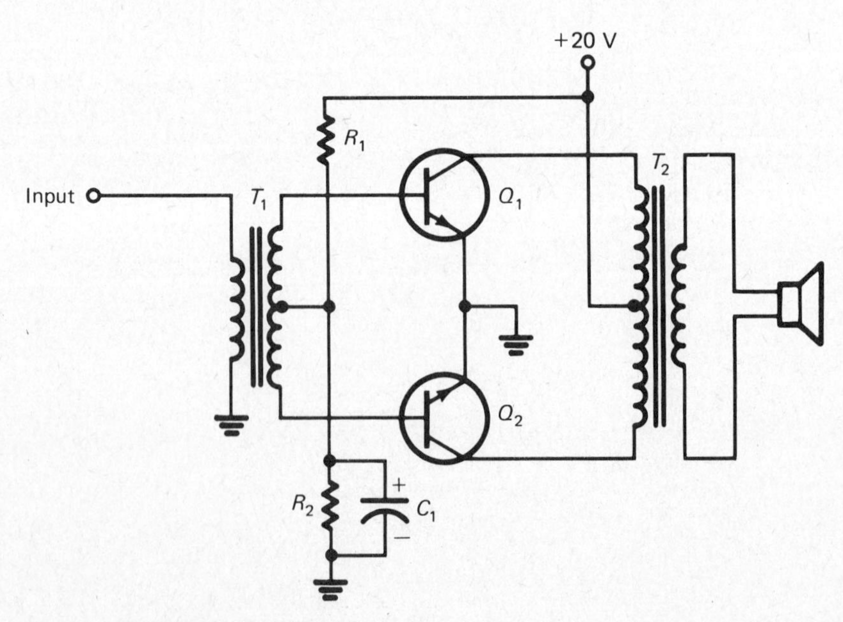

Fig. 8-1 Circuit for Questions 16 to 20.

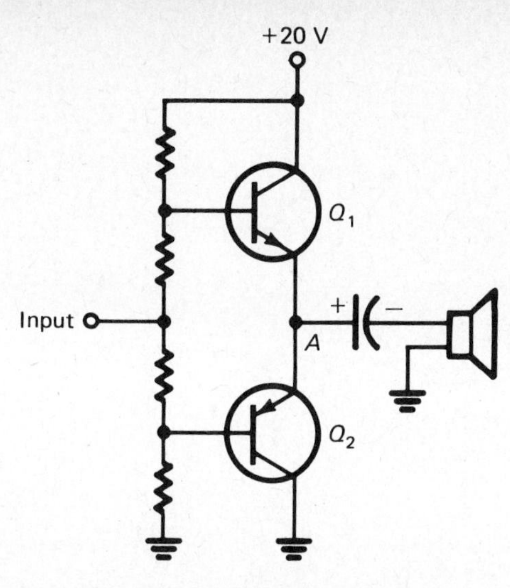

Fig. 8-2 Circuit for Questions 21 to 25.

Questions 21 to 25 refer to Fig. 8-2.

21. The amplifier shown is
   a. Transformer-coupled
   b. Complementary symmetry
   c. Push-pull common-emitter
   d. All of the above

22. If the input signal is positive-going
   a. Point *A* will be negative-going
   b. Point *A* will be positive-going
   c. Transistor Q_1 will be turning off
   d. Transistor Q_2 will be turning on harder

23. What is the configuration of Q_1 and Q_2?
   a. Common-emitter
   b. Common-base
   c. Emitter-follower
   d. None of the above

24. Because of age, the capacitor loses most of its capacity. The symptom will be
   a. Crossover distortion
   b. Transistor Q_2 will run hot
   c. Transistor Q_1 will be destroyed
   d. Poor low-frequency response

25. There is no input signal. A voltmeter shows point *A* resting at 0 V.
   a. This is normal with no signal
   b. Transistor Q_1 may be shorted from collector to emitter
   c. Transistor Q_2 may be shorted from collector to emitter
   d. The speaker is burned out

26. Which amplifier class has the smallest conduction angle?
   a. A
   b. B
   c. C
   d. AB

27. Why do class C amplifiers often use tank circuits?
   a. To forward-bias the base-emitter junction
   b. To restore the sine-wave signal
   c. To reverse-bias the base-emitter junction
   d. To decrease the conduction angle

28. A tank circuit uses a 220-pF capacitor in parallel with a 1-μH coil. What is its resonant frequency?
   a. 455 kHz
   b. 10.7 MHz
   c. 21.3 MHz
   d. 30 MHz

ACTIVITY 8-2
LAB EXPERIMENT: AMPLIFIER CLASSES

PURPOSE

To study the characteristics of different classes of amplifiers and several large-signal amplifier circuits.

MATERIALS

Qty.	
2	multimeters
1	oscilloscope with ÷10 probe
1	audio-signal generator
1	8-Ω loudspeaker
1	dc power supply, variable to 15 V
1	4.7-Ω ½-W resistor
2	10-Ω ½-W resistors
1	33-Ω ½-W resistor
2	100-Ω ½-W resistors
2	1-kΩ ½-W resistors
2	10-kΩ ½-W resistors
1	18-kΩ ½-W resistor
1	500-kΩ 2-W linear-taper potentiometer
1	0.05-μF paper or Mylar capacitor

Qty.	
1	0.5-μF paper or Mylar capacitor
1	25-μF 15-V, electrolytic capacitor
1	500-μF 25-V, electrolytic capacitor
2	2N4401 transistors or equivalent
1	2N4403 transistor or equivalent
1	30-mH RF choke (not critical)
1	transistor-type output transformer
1	transistor-type driver transformer

INTRODUCTION

This experiment has been designed to emphasize the important concepts of the various classes of amplification. It also provides experience with power amplifiers. Work carefully to obtain the best understanding possible. Check all connections and polarities before turning on the power. Mistakes can damage components. When in doubt, ask your instructor.

The experiment is divided into four parts. Be sure to record all data and answer the questions before moving to the next part. The parts need not be completed in any particular order.

PROCEDURE

Part 1

1. Construct the circuit shown in Fig. 8-3. Set the meter to a 100-mA dc current range and connect as shown. The meter will be switched to a 10-mA range later. Be sure the transformer is *the output transformer.* The center-tap connection will not be used in this part of the experiment.
2. Turn the amplitude of the signal generator all the way down to zero. Adjust the 500-kΩ potentiometer for a meter reading of about 8 mA. Now, switch the meter to the 10-mA range for better accuracy.

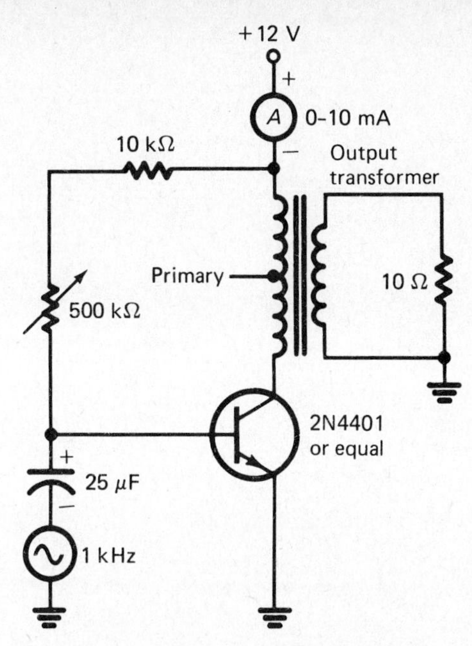

Fig. 8-3 Transformer-coupled amplifier.

3. Connect your oscilloscope across ground and the collector of the transistor. Slowly increase the amplitude of the input signal until a collector signal of about 4 V peak-to-peak is noted on the oscilloscope. Is the collector signal a good replica of the input signal?
4. Continue increasing the amplitude until the collector wave shows signs of clipping. (Clipping in a transformer-coupled amplifier may appear a little different from the clipped waveforms you have seen. If the clipping or distortion is not appearing at the top and bottom of the waveform in equal fashion, try a slight adjustment of the 500-kΩ potentiometer. This will help you select the optimum *Q* point for your amplifier.)
   a. What is the maximum peak-to-peak collector swing when the clipping just begins?
   b. Why is the collector swing greater than the power supply voltage?
5. Decrease the amplitude until the clipping stops. Measure the swing across the collector and ground. Now move your oscilloscope probe to the top of the 10-Ω load resistor. Why is the signal across the load smaller than the collector signal?
6. Watch the millammeter closely and decrease the amplitude to zero.
   a. What happens to the current?
   b. Does the above observation prove class A operation?
7. Remove the 10-Ω resistor and connect an 8-Ω loudspeaker in its place. Increase the amplitude until a comfortable tone level is heard. Turn off the power. Be careful not to change any control settings, and take the transformer out of the circuit. Connect the speaker in place of the transformer primary. Turn the power back on. What happens to volume or level of the tone? Why?

PROCEDURE

Part 2

1. Build the circuit shown in Fig. 8-4. Do *not* connect the 18-kΩ

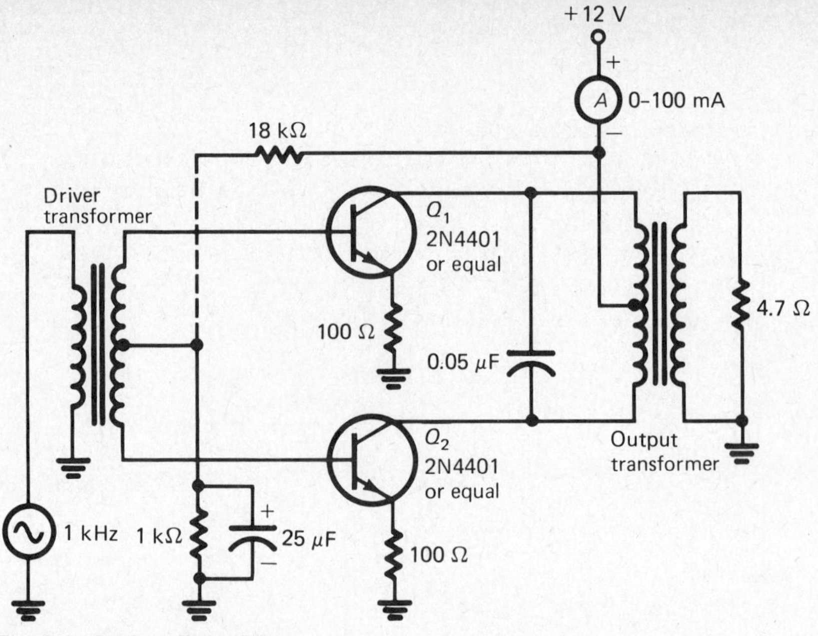

Fig. 8-4 Push-pull amplifier.

resistor yet. It will be connected later. Be sure to use the correct transformers. The driver transformer is different from the output transformer. Set your meter for 100 mA dc and connect as shown. Make sure the amplitude of the signal generator is turned all the way down. Turn on the power. How much current does the amplifier draw at zero signal level? Why?

2. Connect your oscilloscope across the 4.7-Ω load resistor. Set it for high vertical sensitivity (about 0.01 V/div). Slowly increase the amplitude of the signal generator until about 4 divisions (0.4 V peak-to-peak with the probe) are seen on the scope.
   a. Is the signal a good replica of the input? Why?
   b. What happened to the milliammeter reading? Why?
3. Increase the amplitude until the oscilloscope shows an output signal of about 8 divisions.
   a. Is the distortion worse or better? Why?
   b. What happened to the milliammeter reading? Why?
4. Observe the output waveform and disconnect either of the transistor base leads. Observe the effect on the waveform. Reconnect it and then disconnect the other base lead. Again observe the effect on the waveform. What happens to the output waveform? Why?
5. Reduce the amplitude of the signal generator to zero. Connect the 18-kΩ resistor as shown in Fig. 8-4. What happens to the milliammeter reading? Why?
6. Increase the amplitude of the signal generator for an output of about 4 divisions on the oscilloscope.
   a. How does the output signal look compared with the signal obtained with the 18-kΩ resistor disconnected?
   b. How does the current drain compare with previous readings?
   c. Would you agree that class AB eliminates distortion at the price of some efficiency?

PROCEDURE

Part 3

1. Build the circuit shown in Fig. 8-5. Be sure to use the correct transistors, *one NPN and one PNP, as shown.* Set the amplitude of the signal generator to zero. Turn on the power and measure the dc voltage at point *D* with respect to ground.
   a. Is the voltage about half the power-supply voltage? If not, you have an error or a defective component.
   b. What is the no-signal current drain?

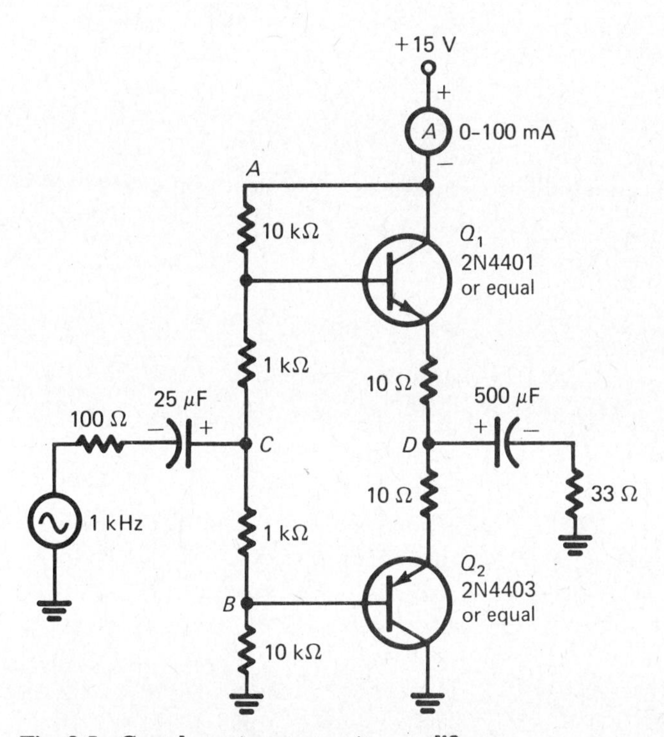

Fig. 8-5 Complementary-symmetry amplifier.

2. Measure the base-emitter voltage on both transistors. Note both polarity and magnitude. Are both transistors biased for linear operation? Are the base-emitter polarities correct for both transistors?
3. Connect your oscilloscope across the 33-Ω load resistor. Increase the amplitude of the signal generator until the scope shows an output of 6 V peak-to-peak.
   a. Is the output signal a good replica of the input?
   b. What is the current drain of the amplifier now?
   c. What class is the amplifier operating in?
   d. Compare the *phase* of the signal at point *C* to the *phase* of the output signal. What is the phase relationship? Why?
   e. Compare the amplitude of the signal at point *C* to the amplitude of the output signal. What is the voltage gain of this circuit?
   f. Why is the voltage gain less than 1?
4. Set up your multimeter for a sensitive ac voltage range. Measure the ac voltage across the 100-Ω resistor. The output signal should still be 6 V peak-to-peak.
   a. What is the ac voltage drop across the 100-Ω resistor?

b. Use Ohm's law and calculate the signal current through the 100-Ω resistor. What is the signal current through the 100-Ω resistor?
c. Calculate the signal input power to the amplifier. It can be found by multiplying the signal voltage at point *C* by the signal current. What is the signal-power input to the amplifier?
d. Calculate the signal output power from the amplifier. There is 6 V peak-to-peak across 33 Ω. Change peak-to-peak to rms. Then use $P = V^2/R$. What is the signal output power from the amplifier?
e. Calculate the power gain of the amplifier. Use the input power and divide it into the output power. What is the power gain of the amplifier?
f. This amplifier shows no voltage gain. In fact, it shows a voltage loss. Yet is is useful. Why?

5. Disconnect the 10-kΩ resistors from the circuit of Fig. 8-5 at points *A* and *B*.
   a. What happens to the output signal?
   b. What class is the amplifier in now?
   c. Which class (AB or B) is best for low distortion?

PROCEDURE

Part 4

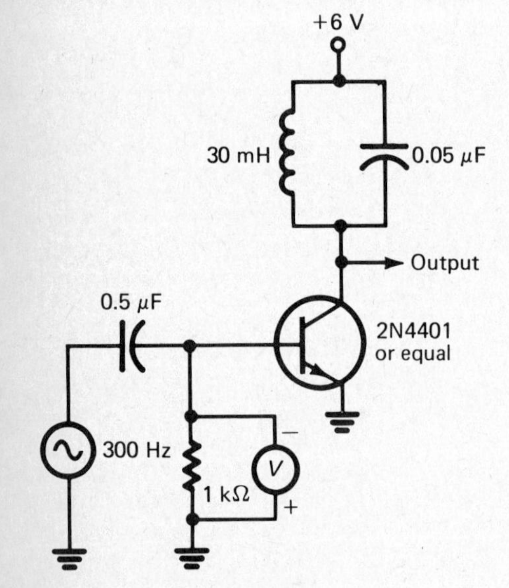

Fig. 8-6 Class C amplifier.

1. Set up the circuit shown in Fig. 8-6. Connect your oscilloscope across the output and ground. Set the time per division to 200 μs and the vertical to 0.2 V/div. The meter should be set to a 20-V dc range. Decrease the amplitude of the signal generator to zero. What base-emitter bias is shown?
2. Increase the amplitude of the signal generator until the scope shows an output signal of about 4 divisions.
   a. What happens to the base-emitter bias?
   b. What is producing it?
3. Increase the amplitude again for an oscilloscope display of 8 divisions.
   a. Does the base-emitter bias increase? Why?
   b. Explain the output waveform from the amplifier.
   c. What class is the amplifier operating in?
4. Try switching your signal generator from sine-wave output to square or triangle if available.
   a. Is the output signal affected? Why?
   b. Use the resonance equation and calculate the reasonant frequency of the tank circuit. Use 30 mH and 0.05 μF.
5. Change the frequency of the signal generator to the resonant frequency of the tank circuit. Decrease the amplitude until a good sinusoidal output is seen on the oscilloscope. Compare the waveform with that described in step 3b.

ACTIVITY 8-3
CONSTRUCTION PROJECT: BOOSTER AMPLIFIER

INTRODUCTION

A booster amplifier will fill a need for boosting the output of an inexpensive AM/FM radio or tape player to about 10 W. It is designed to plug into the external speaker jack or headphone jack found on most radios and tape players. It will provide high volume when connected to a reasonably efficient speaker system.

Parts List

Part Numbers	Description
C_1	1-mF 50-V electrolytic capacitor
C_2, C_5	4.7-μF 25-V electrolytic capacitor
C_3	220-pF ceramic disc capacitor
C_4	25-μF 50-V electrolytic capacitor
C_6	100-pF ceramic disc capacitor
C_7	1-mF 25-V electrolytic capacitor
C_8	470-pF ceramic disc capacitor
D_1–D_4	IN5392 diode or equivalent
D_5, D_6	IN4001 diode or equivalent
F_1	1-A 120-V 3AG slow-blow fuse
L_1	4.7-μH RF choke
S_1	2-A 120-V SPST switch
T_1	25.2-V 1-A Stancor P-6469 power transformer or equivalent
R_1	10-Ω ¼-W, 10% resistor
R_2	1.2-kΩ ¼-W, 10% resistor
R_3	10-kΩ ¼-W, 10% resistor
R_4	39-Ω ¼-W, 10% resistor
R_5	2.7-kΩ ¼-W, 10% resistor
R_6, R_{12}	330-Ω ¼-W, 10% resistor
R_7	47-kΩ ¼-W, 10% resistor
R_8	18-kΩ ¼-W, 10% resistor
R_9	47-Ω ¼-W, 10% resistor
R_{10}	1-kΩ ¼-W, 10% resistor
R_{11}	6.8-Ω ¼-W, 10% resistor
R_{13}, R_{14}	0.47-Ω ¼-W, 10% resistor
R_{15}	27-Ω ¼-W, 10% resistor
Q_1, Q_2	2N3903 transistors or equivalent
Q_3	2N3905 transistor or equivalent
Q_4	2N4921 transistor or equivalent
Q_5	2N4918 transistor or equivalent
Misc.	Chassis, cabinet, hardware, input jack, speaker terminals, heat sink, fuse holder, circuit board, wire

Figure 8-7 on the next page shows the schematic for the booster amplifier. Transistors Q_4 and Q_5 form a complementary-symmetry power amplifier, which provides good performance and eliminates the need for expensive transformers. Both dc and ac (signal) feedback are used for stability of the operating point and low distortion.

Resistor R_1 in Fig. 8-7 acts as the load for the audio amplifier in the radio or tape player. If a high-impedance amplifier is desired, R_1 can be eliminated. The input impedance of the booster amplifier, without R_1, will be around 22 kΩ. Thus, it may be possible to take the audio signal from an earlier stage in the radio or tape player. There will be less distortion by eliminating the output amplifier in the radio. The disadvantage is that it is less convenient to use.

CAUTION! ***If you intend to modify the wiring of your radio or tape player, use good safety procedures. Line-operated devices can be dangerous. If you are in doubt, ask your instructor.***

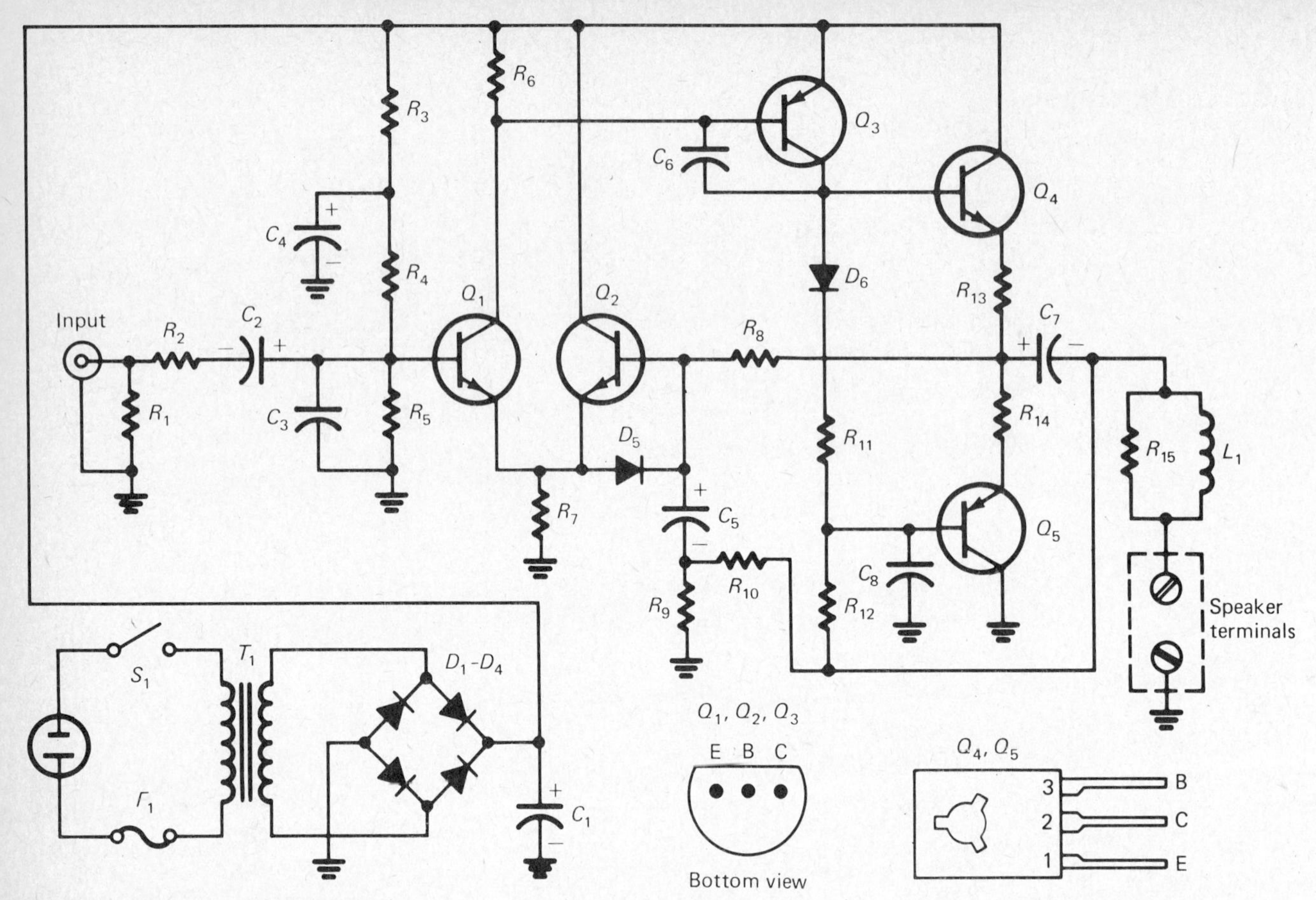

Fig. 8-7 Booster-amplifier schematic.

There is no volume control on the booster amplifier. It is designed to follow the volume control in the unit to be boosted. If you want a separate volume control, use a 50-kΩ potentiometer with audio taper. Connect it across the input with the wiper arm going to R_2. Be sure to arrange it so that turning the control clockwise increases the volume.

The booster amplifier will drive 4-, 8-, or 16-Ω speakers. The output power will be reduced if used to drive a 16-Ω speaker. Never short the speaker terminals when the amplifier is on. The transistors may be damaged. Be on the safe side: *always* turn the power off when making or breaking connections.

Do not use this amplifier with small speakers. The output power is high and may damage them. Use speakers that are rated at 15 W or more.

CONSTRUCTION DETAILS

Transistors Q_4 and Q_5 must be provided with a heat sink. If a cabinet is to be included in your design, make provision for an aluminum rear panel. Mount the transistors on the rear panel using mica washers, insulating bushings, and silicon grease. Make absolutely certain that the transistors are insulated electrically from the panel. Consult Appendix B for information on heat sinks.

Wire the amplifier using circuit-board material and insulated tie points. You may wish to design and prepare a printed circuit board. Check your wiring carefully. Check all components. Make sure the diodes and electrolytic capacitors are properly installed. Check your transistors and their leads. Have another person check your wiring.

Be prepared with a voltmeter when the amplifier is ready for testing. Connect it across C_1. Connect a 6.8-Ω 2-W resistor across the speaker terminals. Momentarily turn on the power. The meter should show about 36 V. Any large error must be investigated *before* turning the power on again. If this voltage is correct, connect your voltmeter from the junction of R_{13} and R_{14} to ground. The negative lead of the meter is to be grounded. Momentarily turn on the power. The meter should show about 18 V. Any large error must be investigated before turning the power on again.

If the above voltage checks are good, you are ready to test the amplifier with a signal. Connect a speaker and an input cable. Turn the volume on the radio or signal source all the way down. Turn on the booster amplifier. It is normal to hear a thump in the speaker. Slowly advance the volume. You should begin to hear output from the speaker.

CHAPTER 9

Operational Amplifiers

ACTIVITY 9-1 TEST: DIFFERENTIAL AND OPERATIONAL AMPLIFIERS

Choose the letter that best completes the statement or answers the question.

Questions 1 through 13 refer to Fig. 9-1.

1. An unwanted signal could be rejected by this amplifier if it appeared
   a. At both inputs as a common-mode signal
   b. At the left input as a differential signal
   c. At the right input as a differential signal
   d. At both inputs as a differential signal
2. How much current flows in R_E?
   a. 1.13 mA
   b. 1.68 mA
   c. 2.25 mA
   d. 3.99 mA
3. Find V_{R_L}
   a. 3.33 V
   b. 4.75 V
   c. 6.78 V
   d. 9.00 V
4. Find V_{CE}
   a. 1.31 V
   b. 5.92 V
   c. 8.85 V
   d. 11.3 V
5. The amplifier is biased
   a. Too close to saturation for linear operation
   b. Too close to cutoff for linear operation
   c. Just about right for linear operation
   d. None of the above
6. Find V_B
   a. 0 V
   b. 76.3 mV
   c. 115 mV
   d. 438 mV

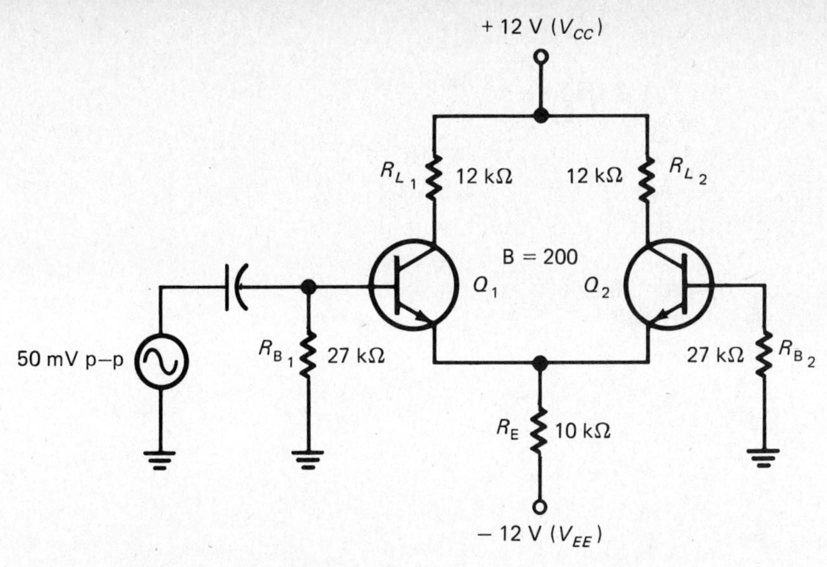

Fig. 9-1 Circuit for Questions 1 to 13.

7. Find r_E (using 50 mV)
   a. 12.7 Ω
   b. 22.6 Ω
   c. 39.0 Ω
   d. 88.5 Ω
8. Find the differential voltage gain
   a. 12.8
   b. 36.2
   c. 67.8
   d. 100
9. Find the common-mode voltage gain
   a. 0.6
   b. 0.9
   c. 1.5
   d. 5.9
10. What is the common-mode rejection ratio (CMRR)?
    a. 33 dB
    b. 41 dB
    c. 50 dB
    d. 83 dB
11. What signal will be found at the collector of Q_2?
    a. 0
    b. 1.81 V peak-to-peak
    c. 3.39 V peak-to-peak
    d. 5.00 V peak-to-peak
12. How will the signal at the collector of Q_2 compare with the input signal?
    a. It will be much larger and in phase
    b. It will be much larger and out of phase
    c. It will be much smaller and out of phase
    d. None of the above
13. What is the differential output of the amplifier?
    a. 0
    b. 3.62 V peak-to-peak
    c. 6.78 V peak-to-peak
    d. 10 V peak-to-peak

14. Most operational amplifiers have
   a. A differential output
   b. A single-ended output
   c. A single-ended input
   d. Very low CMRR
15. Most operational amplifiers have two input terminals, called
   a. Differential and common-mode
   b. High-impedance and low-impedance
   c. Inverting and noninverting
   d. Offset null plus and offset null minus
16. An operational amplifier has a slew rate of 10 V/μs. What is the maximum peak-to-peak swing from this amplifier for a frequency of 500 kHz?
   a. 20 V peak-to-peak
   b. 10 V peak-to-peak
   c. 5 V peak-to-peak
   d. 1 V peak-to-peak
17. General-purpose op amps are considered to be
   a. Excellent low-frequency amplifiers
   b. Extremely wide-band devices
   c. Very good RF amplifiers
   d. Low-gain devices

Questions 18 to 21 refer to Fig. 9-2.

18. Compared with the input signal, the output signal will be
   a. Smaller in amplitude
   b. In phase
   c. Double in frequency
   d. Out of phase
19. The voltage gain will be
   a. 0.01
   b. 10
   c. 100
   d. 1
20. The input impedance will be
   a. 0 Ω
   b. 75 Ω
   c. 10 kΩ
   d. 50 kΩ

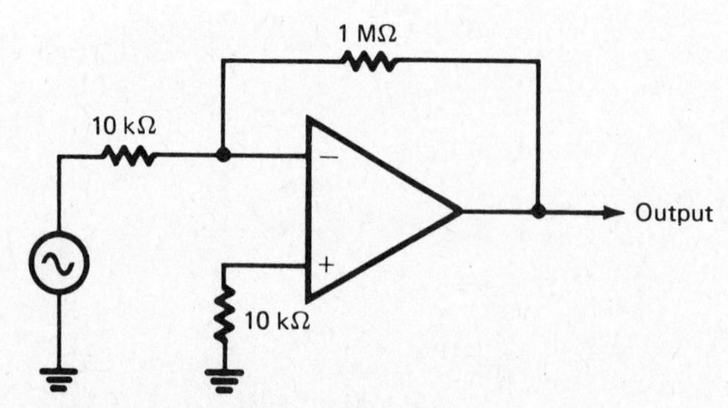

Fig. 9-2 Circuit for Questions 18 to 21.

21. Changing the 1-MΩ resistor to a 100-kΩ resistor will
  a. Increase the voltage gain
  b. Decrease the voltage gain
  c. Not affect the voltage gain
  d. Change the input impedance

Questions 22 to 25 refer to Fig. 9-3.

22. Compared with the input signal, the output signal will be
  a. Smaller in amplitude
  b. In phase
  c. Half the frequency
  d. Out of phase
23. The voltage gain will be
  a. 1.1
  b. 11.1
  c. 101
  d. Impossible to predict
24. The input impedance will be
  a. 10 Ω
  b. 100 Ω
  c. 1 kΩ
  d. 1 MΩ
25. Changing the 100-kΩ resistor to a 10-kΩ resistor will
  a. Increase the voltage gain
  b. Increase the amplifier bandwidth
  c. Both of the above
  d. Decrease the input impedance by a factor of 10

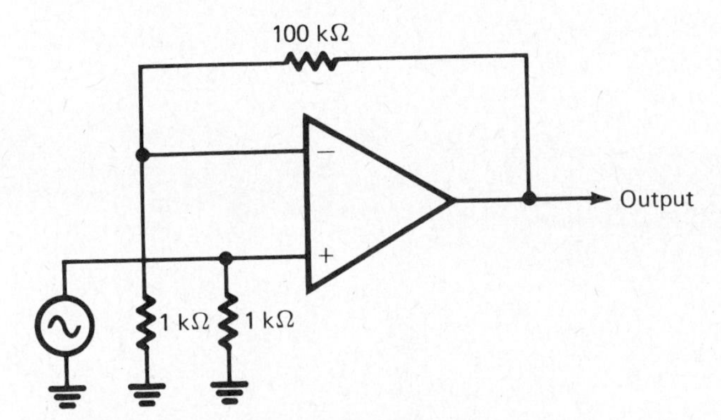

Fig. 9-3 Circuit for Questions 22 to 25.

Questions 26 to 31 refer to Fig. 9-4, shown on next page.

26. Graphs of this type are called
  a. Bode plots
  b. Sine-cosine plots
  c. Impedance plots
  d. Slew-rate calculators
27. What is the open-loop break frequency?
  a. 6 Hz
  b. 10 Hz
  c. 1 kHz
  d. 1 MHz

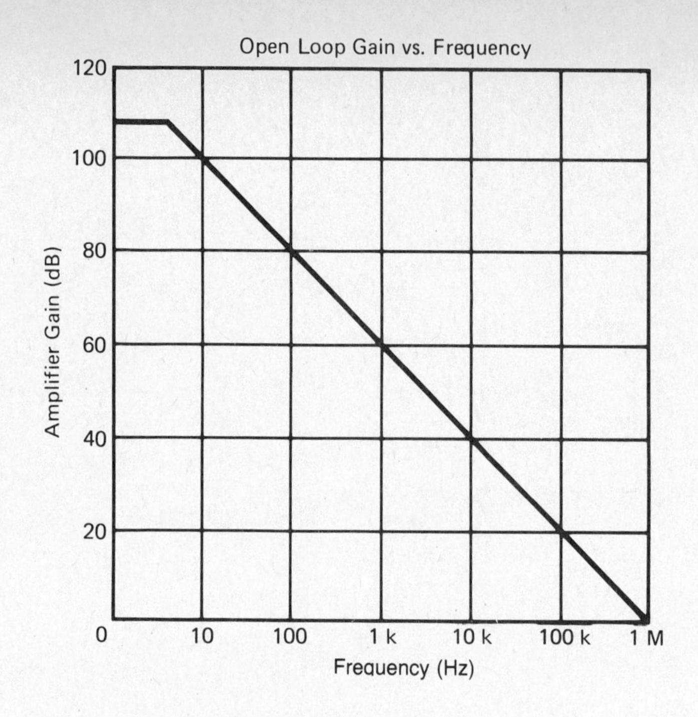

Fig. 9-4 Graph for Questions 26 to 31.

28. The amplifier is to be run closed-loop with a gain of 60 dB. Where is the break frequency?
    a. 6 Hz
    b. 1 kHz
    c. 10 kHz
    d. 1 MHz
29. A 10-dB gain is needed at a frequency of 1 MHz. What does the graph predict?
    a. The amplifier will have to be run open-loop
    b. The amplifier will have to be run closed-loop
    c. Heavy negative feedback will be required
    d. It cannot be achieved
30. The amplifier is to be run with a closed-loop gain of 40 dB. What is the actual gain going to be at a frequency of 1 kHz?
    a. 108 dB
    b. 50 dB
    c. 40 dB
    d. 37 dB
31. The amplifier is to be run with a closed-loop gain of 60 dB. What is the actual gain going to be at a frequency of 1 kHz?
    a. 60 dB
    b. 57 dB
    c. 50 dB
    d. 38 dB

Questions 32 to 34 refer to Fig. 9-5.

32. If V_1 = +0.2 V and V_2 = +0.3 V, what is the output voltage?
    a. +0.5 V
    b. +0.1 V
    c. −0.5 V
    d. −5.0 V

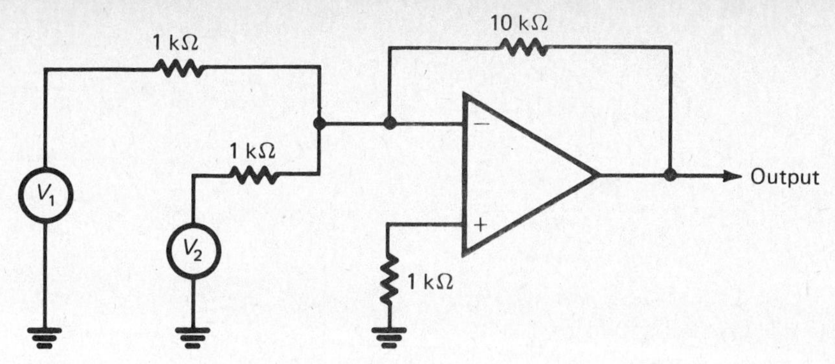

Fig. 9-5 Circuit for Questions 32 to 34.

33. What isolates V_1 from V_2?
    a. The inverting input is a virtual ground
    b. The high impedance of the resistors
    c. The common grounds
    d. None of the above

34. Can the amplifier *scale* the input voltages?
    a. Yes, by changing the resistor in series with V_1
    b. Yes, by changing the resistor in series with V_2
    c. Yes, by changing either of the above resistors
    d. No

35. A filter circuit that uses an operational amplifier to simulate inductance is classified as
    a. An active filter
    b. A passive filter
    c. An integrated filter
    d. A discrete filter

36. An operational amplifier that uses a capacitor feedback from output to the inverting input and is used for summation is called
    a. A summing amplifier
    b. An integrator
    c. A Schmitt trigger
    d. A comparator

37. An op amp that runs open-loop and switches its output state from maximum positive to maximum negative (or the reverse) when an input signal crosses a threshold voltage is called
    a. A difference amplifier
    b. An integrator
    c. A Schmitt trigger
    d. A comparator

38. Which of the following circuits exhibits hysteresis?
    a. An active filter
    b. An A/D converter
    c. A Schmitt trigger
    d. A comparator

39. What is an application for a circuit with hysteresis?
    a. Conditioning a noisy signal
    b. Eliminating low-frequency components from a signal
    c. Rejection of common-mode hum
    d. All of the above

ACTIVITY 9-2
LAB EXPERIMENT: DIFFERENTIAL AND OPERATIONAL AMPLIFIERS

PURPOSE

To get experience with differential and operational amplifiers and their application.

INTRODUCTION

This experiment demonstrates several important ideas concerning differential and operational amplifiers. Work slowly and carefully to obtain the best understanding. Double-check your components and connections before applying power. The IC op amps used in this experiment can be destroyed by improper connection or by reverse polarity. Ask your instructor to check your circuit before turning on the power.

Be sure to record the data and answer the questions before moving on to the next part of the experiment. The parts need not be completed in numerical order.

Part 1

MATERIALS

Qty.		*Qty.*	
1	multimeter	1	390-Ω ½-W resistor
1	oscilloscope with ÷10 probe	1	220-Ω ½-W resistor
1	audio-signal generator	1	100-Ω linear potentiometer
1	20-V bipolar dc power supply or single supply and 9-V battery	1	0.01-μF Mylar or paper capacitor
2	15-kΩ ½-W resistors	2	25-μF 15-V electrolytic capacitors
2	10-kΩ ½-W resistors	1	SPST switch
2	5.1-kΩ ½-W resistors	1	driver transformer
2	4.7-kΩ ½-W resistors	1	1N4733 zener diode or equivalent
1	2.2-kΩ ½-W resistor	3	2N4401 transistors or equivalent
2	1-kΩ ½-W resistors		

PROCEDURE

1. Build the circuit shown in Fig. 9-6. Don't connect transformer T_1 or the 0.01-μF capacitor, which you will add later. Close S_1. Turn the amplitude of the signal generator all the way down. Adjust the 100-Ω potentiometer to midrange. Turn on the dc power supply. Use your voltmeter and measure the collector voltages of Q_1 and Q_2 (with respect to ground).
   a. What is V_C for Q_1?
   b. What is V_C for Q_2?

2. It should be possible to balance the collector voltages. Connect your voltmeter from the collector of Q_1 to the collector of Q_2. Adjust the 100-Ω potentiometer for a reading of 0 V.
   a. When the meter reads 0 V across the collectors, what is the *differential* dc output voltage?
   b. When there is no differential input voltage, what is the differential output?

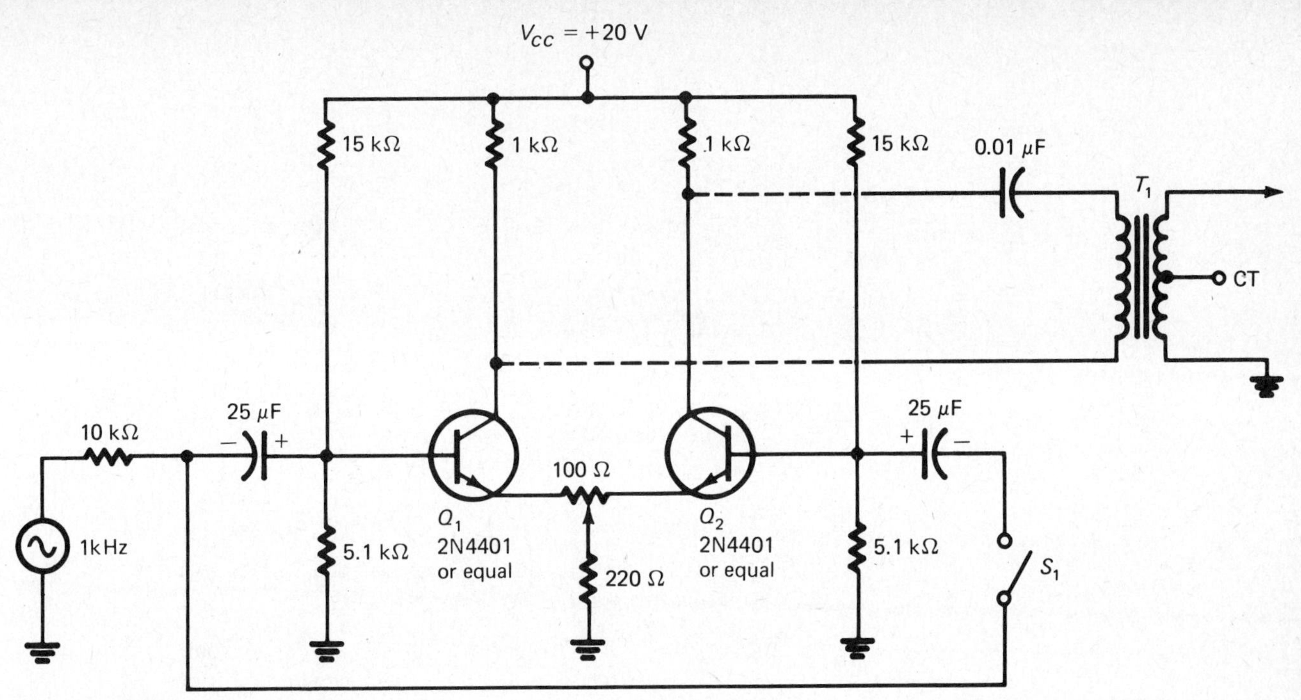

Fig. 9-6 Differential amplifier.

3. Open S_1. Connect the oscilloscope across ground and the collector of Q_1. Increase the signal-generator amplitude until the display shows 10 V peak-to-peak. Now check the collector of Q_2 with the oscilloscope.
   a. Why is there a signal at Q_2 when the switch is open?
   b. What is the phase relationship from collector to collector?
   c. How much signal swing is available if the differential output is taken?
4. Close S_1. This applies a common-mode signal to the amplifier. Again, check the signal phase from Q_1 to Q_2. What happens to the collector signals when a common-mode signal is applied?
5. Connect T_1 and the 0.01-μF capacitor. Connect the oscilloscope across the output of the transformer. Carefully adjust the 100-Ω potentiometer. It should be possible to reduce the differential output to zero or near zero. Is a common-mode input signal rejected in the differential output of this amplifier?
6. Open S_1. The input is now differential since only Q_1 is driven.
   a. Does the oscilloscope show a substantial differential output?
   b. Does the amplifier appear to have a reasonable CMRR?
7. The experimental circuit shown in Fig. 9-6 is not practical because of the transformer. It would be better to follow the amplifier with a second differential amplifier to achieve an acceptable CMRR. Figure 9-7 on the next page shows a differential amplifier circuit that uses a *bipolar supply.* This circuit will give a reasonable CMRR *for either single-ended output* thanks to the relatively large value of the emitter resistor.
8. Build the circuit shown in Fig. 9-7. Do not connect the signal generator yet. Be sure to arrange the bipolar supply properly. Make a copy of Table 9-1. Calculate the direct current and voltages (I_E through V_C) and record the values in the table. These values are for either transistor since we assume balance in a differential amplifier. Next, for either Q_1 or Q_2, measure and record all the dc

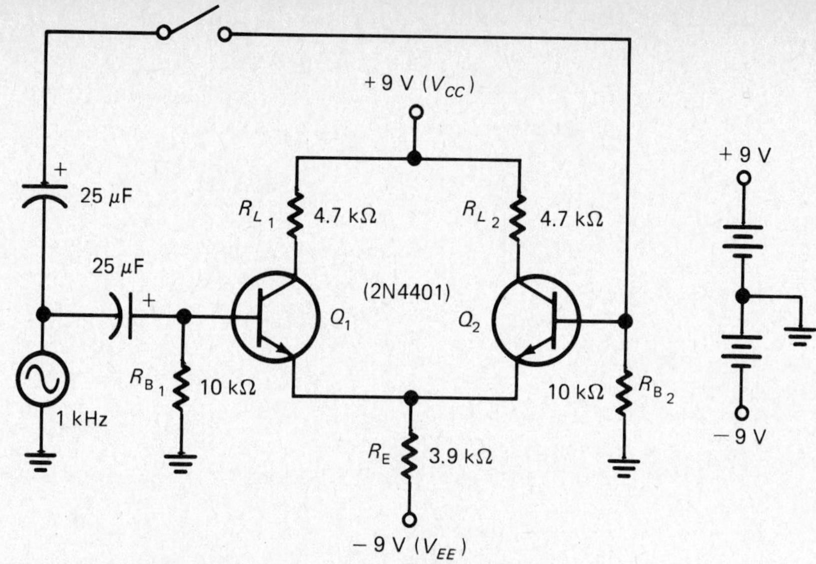

Fig. 9-7 Differential amplifier with a bipolar supply.

table values (V_B through V_C). Any large discrepancy indicates a calculation error, a circuit error, or measurement error. All dc errors must be corrected before proceeding.

9. Calculate r_E (using 50 mV) and the remaining ac values shown in the table. Be sure to record your results. Connect the signal generator to the input of the amplifier. Open the switch. Connect the oscilloscope across ground and the collector of Q_2. Adjust the amplitude of the signal generator for a display of 6 V peak-to-peak. There should be no distortion. Now, measure the signal at the base of Q_1. Compute the differential gain of the amplifier by dividing the base signal voltage into 6 V peak-to-peak. Record this differential gain in your copy of the table.
10. Close the switch. The signal applied to the amplifier is now common-mode. Measure the signal at the collector of Q_1. It should be far

Table 9-1

	Calculated or Assumed	Measured
V_B	0 V	
V_E	−0.7 V	
I_E		
V_{R_L}		
V_C		
r_E		N.A.
$A_{V(diff)}$		
$A_{V(com)}$		
CMRR (dB)		

less than 6 V peak-to-peak. Divide the signal input voltage (measure at either base) into the collector signal voltage. The result is the common-mode gain of the amplifier and should be recorded in the table. Calculate the CMRR and record the result in the table:

$$\text{CMRR (dB)} = 20 \times \log \frac{A_V(\text{diff})}{A_V(\text{com})}$$

11. The circuit shown in Fig. 9-7 is adequate when a moderate CMRR is needed for either single-ended output. Figure 9-8 shows a circuit that produces excellent CMRR for either single-ended output. The CMRR is high in this circuit because of the large impedance of the current source.
12. Modify your circuit to that shown in Fig. 9-8 by replacing the 3.9-kΩ resistor with the current source. Open the switch. Adjust the signal-generator amplitude, if necessary, for a signal at the collector of Q_2 of 6 V peak-to-peak. Verify that the differential gain has *not* changed from what it was in the last circuit by measuring the signal voltage at the base of Q_1. Now, close the switch. The collector of Q_2 should show almost no ac signal. This amplifier does an excellent job of canceling the common-mode signal at either single-ended output.
13. It is difficult to measure the CMRR for the amplifier of Fig. 9-8 because it is so high. If your instructor assigns this step, or if you want to attempt it, here are some tips. Turn the power off. Bypass both V_{CC} and V_{EE} to ground with electrolytic capacitors. Use 50-μF units and *be sure to observe polarity.* These capacitors will remove some of the noise from the output and make measurement a little easier. Turn the power back on. Make sure the switch is still closed. Connect the oscilloscope to the collector of Q_2. Increase

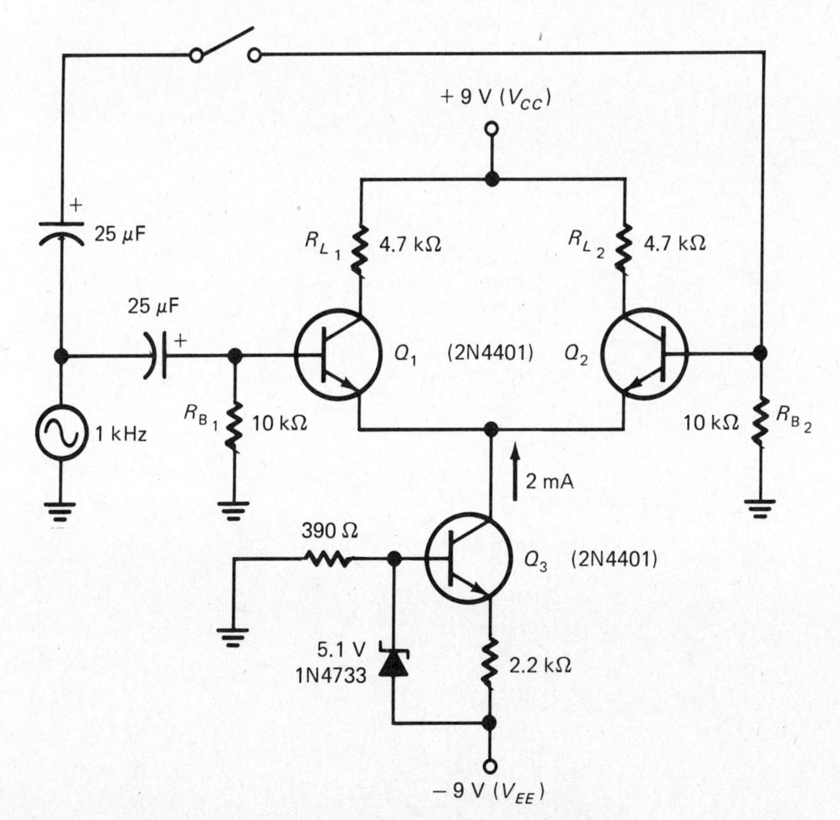

Fig. 9-8 Differential amplifier with current source biasing.

the vertical sensitivity of the oscilloscope to maximum. Slowly increase the amplitude of the signal generator while watching the oscilloscope. You can continue to increase amplitude until the signal shows distortion. At this point you have exceeded the common-mode range of the amplifier and it is now overdriven. Decrease the amplitude until the distortion just disappears. Record the ac signal at the collector. Now, measure the signal at either base. It will be much larger than the collector signal. Calculate the CMRR. It can be greater than 80 dB for this circuit! Here are some typical results:

$$V_{in} = 6.7 \text{ V peak-to-peak}$$

$$V_{out} = 20 \text{ mV peak-to-peak}$$

$$A_{V(com)} = 2.99 \times 10^{-3}$$

$$A_{V(diff)} = 45$$

$$\text{CMRR} = 20 \times \log \frac{45}{2.99 \times 10^{-3}} = 83.6 \text{ dB}$$

Part 2

MATERIALS

Qty.	
1	multimeter
1	oscilloscope with ÷10 probe
1	audio-signal generator
1	20-V dc power supply
1	μA741CP IC op amp or equivalent
1	220-kΩ ½-W resistor
3	100-kΩ ½-W resistors
1	10-kΩ ½-W resistor
1	4.7-kΩ ½-W resistor
1	1 kΩ ½-W resistor
2	25-μF 15-V electrolytic capacitors
1	0.02-μF paper or Mylar capacitor

PROCEDURE

1. Build the circuit shown in Fig. 9-9. Turn the amplitude of the signal generator all the way down to zero. Use your voltmeter and measure the dc voltage at the noninverting input (pin 3) of the op amp. Also measure the dc voltage at the output (pin 6) of the op amp. Is the dc voltage about half the power-supply voltage? Why?
2. Increase the amplitude of the signal generator until the oscilloscope shows an output signal of about 10 V peak-to-peak.
   a. Measure and record the voltage gain and the phase performance of the amplifier.
   b. Is this an inverting amplifier?
3. Replace the 4.7-kΩ feedback resistor with a 10-kΩ resistor.
   a. Measure and record the voltage gain.
   b. Does the feedback resistor help determine the voltage gain in this type of amplifier?
4. Set your oscilloscope to a sweep speed of 1 μs/div and a vertical sensitivity of 0.1 V/div. Change the signal generator to square-wave output. Adjust the amplitude to zero and the frequency of the generator to 1 MHz. Slowly increase the amplitude until a triangle waveform is seen on the screen. The oscilloscope is connected to the output (pin 6) of the op amp.
   a. Why is a triangle wave seen on the screen?
   b. What is the slew rate of the op amp?

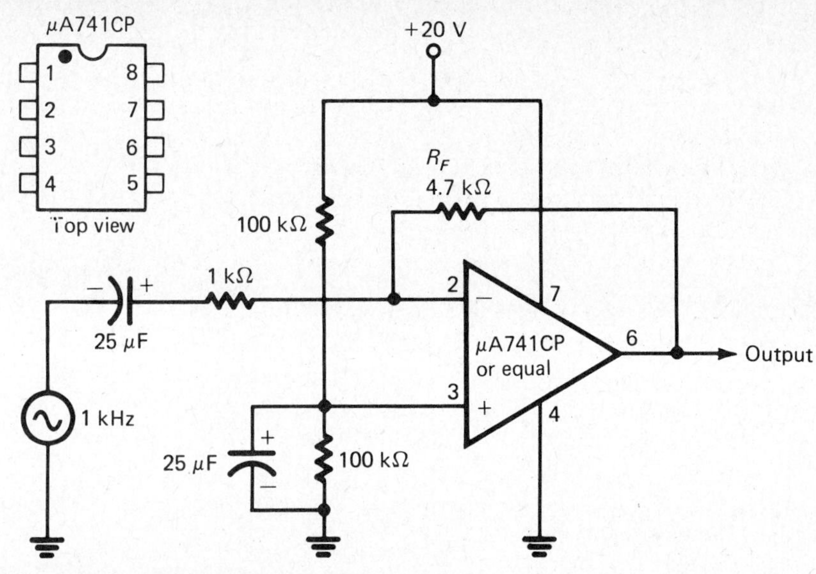

Fig. 9-9 Inverting op amp.

5. Refer to Fig. 9-4. Verify this plot by setting the op-amp gain to 20 dB and then to 40 dB. This is done by choosing the proper feedback resistor. A 10-kΩ resistor will give a voltage gain of 10 times, or 20 dB. A 100-kΩ resistor will give a voltage gain of 100 times, or 40 dB.
6. Reset the signal generator for sinusoidal output. Start at a frequency of 1 kHz. Adjust the amplitude on the generator for an output from the op amp of 1 V peak-to-peak. Note that when the output drops to 0.7 V peak-to-peak, the output is down 3 dB.
   a. With a gain of 20 dB, at what frequency does the gain drop 3 dB?
   b. With a gain of 40 dB, at what frequency does the gain drop 3 dB?
   c. What is the rate of gain decrease above the break frequency?
   d. More gain can be had from the op amp at the sacrifice of what amplifier specification?
7. Build the circuit shown in Fig. 9-10. Connect your oscilloscope to

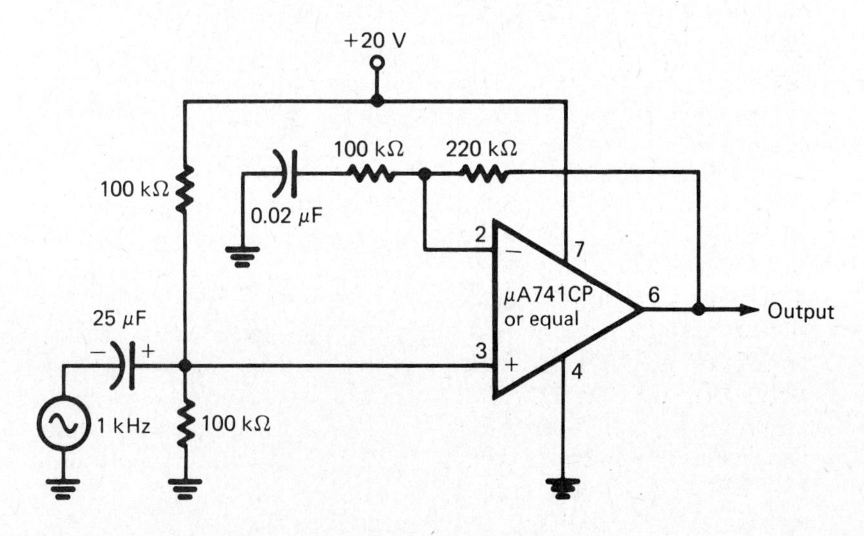

Fig. 9-10 Noninverting op amp.

the op amp output (pin 6). Adjust the amplitude of the signal generator for an output signal of 10 V peak-to-peak.

a. What is the voltage gain of the op amp?

b. What is the phase relationship from the input of the amplifier to the output of the amplifier?

8. Replace the 220-kΩ feedback resistor with a 1-MΩ resistor and repeat step 7.

a. What is the voltage gain of the op amp?

b. Does the feedback help determine the voltage gain in this circuit?

Part 3

MATERIALS

Qty.	
1	oscilloscope with ÷10 probe
1	audio-signal generator
1	0- to 15-V bipolar dc power supply or single supply and 9-V battery
1	digital frequency counter (optional)
1	μA741CP IC op amp or equivalent
1	510-kΩ ½-W resistor
1	270-kΩ ½-W resistor
1	220-kΩ ½-W resistor
3	100-kΩ ½-W resistors
1	1.3-kΩ ½-W resistor
1	1-kΩ ½-W resistor
1	820-Ω ½-W resistor
1	1-kΩ linear potentiometer
1	25-μF 15-V electrolytic capacitor
2	0.1-μF Mylar or paper capacitors
2	0.02-μF Mylar or paper capacitors
1	0.002-μF Mylar capacitor
2	0.001-μF Mylar capacitors

PROCEDURE

Note: The circuits in this section are sensitive to component tolerance. Use an accurate ohmmeter to verify the resistors. If several are available, choose the most accurate. Capacitors should be of the Mylar or paper type with good accuracy. Ceramic capacitors are a poor choice for circuits of this type. Use a digital frequency counter, if available, for an accurate display of frequency.

1. Build the circuit shown in Fig. 9-11. Set your signal generator for a frequency of 600 Hz. Connect the oscilloscope to the output of the op amp (pin 6). Adjust the signal amplitude for an output of 6 V peak-to-peak. Now, vary the frequency of the signal generator slightly above and below 600 Hz. You should be able to watch the signal peak sharply on the oscilloscope. Find the setting of frequency where the amplitude is maximum. Now, readjust the generator amplitude for an output of exactly 10 V peak-to-peak.

2. Obtain a sheet of semilog paper similar to that shown in Fig. 9-12 for plotting the frequency-response curve of the circuit. You are now set at an output of 10 V peak-to-peak. Read the output frequency of the signal generator and locate the point on the graph. Note that the horizontal axis is logarithmic. The line to the right of 100 Hz is 200 Hz. The line to the right of 1 kHz is 2 kHz and so on.

3. Vary the output frequency of the signal generator and carefully plot the frequency response curve of the circuit on your graph paper.

a. Identify the circuit of Fig. 9-11.

b. Is the circuit an active filter or a passive filter?

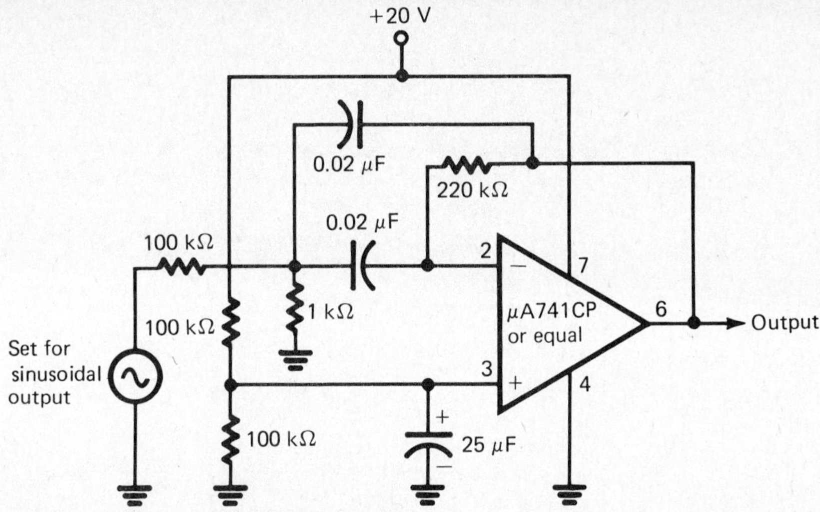

Fig. 9-11 Filter circuit for Part 3, Step 1.

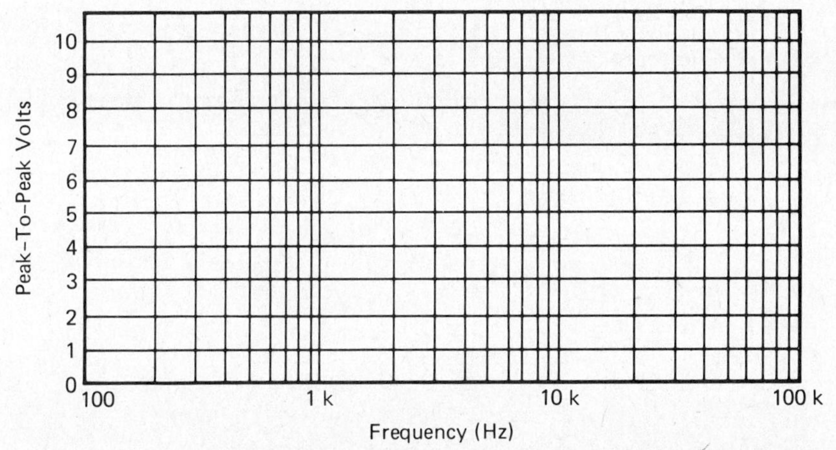

Fig. 9-12 An example of semilog graph paper used for a frequency-response curve.

4. Build the circuit shown in Fig. 9-13 on the next page. If you do not have access to a bipolar power supply or two separate supplies, you can use one dc power supply and one 9-V battery (this circuit will work with a ±9-V supply). Set your signal generator for a 60-Hz sine-wave output. Connect the oscilloscope across V_{out} and ground of the filter circuit. Adjust the 1-kΩ potentiometer for the *smallest* output signal. There should be a definite *null* as you adjust the potentiometer. Shift the frequency of the signal generator up and down a little to find the best null. Readjust the potentiometer for the smallest possible output signal.
5. Change the frequency of the generator to 40 Hz. Adjust the amplitude so that the oscilloscope shows an output signal of 6 V peak-to-peak. Figure 9-14 on the next page shows an example of graph paper to plot the frequency-response curve for the filter. Take enough readings to produce an accurate graph.

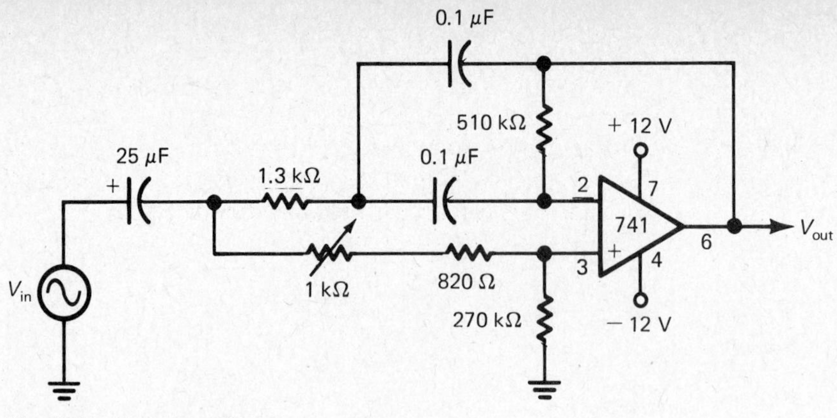

Fig. 9-13 Bandstop filter.

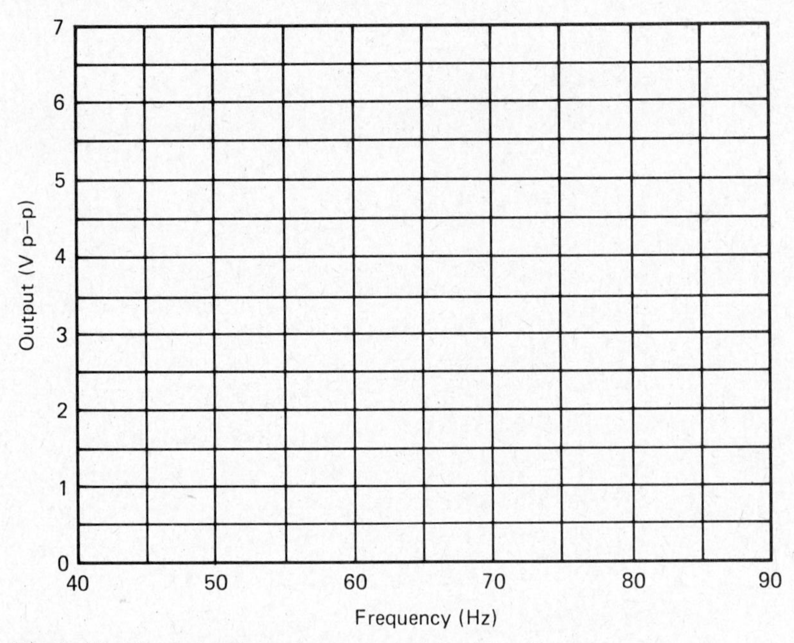

Fig. 9-14 Example of graph paper used to plot a frequency-response curve.

Part 4

MATERIALS

Qty.		*Qty.*	
1	oscilloscope with ÷10 probe	1	12-kΩ ½-W resistor
1	multimeter	1	10-kΩ ½-W resistor
1	±15-V bipolar dc power supply or equivalent	2	1-kΩ ½-W resistors
1	frequency counter (optional)	1	1-kΩ linear-taper potentiometer
2	μA741CP IC op amps or equivalent	1	25-μF 15-V electrolytic capacitor
1	2N4401 transistor or equivalent	1	0.01-μF Mylar capacitor
3	100-kΩ ½-W resistors	1	0.01-μF ceramic-disc capacitor
		1	IN4001 diode or equivalent

PROCEDURE

1. Build the circuit shown in Fig. 9-15. If a dual power supply is not available, two power supplies can be used. Connect a counter to the output to measure the output frequency of the circuit. If a frequency counter is not available, use your oscilloscope to measure the output period. This can be converted to frequency by

$$\text{Frequency} = \frac{1}{\text{period}}$$

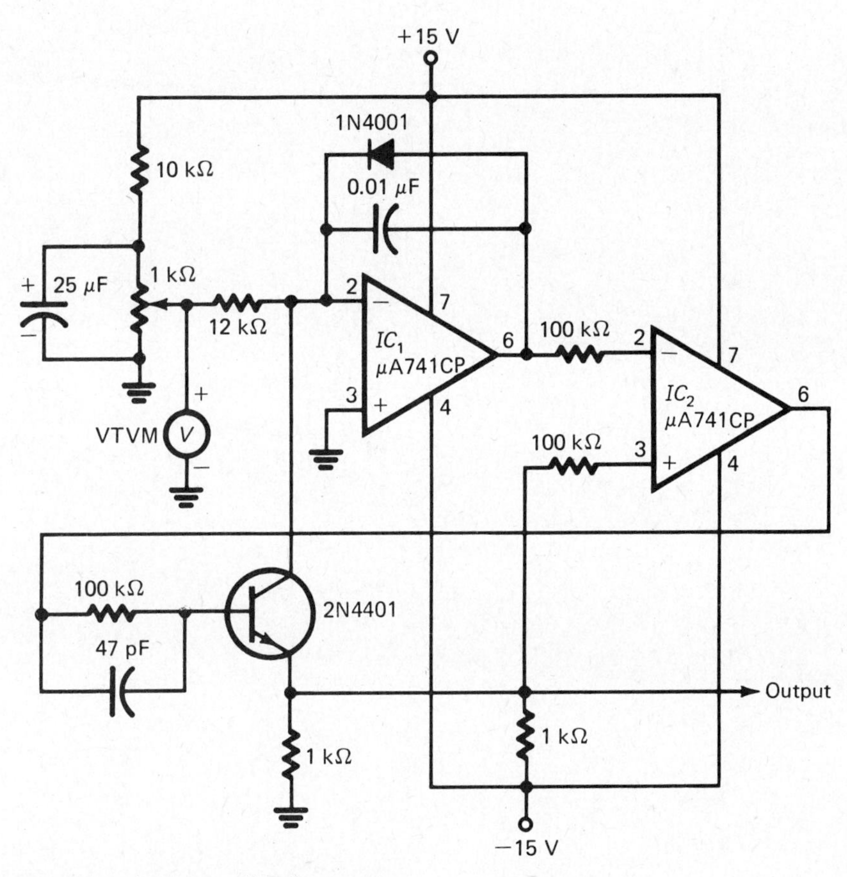

Fig. 9-15 Analog-to-digital converter.

2. Set the 1-kΩ potentiometer to about midrange. This applies about 0.7 V dc to the input of the integrator. Use your oscilloscope and check the waveform at pin 6 of IC_1. You should see a sawtooth signal. Check the waveform at the output. You should see a pulse signal.
3. Use graph paper similar to that shown in Fig. 9-16 on the next page to plot the performance of the circuit. The potentiometer is adjusted for the various input voltages that make up the horizontal axis. The output frequency is plotted along the vertical axis.

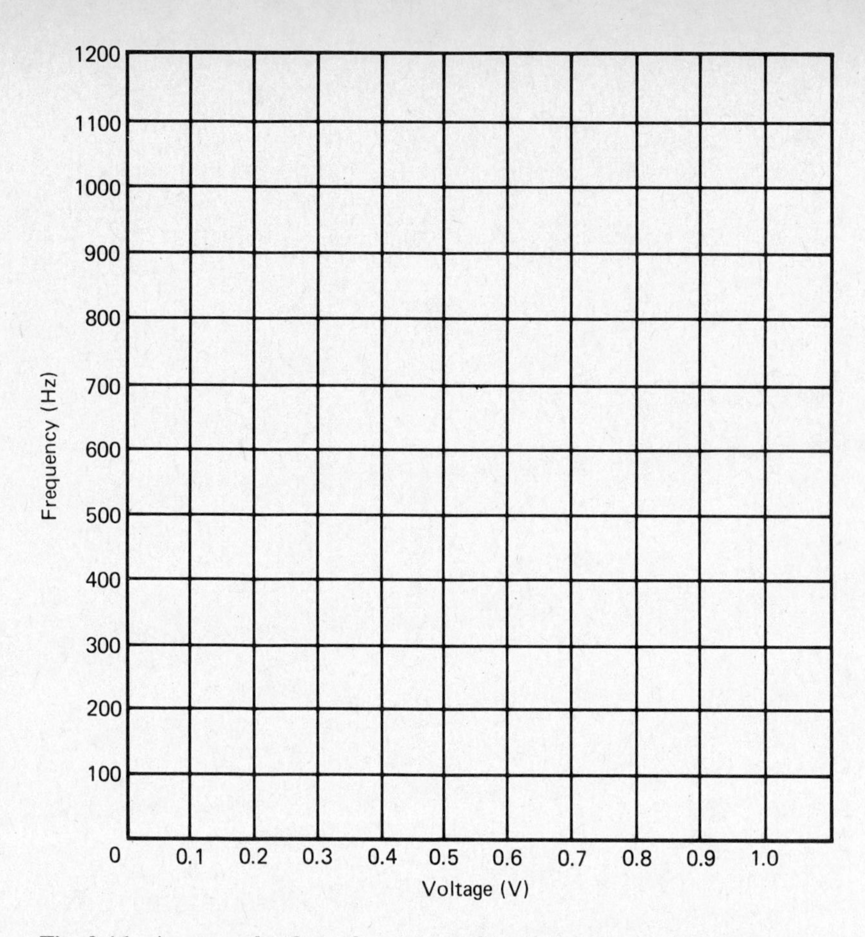

Fig. 9-16 An example of graph paper used to plot the converter-response curve.

CHAPTER 10

Amplifier Troubleshooting

ACTIVITY 10-1
TEST: AMPLIFIER TROUBLESHOOTING

Choose the letter that best completes the statement or answers the question.

1. When troubleshooting an audio amplifier, one of the very first steps would be to
   a. Use signal injection into the last stage
   b. Use signal injection into an early stage
   c. Verify proper connections and control settings
   d. Measure various voltages on the transistors

2. If the power lamp will not come on, the problem could be
   a. A burned-out lamp
   b. A blown fuse or tripped circuit breaker
   c. A defective off-on switch
   d. Any of the above

3. Why is it possible to get a shock from a piece of equipment that is not plugged into the power outlet?
   a. Coils can store a charge
   b. Ground loops with test equipment
   c. The circuit-board ground may be cracked
   d. None of the above

4. A resistor is burned black in a piece of equipment. The correct procedure is to
   a. Replace the resistor with one that has a higher wattage
   b. Replace the resistor with one that has more resistance
   c. Find the cause of the overload
   d. Take it out of the circuit and measure its resistance

5. The *first* electrical check that should be made when troubleshooting is
   a. Signal injection
   b. Verification of power-supply voltages
   c. Testing all transistors
   d. Testing all ICs

6. The purpose of the isolation transformer as used in troubleshooting is to
   a. Bypass the power transformer in the unit under test
   b. Change the ac line to direct current
   c. Prevent the power supply from shorting out
   d. Reduce shock hazard and equipment damage
7. A loudspeaker is suspected of causing a distorted sound. The best check for this speaker is to
   a. Click-test it with a battery or a dry cell
   b. Click-test it with an ohmmeter
   c. Substitute with a known good speaker
   d. Any of the above
8. An amplifier has no audio output from the speaker. The problem probably is
   a. No input signal
   b. A defective stage of amplification
   c. A defective speaker
   d. Any of the above
9. Signal injection is to be used to find the break in the signal chain. The first place to inject signal is
   a. At the input to the last stage
   b. At the input to an intermediate stage
   c. At the input to the first stage
   d. Any of the above
10. Signal injection is to be used for troubleshooting an audio amplifier. The injection frequency should be
    a. 10 Hz
    b. 1 kHz
    c. 20 kHz
    d. 100 kHz
11. Signal injection is used to troubleshoot a four-stage amplifier. Normal output occurs when the signal is injected at the input of the fourth stage, but there is no output when the signal is injected at the input of the third stage. The problem is
    a. A defective power supply
    b. A defective fourth stage
    c. A defective third stage
    d. In the first or second stage
12. It is best to capacitively couple the ac signal when using injection because
    a. A ground connection is not needed
    b. Hum voltage will be avoided
    c. The frequency response will be improved
    d. The dc bias will not be upset
13. Click tests are similar to
    a. Signal injection
    b. Signal tracing
    c. Voltage analysis
    d. Waveform analysis
14. When using signal tracing to troubleshoot an amplifier, it is best to start at the
    a. Amplifier input
    b. Output of the second stage
    c. Input of the last stage
    d. Output of the last stage

Questions 15 to 25 refer to Fig. 10-1.

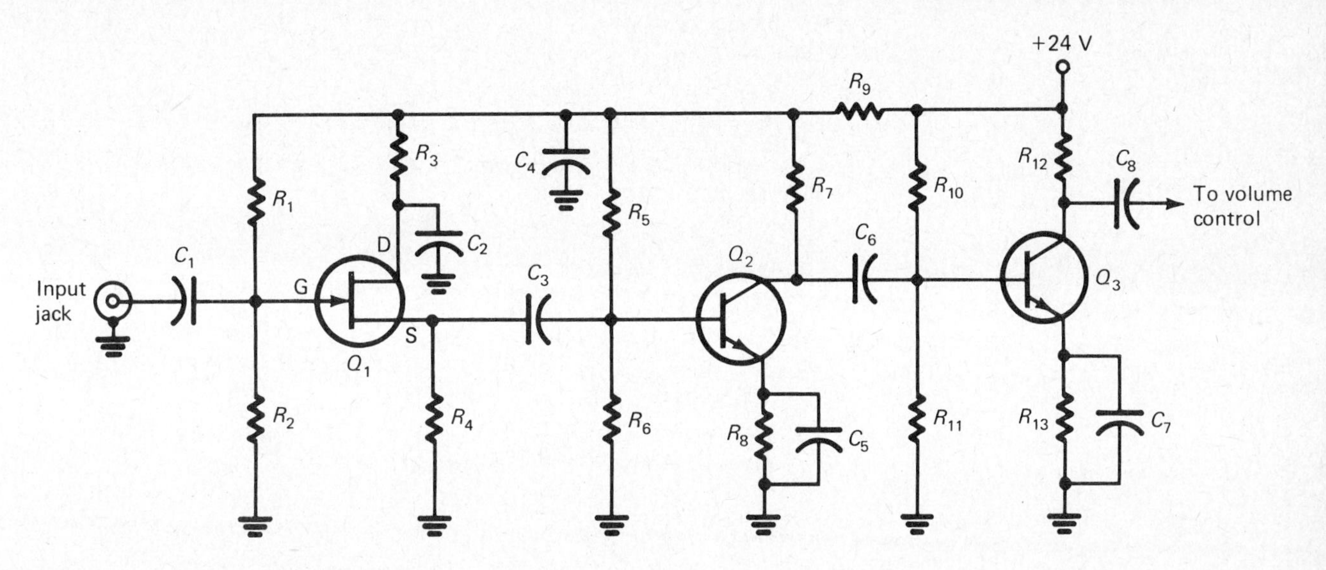

Fig. 10-1 Circuit for Questions 15 to 25.

15. How much voltage gain can be expected from the first stage Q_1?
    a. About 1
    b. About 10
    c. About 100
    d. About 300
16. Normal drain voltage at transistor Q_1 is 18 V. Suppose it measures 24 V. What is wrong?
    a. Resistor R_4 is open
    b. Transistor Q_1 is open
    c. Either of the above
    d. None of the above
17. The drain voltage of Q_1 and the collector voltage of Q_2 are both low. Transistor Q_3 shows normal voltages. What is wrong?
    a. The 24-V supply is low
    b. Resistor R_3 is open
    c. Resistor R_9 is shorted
    d. Capacitor C_4 is leaky
18. Capacitor C_5 is open. What is the most likely symptom?
    a. The collector voltage of Q_2 will be wrong
    b. The base voltage of Q_3 will be high
    c. Severe distortion
    d. Lack of gain
19. Capacitor C_7 is shorted. What will voltage analysis show?
    a. The base voltage of Q_3 will be low
    b. The emitter voltage of Q_3 will be low
    c. The collector voltage of Q_3 will be low
    d. All of the above
20. The amplifier has severe distortion. A voltage check shows that the collector of Q_3 is only around 3 V. It is supposed to be 14 V. What is wrong?
    a. Transistor Q_2 is defective
    b. Capacitor C_6 is shorted
    c. Capacitor C_8 is open
    d. Resistor R_{10} is open

21. The amplifier has a loud hum in the output. The setting of the volume control has no effect on the hum. Where is the problem likely to be?
a. In C_4
b. In Q_1
c. In Q_2 or Q_3
d. In a stage after the volume control

22. The collector of Q_3 is supposed to measure 14 V. What will it measure if R_{11} opens?
a. Low
b. Normal
c. High
d. The full power supply (24 V)

23. Resistor R_{10} opens. What will happen to the collector voltage of Q_3?
a. It will go to 14 V
b. It will go to 24 V
c. It will go to 0 V
d. None of the above

24. All dc readings are normal. Signal injection at the base of Q_3 produces an output signal. Injection at the base of Q_2 will not produce an output signal. What is the problem?
a. R_7 is open
b. C_6 is open
c. R_5 is open
d. Q_2 is shorted

25. Suppose that C_6 loses most of its capacity. What would be the most likely symptom?
a. Q_2 would overheat
b. Q_3 would short out
c. Loss of gain and poor low-frequency response
d. The fuse would blow

26. An oscilloscope is used to measure the audio voltage across an 8-Ω load resistor. The scope shows a sine wave of 25 V peak-to-peak. What is the rms power output of the amplifier driving the resistor?
a. 25.00 W
b. 18.03 W
c. 9.76 W
d. 4.32 W

27. What could cause a loss of gain in an RF amplifier?
a. An open bypass capacitor
b. An AGC problem
c. Misalignment
d. Any of the above

28. Which of the following defects will be *least* likely to produce hum in the output of an amplifier?
a. An open coupling capacitor
b. A defective filter capacitor
c. A broken shield on an input cable
d. An open ground

29. Why is a triangle wave often preferred for checking an audio amplifier for distortion?
a. It is easy to see clipping
b. It is easy to see crossover distortion
c. Both of the above
d. It is easier to generate than a sine wave

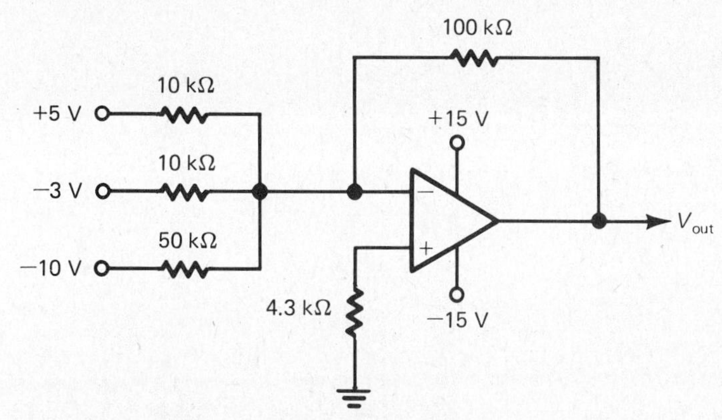

Fig. 10-2 Circuit for Questions 30 to 32.

Questions 30 to 32 refer to Fig. 10-2.

30. Find the normal value of V_{out}
a. 0 V
b. +2.5 V
c. −2.5 V
d. +14 V

31. Find V_{out} if the +5 V input is in error and is actually +6 V
a. 0 V
b. −10 V
c. −14 V
d. +14 V

32. Find V_{out} if the 50-kΩ resistor is open
a. 0 V
b. −20 V
c. +20 V
d. −14 V

33. The output of an op amp is stuck at the positive rail. The problem could be
a. A dc error at one of its inputs
b. A defective op amp
c. Latch-up
d. Any of the above

ACTIVITY 10-2
LAB EXPERIMENT: AMPLIFIER TROUBLESHOOTING AND REPAIR

PURPOSE

To gain practical experience in troubleshooting and repairing amplifiers.

MATERIALS

Qty.

- 1 multimeter
- 1 oscilloscope with ÷10 probe
- 1 audio-signal generator
- 1 audio-signal tracer
- 1 isolation transformer (ac line)
- 1 defective amplifier with schematic and service notes

Qty.

- • Assorted screwdrivers and nutdrivers, soldering and desoldering tools, wire cutters and strippers, pliers, etc.

PROCEDURE

This activity involves actual experience in amplifier troubleshooting and repair. Your instructor may furnish circuits for this activity. You may also be instructed to bring in defective amplifiers.

It is important to have the schematic and service literature on hand for this activity. It may be possible to repair some equipment without these materials from time to time, but if the defect is not found in the preliminary checks, the chance of doing so is small.

Service literature is sold for most makes and models at electronics parts distributors. Your school may have a good file of matcrials on hand. Ask your instructor for a recommendation for obtaining what you need.

You must work safely. Review the use of the isolation transformer and other safety procedures. If there is any doubt concerning a connection, a test, or a procedure *be sure to ask your instructor first.*

Use Fig. 10-3 as a guide for the proper troubleshooting procedures. Prepare a similar chart for each job assigned (it not only helps you organize your work but also provides a record of the tests and repairs you have performed).

ACTIVITY 10-3 CONSTRUCTION PROJECT: SIGNAL TRACER

INTRODUCTION

A signal tracer is a valuable troubleshooting instrument. It is a high-gain amplifier complete with its own speaker and power supply. It gives the technician an easy way to listen to signals. In some cases, it can provide more information than conventional instruments.

Parts List

Part Numbers	Description
B_1	9-V Eveready 1222 battery or equivalent
C_1	0.02-μF 600-V Mylar or paper capacitor
C_2, C_3	0.5-μF 50-V Mylar or paper capacitor
C_4, C_7	100-μF 15-V electrolytic capacitor
C_5	4.7-μF 15-V electrolytic capacitor
C_6	0.05-μF 50-V ceramic capacitor
J_1	Shielded audio-type jack
R_1	10-MΩ ¼-W 5% resistor
R_2	1-MΩ ¼-W 5% resistor
R_3	4.7-kΩ ¼-W 5% resistor
R_4	1-kΩ ¼-W 5% resistor

Parts List, *(Continued)*

Part Numbers	Description
R_6	10-Ω ¼-W 5% resistor
R_5	10-kΩ audio-taper potentiometer
IC_1	LM386 low-voltage amplifier
Q_1	2N4220 transistor or equivalent
S_1	SPST switch
SP_1	Miniature 8-Ω speaker
Misc.	Wire, hardware, battery clip, knob, circuit board, cabinet

Customer:	Job No.	Date:	Technician:
Customer Address:		Customer Complaint:	
PRELIMINARY CHECKS			
Cabinet		Volume Control	
Power Cord		Tone/Loudness	
Fuses		Source Selector	
Circuit Breakers		Speakers	
Connectors		Tape Monitor	
Lamps		Stereo/Balance	
Cables		Mute	
Other		Others	
VISUAL CHECKS			
Broken Parts		Broken Wires	
Burned Parts		Foreign Objects	
Circuit Board Damage		Other	
ELECTRICAL CHECKS			
Supply Voltages		Heat Sensitive	
Signal Checks		Vibration	
Defective Stage		Distortion	
Noise/Hum		Others	
SUMMARY			
Fault or Faults			
How Corrected			
Parts Replaced			

Fig. 10-3 An example of a troubleshooting job sheet.

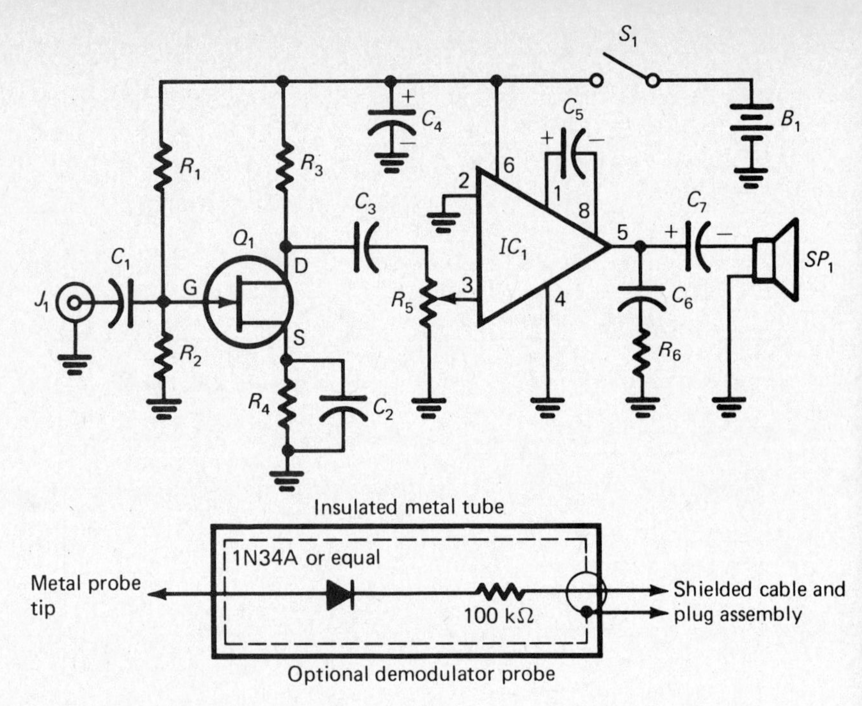

Fig. 10-4 Signal-tracer schematic.

Figure 10-4 shows the schematic diagram for this project. Transistor Q_1 is an N-channel JFET and serves as the preamplifier. The JFET gives a moderate voltage gain and has a high input impedance. IC_1, a low-voltage audio-power amplifier, provides 46 dB of gain and can deliver several hundred milliwatts of audio power to the speaker.

CONSTRUCTION DETAILS

To build this project you must plan ahead. Obtain your parts and plan a neat layout. Using a circuit board is a good way to construct the signal tracer. There is quite a bit of gain in the circuit, and short leads with good ground connections are important. The circuit must also be laid out in such a way that the output is as far away from the input as possible. Capacitor C_4 is very important in Fig. 10-4 for amplifier stability. Use a good-quality electrolytic capacitor and keep the leads short.

The gain of the signal tracer is such that the input cable must be shielded. Use shielded audio cable or miniature coaxial cable (such as RG/174U). Fit a mating audio plug at one end of the cable and an insulated test probe at the other. The end with the probe must also be provided with a grounding clip.

You may wish to use your signal tracer for radio servicing as well. Even though it is designed for audio applications, it can serve as an RF signal tracer by adding a demodulator probe. This probe is shown in Fig. 10-4. It will demodulate (detect) AM signals. It will not detect FM signals. Detection in an FM system requires a more elaborate circuit.

When building the demodulator probe, be sure to insulate the metal case. You may be able to find a plastic tube that will slip over the metal tube housing the diode and resistor. Or you can wrap the metal tube with several layers of high-quality plastic electrical tape. In either case, *be very careful to do a good job of insulating.*

The metal tip of the demodulator probe must not touch the metal tube. This would short the diode out of the circuit, and the probe would not work. You can use a small grommet to insulate the metal tip from the tube.

OPERATION

Signal tracers are easy to use. Locate the common ground in the circuit under test and ground the test probe with the clip. Now, probe those circuit points where you wish to listen to the signal. Adjust the gain of the signal tracer as necessary. Signal tracing is relatively safe in low-voltage amplifiers.

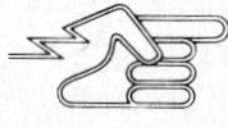 **CAUTION!** ***Some circuits use lethal voltages.***

CHAPTER 11

Oscillators

ACTIVITY 11-1
TEST: OSCILLATORS

Choose the letter that best completes the statement or answers the question.

1. How can an oscillator circuit be described?
   a. An electronic circuit that changes dc to ac
   b. An amplifier that supplies its own input signal
   c. An amplifier with regenerative feedback
   d. All of the above
2. When will an amplifier oscillate?
   a. When the gain is greater than the loss
   b. When the feedback is in phase
   c. When both the above conditions are met
   d. When the feedback is out of phase

Questions 3 to 7 refer to Fig. 11-1.

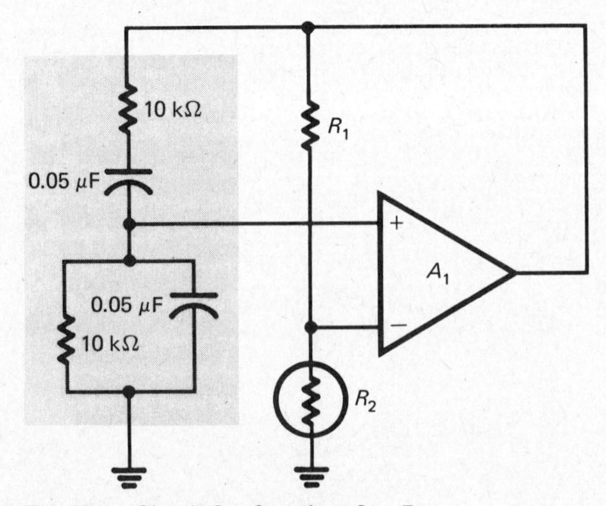

Fig. 11-1 Circuit for Questions 3 to 7.

3. What is the circuit shown?
   a. Phase-shift oscillator
   b. Wien bridge oscillator
   c. Twin-T oscillator
   d. Clapp oscillator
4. What is the expected output waveform?
   a. Square wave
   b. Sine wave
   c. Sawtooth wave
   d. None of the above
5. What is the portion of the circuit enclosed in the shaded area?
   a. Lead-lag network
   b. Phase-shift network
   c. Twin-T network
   d. Relaxation network
6. What is the expected output frequency?
   a. 123 Hz
   b. 246 Hz
   c. 318 Hz
   d. 922 Hz
7. What is the function of R_2?
   a. It helps determine f_r
   b. It sets the output frequency
   c. It stabilizes amplifier gain
   d. All of the above
8. Assume that a common-base amplifier is to be used as an oscillator. What will be required of the feedback network?
   a. A 0° phase shift
   b. A 60° phase shift
   c. A 90° phase shift
   d. A 180° phase shift

Questions 9 to 14 refer to Fig. 11-2.

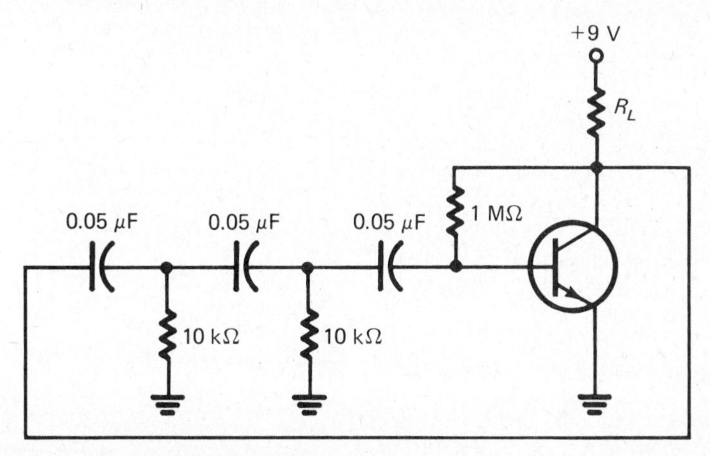

Fig. 11-2 Circuit for Questions 9 to 14.

9. What is the circuit shown?
   a. Phase-shift oscillator
   b. Wien bridge oscillator
   c. Twin-T oscillator
   d. Relaxation oscillator

10. What phase shift is provided by the feedback network?
    a. 0°
    b. 90°
    c. 120°
    d. 180°
11. The amplifier has a voltage gain of 100. What load does the 1-MΩ resistor present to the feedback signal?
    a. 10 kΩ
    b. 22.7 kΩ
    c. 100 kΩ
    d. 1 MΩ
12. What is the expected output frequency?
    a. 60 Hz
    b. 130 Hz
    c. 846 Hz
    d. 1.2 kHz
13. What is the expected output waveform?
    a. Square wave
    b. Sawtooth wave
    c. Sinusoidal wave
    d. Pulse-type waveform
14. How many frequencies will arrive exactly in phase at the amplifier input?
    a. 0
    b. 1
    c. 2
    d. 3
15. Which of the following can be used to control the frequency of an oscillator?
    a. *RC* networks
    b. *LC* networks
    c. Crystals
    d. All of the above

Questions 16 to 21 refer to Fig. 11-3.

16. What is the circuit?
    a. Colpitts oscillator
    b. Hartley oscillator
    c. Clap oscillator
    d. Crystal oscillator
17. What is the purpose of the capacitor from base to ground?
    a. It provides signal feedback
    b. It sets f_r
    c. It determines the output frequency
    d. None of the above
18. What configuration is the amplifier operating in?
    a. Common-emitter
    b. Common-collector
    c. Common-base
    d. None of the above
19. What is the required phase shift in the feedback circuit of the oscillator?
    a. 0°
    b. 60°
    c. 90°
    d. 180°

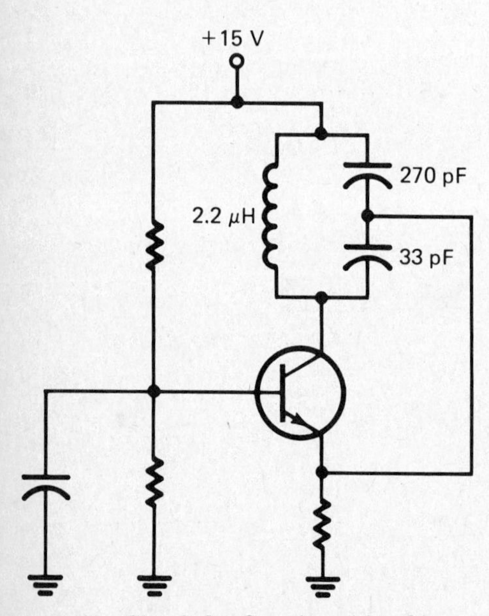

Fig. 11-3 Circuit for Questions 16 to 21.

20. What is the *effective* capacity of the tank circuit of the oscillator?
  a. 29.4 pF
  b. 33 pF
  c. 270 pF
  d. 303 pF
21. What is the expected output frequency?
  a. 489 kHz
  b. 3.6 MHz
  c. 12.1 MHz
  d. 19.8 MHz
22. Some oscillators use crystals for
  a. Amplification
  b. Temperature control
  c. Frequency control
  d. All the above
23. The major advantage to the use of a crystal-controlled oscillator is
  a. Low cost
  b. Simplicity
  c. Frequency stability
  d. Small size
24. Overtone crystals operate
  a. In the series-resonant mode
  b. In the parallel-resonant mode
  c. Below their fundamental frequency
  d. At extremely low frequencies
25. How is it possible to force a crystal oscillator to operate on the correct overtone?
  a. By tuning *RC* networks to the desired overtone
  b. With a tank circuit resonant for the desired overtone
  c. By increasing the positive feedback to the collector
  d. By using a trimmer in series with the crystal

Questions 26 to 30 refer to Fig. 11-4

26. Device Q_1 is
  a. An N-channel FET
  b. A P-channel FET
  c. An IC
  d. A UJT
27. The intrinsic standoff ratio is near 0.63. What is the value of the output frequency?
  a. 984 Hz *c.* 4.7 kHz
  b. 1.59 kHz *d.* 10.6 kHz
28. What is the waveform from terminal E to ground?
  a. A sawtooth *c.* A sinusoid
  b. A pulse *b.* A square
29. What is the waveform from terminal B_1 to ground?
  a. A sawtooth *c.* A sinusoid
  b. A pulse *d.* A straight line (dc)
30. What is the similarity between this circuit and an astable multivibrator?
  a. Both are controlled by *RC* time constants
  b. Both are considered relaxation oscillators
  c. Both produce nonsinusoidal outputs
  d. All of the above

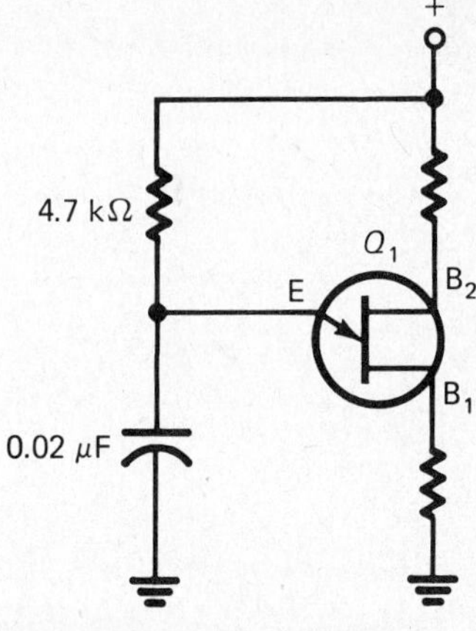

Fig. 11-4 Circuit for Questions 26 to 30.

31. What controls the square-wave symmetry in an astable multivibrator?
   a. The power-supply voltage
   b. The tank circuit
   c. The *RC* timing components
   d. None of the above
32. An amplifier uses negative feedback. Why would the feedback become positive at an extremely high frequency?
   a. Gain tends to increase with frequency
   b. Phase error within the amplifier increases with frequency
   c. Amplifier gain decreases as frequency increases
   d. Transistor gain
33. The condition described in question 32 may cause unwanted oscillations. What can be done to prevent this?
   a. Use frequency compensation
   b. Use more gain
   c. Use positive feedback
   d. All of the above
34. Unwanted feedback can be reduced in electronic circuits by using
   a. Shielding
   b. Bypassing
   c. Separate ground paths
   d. All of the above
35. An RF transistor amplifier will use feedback to cancel the feedback signal within the transistor itself. What is this technique called?
   a. Regeneration
   b. Demodulation
   c. Neutralization
   d. Lead-lag phasing
36. A technician is troubleshooting an oscillator circuit and notes that connecting the oscilloscope probe lowers the output frequency. What is this due to?
   a. A faulty tank circuit
   b. Loading effect
   c. A low-gain oscillator transistor
   d. Incorrect supply voltage
37. Frequency instability in an oscillator can be caused by
   a. Temperature changes
   b. Power-supply voltage changes
   c. Poor connections
   d. Any of the above

ACTIVITY 11-2
LAB EXPERIMENT: OSCILLATOR CIRCUITS

PURPOSE

To construct and analyze several popular oscillator circuits.

INTRODUCTION

The experience you gain for each oscillator circuit will be important for your understanding of electronic circuitry. For this reason, you should work slowly and carefully and try to get the best results. High-frequency oscillator circuits should be breadboarded using the shortest possible leads. Double-check your connections and components before turning on the power.

Be sure to record the data and answer the questions before moving on to the next part of the experiment. The parts may be completed in any order.

Part 1

MATERIALS

Qty.		*Qty.*	
1	oscilloscope with probe	1	150-Ω ½-W resistor
1	digital frequency counter (optional)	1	0.05-μF capacitor
1	±15-V dual-voltage dc power supply	2	0.01-μF paper or Mylar capacitors
2	100-kΩ ½-W resistors	2	1-nF paper or Mylar capacitors
1	500-Ω potentiometer, linear taper	1	μA741CP IC op amp or equivalent

PROCEDURE

1. Build the circuit shown in Fig. 11-5. Connect your oscilloscope probe to the circuit output. Turn on the power. Adjust the oscilloscope for a good stable display. Now, adjust the 500-Ω potentiometer for an undistorted sinusoidal output. Note that the setting is critical. Be patient and try to obtain the best possible waveform. If you have access to a digital frequency counter, connect this instrument to the output of the oscillator.

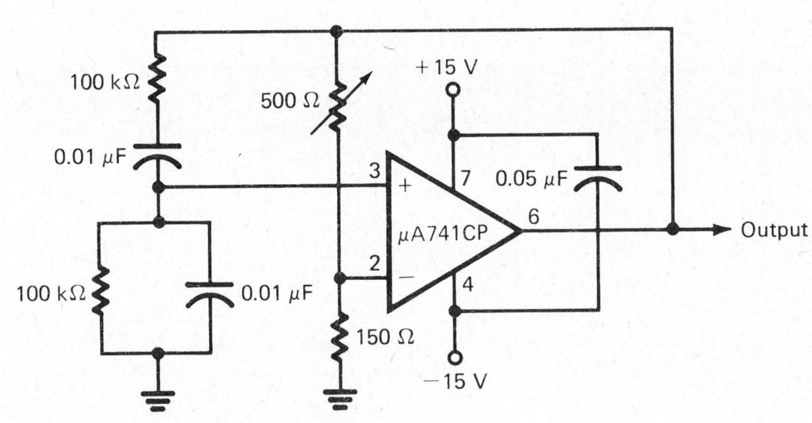

Fig. 11-5 Wien-bridge oscillator.

2. Calculate the resonant frequency of the lead-lag network using

$$f_r = \frac{1}{6.28RC}$$

   a. What is the calculated frequency?
   b. How well does the measured frequency compare with the calculated frequency (use your oscilloscope and convert period to frequency if the counter is not available)?

c. What is the amplitude of the output waveform?

3. Turn off the power. Substitute two 0.001-μF capacitors for the 0.01-μF units in the lead-lag network. Recalculate the resonant frequency.
   a. What is the new resonant frequency?
   b. Turn on the power and measure the frequency. How well does it agree with the calculated frequency?
   c. What is the function of the 500-Ω potentiometer in Fig. 11-5?
   d. Is is possible to obtain a good sine wave from this circuit?
   e. What would be a better way to control the gain of the op amp in this circuit?

Part 2

MATERIALS

Qty.	
1	oscilloscope with probe
1	digital frequency counter (optional)
1	audio-signal tracer (optional)
1	0- to 20-V variable dc power supply
1	470-kΩ ½-W resistor
2	4.7-kΩ ½-W resistors
1	3.3-kΩ ½-W resistor
1	25-μF 25-V electrolytic capacitor
3	0.05-μF paper or Mylar capacitors
1	2N4401 transistor or equivalent

PROCEDURE

1. Build the circuit shown in Fig. 11-6. Connect your oscilloscope probe to the output. Also connect a digital frequency counter if available. Turn on the power supply and slowly increase the output voltage until the circuit starts oscillating. This circuit will show considerable distortion unless the power-supply voltage is adjusted for the minimum useful voltage. This, in effect, controls the gain and keeps the distortion low. Calculate the operating frequency using the formula

$$f_r = \frac{1}{15.39RC}$$

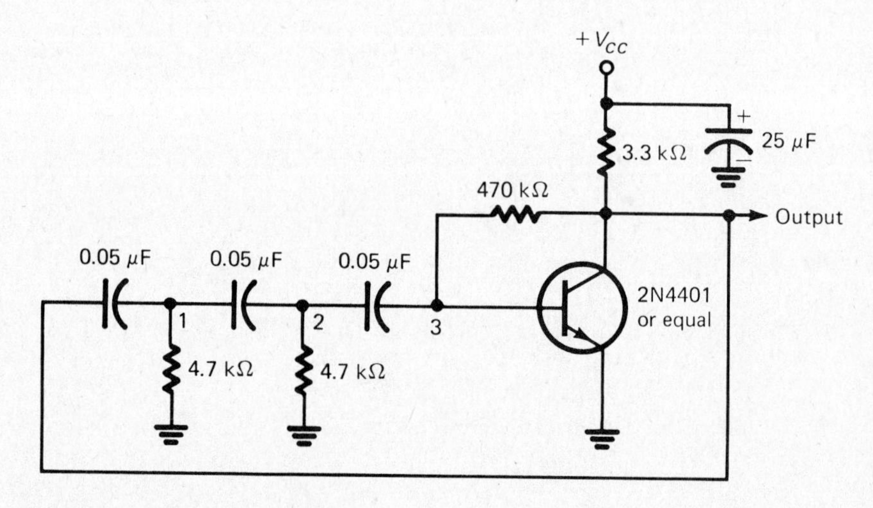

Fig. 11-6 Phase-shift oscillator.

a. What is the calculated frequency?

b. Measure the output frequency using the oscilloscope or the counter. How well does the measured frequency agree with the calculated frequency?

c. Break the feedback path by opening the connection from the collector to the first 0.05-μF capacitor. What happens to the output signal when there is no feedback?

2. Set up your oscilloscope to measure phase. Restore the feedback connection. Check the relative phase and amplitude of the signal at points 1, 2, and 3.

   a. What can you conclude about the way the feedback network operates?

   b. Can you see that the transistor gain must be high in order to sustain oscillations? Why?

3. If a signal tracer (audio type) is available, connect it to the output of the phase-shift oscillator shown in Fig. 11-6. Adjust the gain of the tracer for a moderate output level. Slowly decrease the power-supply voltage until the oscillator stops. Make and break the power-supply connection while listening to the sound from the tracer. You should hear a bongo sound. Experiment with the setting of the power supply and note the effect it has on the sound. It is possible to obtain several musical effects with this circuit.

Part 3

MATERIALS

Qty.		*Qty.*	
1	oscilloscope with probe	1	500-pF mica capacitor
1	digital frequency counter (optional)	1	365-pF variable capacitor
1	dc power supply, 12 V	1	100-pF mica capacitor
1	AM radio receiver	1	Hartley oscillator coil, AM-broadcast-band type
1	270-kΩ ½-W resistor	1	2N4401 transistor or equivalent
1	2.2-kΩ ½-W resistor	1	30-mH RF choke
1	390-Ω ½-W resistor		
1	0.05-μF paper or Mylar capacitor		

PROCEDURE

1. Build the circuit of Fig. 11-7 shown on the next page. Connect the oscilloscope to the output. If a counter is available, connect it to the output also. Turn on the power and adjust the oscilloscope for a stable display. Note that the oscilloscope must have good high-frequency response and a brief sweep period to display the waveform for this Hartley oscillator accurately.

2. The tank circuit in Fig. 11-7 is loaded by the other components connected to it. This means that the actual resonant frequency will be determined to some extent by the transistor and the 100-pF coupling capacitor. The actual range for the tank-circuit capacitance is 75 to 415 pF approximately. The inductance of the Hartley oscillator coil is 146 μH. Use the resonant-frequency equation twice and predict the tuning range of the oscillator:

$$f_r = \frac{1}{6.28\sqrt{LC}}$$

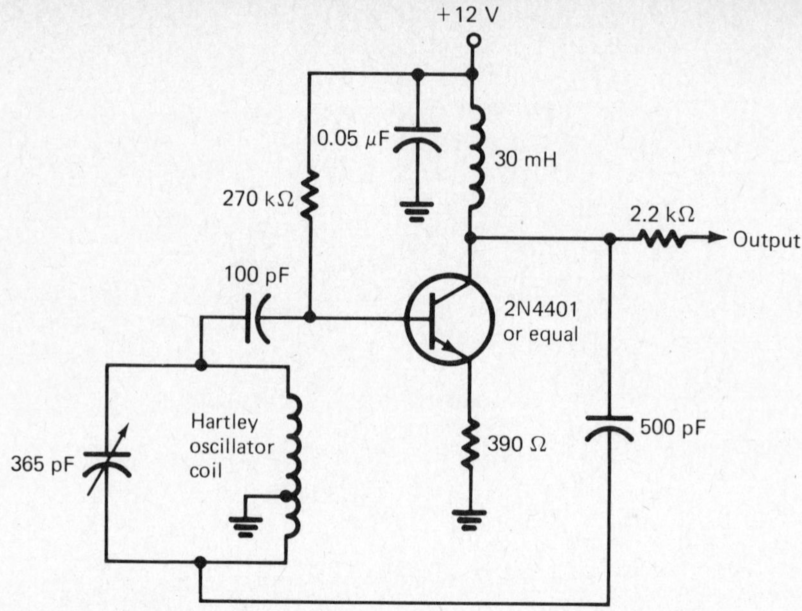

Fig. 11-7 Hartley oscillator.

a. What is the frequency range of the circuit?
b. How does this range compare with the frequency range used for AM radio?

3. Bring an AM radio receiver near the oscillator circuit (about 2 ft). Tune the receiver to a clear place on the dial near 1 MHz. If the radio dial is calibrated in kilohertz, this will be near 1000. Slowly adjust the 365-pF variable capacitor. You should find a setting where the oscillator signal is heard in the AM receiver. Try other settings of the radio dial and see if you can tune the oscillator to those frequencies.
   a. Is the circuit of Fig. 11-7 a fixed-frequency oscillator or a variable-frequency oscillator?
   b. Break the feedback connection at the 500-pF capacitor. What happens to the output signal when the feedback is eliminated?

Part 4

MATERIALS

Qty.		*Qty.*	
1	oscilloscope with probe	1	0.002-μF paper or Mylar capacitor
1	digital frequency counter (optional)	1	500-pF mica capacitor
1	12-V dc power supply	1	250-pF mica capacitor
1	AM radio receiver	1	100-pF mica capacitor
1	270-kΩ ½-W resistor	1	Hartley oscillator coil, AM-broadcast-band type
1	2.2-kΩ ½-W resistor	1	30-mH RF choke
1	390-kΩ ½-W resistor	1	2N4401 transistor or equivalent
1	0.05-μF paper or Mylar capacitor		

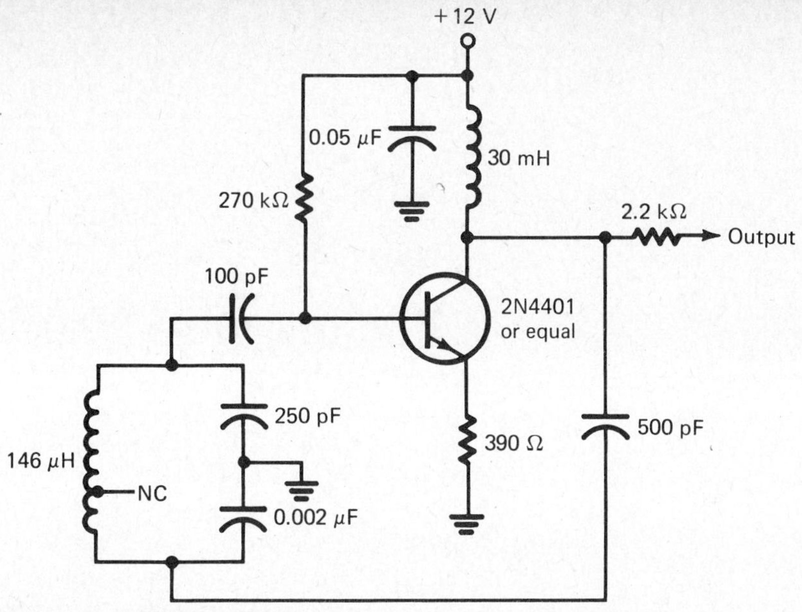

Fig. 11-8 Colpitts oscillator.

PROCEDURE

1. Build the circuit shown in Fig. 11-8. Connect your oscilloscope probe to the output. If a digital frequency counter is available, connect it to the output also.
2. The tank circuit in Fig. 11-8 uses two capacitors, acting in series. From

$$C_{\text{eff}} = \frac{C_1 \times C_2}{C_1 + C_2}$$

What is the effective value of the two tank circuit capacitors?

3. The transistor and the 100-pF coupling capacitor in Fig. 11-8 also add some capacitance to the tank circuit. This additional capacitance, which is on the order of 25 pF, must be added to the effective value calculated above in order to predict the frequency of oscillation more accurately. Use the equation below and do not forget to add 25 pF to the effective value of C to account for circuit-loading effects:

$$f_r = \frac{1}{6.28\sqrt{LC}}$$

What is the frequency of oscillation?

4. If your oscilloscope performs well at high frequencies, it will be possible to measure the period of the output waveform and convert it into a frequency measurement. If the digital counter is available, this method can be used. A third way to measure frequency is to use a radio receiver. Bring an AM receiver near the oscillator circuit and tune the broadcast band. You should be able to find the oscillator signal on the receiver.
   a. Is the output frequency near the calculated frequency?
   b. Is this a fixed or variable-frequency oscillator?
   c. What can be done to change the frequency of oscillation?
   d. Eliminate the feedback by breaking one connection to the 500-pF capacitor in Fig. 11-8. What happens to the output signal from the oscillator?

Part 5

MATERIALS

Qty.		*Qty.*	
1	oscilloscope with probe	1	0.01-μF paper or Mylar capacitor
1	15-V dc power supply	1	500-pF mica capacitor
1	digital frequency counter (optional)	1	150-pF mica capacitor
1	22-kΩ ½-W resistor	1	47-pF mica capacitor
1	2.7-kΩ ½-W resistor	1	3.58-MHz color-television-type crystal
1	2.2-kΩ ½-W resistor	1	2N4401 transistor or equivalent
1	1-kΩ ½-W resistor		
1	220-Ω ½-W resistor		
1	0.05-μF paper or Mylar capacitor		

PROCEDURE

1. Build the circuit shown in Fig. 11-9. Connect the oscilloscope probe and counter (if available) to the oscillator output. Turn on the power. What is the amplitude of the output signal?
2. This oscillator runs higher in frequency than the AM broadcast band. Its signal can be received on a shortwave receiver or an amateur 80-m receiver. The signal should be found at 3.58 MHz. It is also possible to find the second harmonic of the signal at 7.16 MHz (it will be found in the 40-m band on an amateur receiver). You may also wish to check for the third and higher harmonic signals if the receiving equipment is available.
3. If some method of accurately measuring frequency is available, try some of the following: (1) change the power-supply voltage from around 12 to 20 V, (2) bring your hand near the various circuit components, (3) tap the circuit board, (4) move the wires around, and (5) use a little warm air or cool air to change the temperature of the various components. Any or all of the above will usually cause a significant change in an *LC* oscillator circuit. Is the crystal oscillator circuit stable? Why?

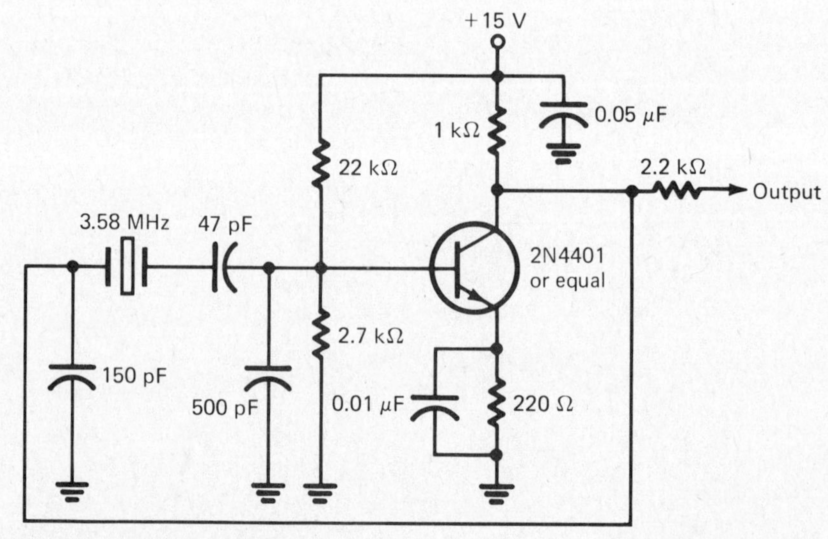

Fig. 11-9 Crystal oscillator.

4. Another experiment that you can perform if accurate frequency measurement is available is to change the 47-pF capacitor. Since this capacitor is often a trimmer type, the crystal oscillator can be set exactly on the desired frequency. It is not possible to produce a large change with this technique. For example, in one circuit the capacitor was changed from 47 to 15 pF and the oscillator changed from 3.579545 to 3.580420 MHz. This represents a change of only 0.024 percent.

Part 6

MATERIALS

Qty.		*Qty.*	
1	oscilloscope with probe	1	0.1-µF paper or Mylar capacitor
1	10-V dc power supply	1	2N2646 UJT or equivalent
1	10-kΩ ½-W resistor		
1	33-Ω ½-W resistor		
1	50-µF 15-V electrolytic capacitor		

PROCEDURE

1. Build the circuit shown in Fig. 11-10. Connect your oscilloscope probe to the emitter terminal E on the transistor. Turn on the power. Adjust the oscilloscope for a good, stable display.

   a. Describe the waveform
   b. Calculate the *RC* time constant for the UJT oscillator

   $$t = RC$$

   c. Measure the period of the waveform. How well does this agree with the calculated time constant?
   d. What transistor parameter can influence the actual operating period for this relaxation oscillator?
   e. Connect the oscilloscope to terminal B_1 on the transistor. Describe the waveform.
   f. What causes the E and B_1 waveforms in this circuit?
2. Turn off the power. Change the capacitor to a 50-µF electrolytic. Observe polarity. The positive lead must go to the emitter of the transistor, and the negative lead must go to ground. Set your oscilloscope to a much slower sweep speed (around 200 ms/div). Turn on the power. What is the effect of using a large timing capacitor in this circuit?

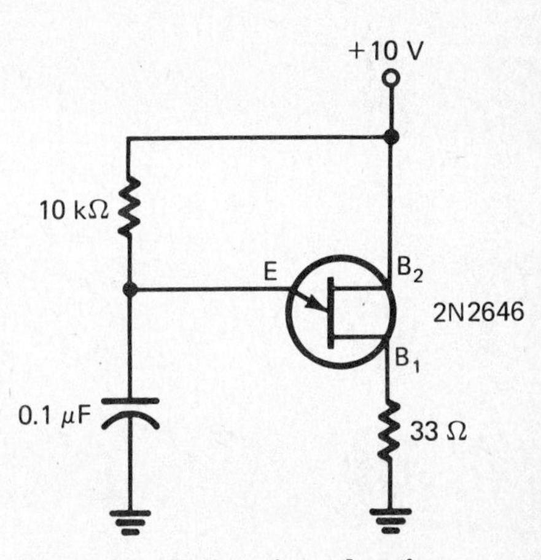

Fig. 11-10 Unijunction relaxation oscillator.

Part 7

MATERIALS

Qty.		*Qty.*	
1	oscilloscope with probe		
1	16-V dc power supply		
2	47-kΩ ½-W resistors	2	0.05-µF paper or Mylar capacitors
2	1-kΩ ½-W resistors	2	2N4401 transistors or equivalent
1	0.1-µF paper or Mylar capacitor		

PROCEDURE

1. Build the circuit shown in Fig. 11-11. Connect the oscilloscope probe to the collector of Q_1. Turn on the power.
   a. What waveform is seen on the oscilloscope?
   b. What is the period of the waveform?
2. The time that each transistor is held in the off condition is determined by the R and C timing components connected in its base circuit. Use $t = 0.69\,RC$ to calculate the off period for each transistor. The waveform period will be equal to twice this amount since in one cycle each transistor is off once.
   a. How well does the calculated waveform period agree with the oscilloscope measurement?
   b. Is this oscillator circuit considered symmetrical or nonsymmetrical?
3. Set up your oscilloscope to measure phase or use a dual-trace scope. Compare the phase of the collector of Q_1 with the collector of Q_2. Are the collector signals in phase or out of phase? If out of phase, by how many degrees?
4. Turn off the power. Change one of the 0.05-μF timing capacitors by replacing it with a 0.1-μF capacitor. Turn on the power and observe the waveform with your oscilloscope. Check both collectors.
   a. Describe the waveform.
   b. Note that in this circuit, when the transistor is on, it is saturated and its collector voltage is very near ground potential. When off, its collector is near 16 V positive. The transistor with the larger base capacitor seems to be held in the off condition twice as long. Why?

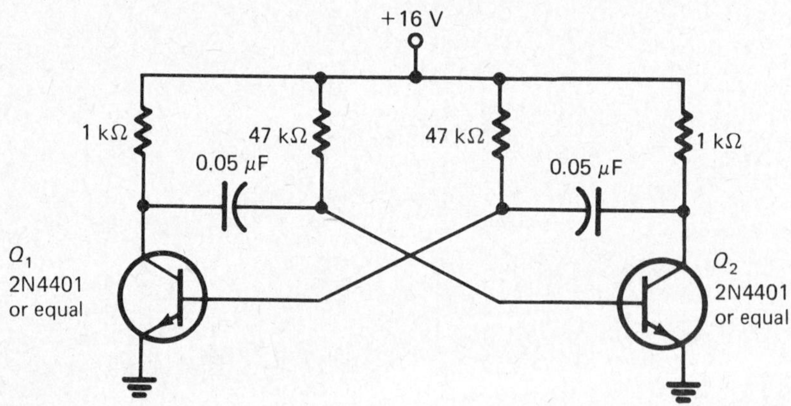

Fig. 11-11 Astable multivibrator.

ACTIVITY 11-3 CONSTRUCTION PROJECT: FUNCTION GENERATOR

INTRODUCTION AND CONSTRUCTION

The term "function generator" refers to an audio oscillator capable of producing at least three waveforms, sine, triangle, and square. Such an instrument is very useful for testing and analyzing various electronic circuits. Thanks to IC technology, function generators are now easy to build.

Figure 11-12 on the next page is a diagram of a practical function generator. Its basic range is 15 to 150 Hz. This can be multiplied by 10, 100, or 1000. Thus, the generator will oscillate at any frequency from 15 Hz to 150 kHz. Capacitors C_1 to C_4 are the range capacitors. The accuracy of each range will be largely determined by the accuracy of these capacitors. If an accurate dial is needed (from range to range), it will be necessary to select these capacitors or to use combinations that will give the required accuracy.

Parts List

Part Numbers	Description
C_1	1-μF 50-V Mylar capacitor
C_2	0.1-μF 50-V capacitor
C_3	0.01-μF 50-V capacitor
C_4	1-nF 50-V Mylar capacitor
C_5	10-μF 15-V electrolytic capacitor
C_6	1-mF 15-V electrolytic capacitor
D_1, D_2	1N4001 diodes or equivalent
Q_1, Q_2	2N4401 transistors or equivalent
Q_3	2N4403 transistors or equivalent
R_1, R_2	270-Ω ¼-W 5% resistor
R_3	680-Ω ¼-W 5% resistor
R_7	1.8-kΩ ¼-W 5% resistor
R_5, R_9	47-Ω ¼-W 5% resistors
R_4	10-kΩ audio-taper potentiometer
R_6	100-kΩ miniature trimmer-type potentiometer
R_{10}	1-kΩ linear-taper audiometer
S_1	Single-pole four-position rotary switch
S_2	Single-pole three-position rotary switch
S_3	SPST switch
IC_1	Intersil 8038 IC or equivalent
Misc.	Wire, cabinet, hardware, battery, battery clip, knobs, jacks, circuit board

For example, if the ×10 range is higher than the dial actually reads, it will be possible to wire a smaller capacitor in parallel with C_2 to pad the frequency down a little.

Resistor R_3 in Fig. 11-12 sets the actual tuning range of R_4. Making R_3 a little lower in value will expand the range. Making R_3 a little higher in value will restrict the range. This makes it possible to adjust the tuning range if necessary.

Resistor R_6 in Fig. 11-12 is for adjusting the sine-wave output. The function switch S_2 should be set in the sine position and the output connected to a good oscilloscope. Select the ×10 frequency range and adjust the oscilloscope for a good stable display. Resistor R_6 can now be adjusted to give the best sine wave. Another way to adjust R_6 is to use an audio distortion meter and set it for the least distortion. It is not possible to produce a perfect sinusoid with this circuit. Distortion from 1 to 2 percent is typical.

The amplifier section (Q_1, Q_2, and Q_3 in Fig. 11-12) is optional. Although it provides no voltage gain, it does provide a low-impedance output. This can be very helpful when troubleshooting certain circuits and devices. For example, this amplifier allows an 8-Ω speaker to be directly driven to a moderate volume level. Many audio-signal generators and function generators will not deliver enough signal into a low-impedance load.

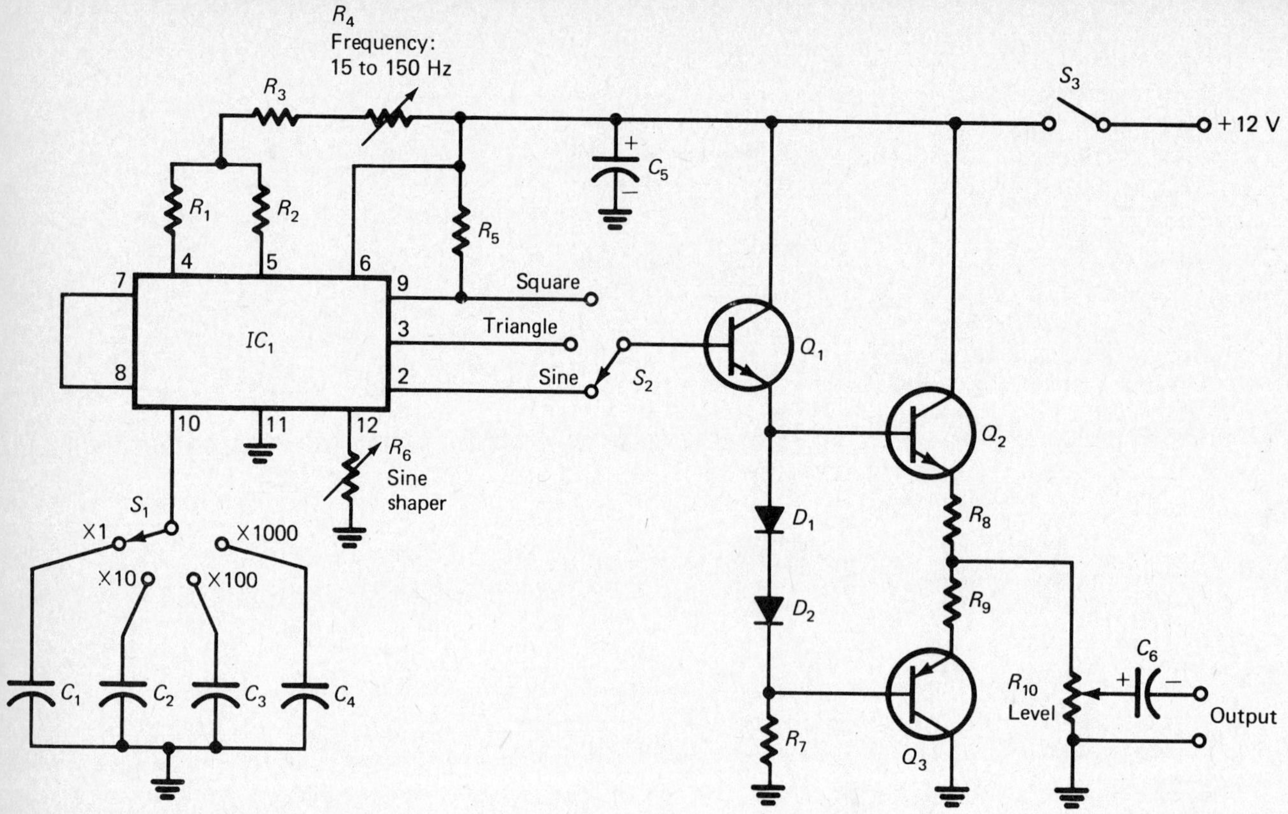

Fig. 11-12 Function-generator schematic.

Capacitor C_6 is high in value so that low-frequency signals will be effectively coupled into low-impedance loads. If this need is not anticipated, C_6 can be lower in value. In fact, when using the generator into high-impedance loads, it is a good idea to use a low-value coupling capacitor in series with the output.

The function generator works well with power supplies that deliver from 12 to 15 V. Battery power is acceptable for occasional use. Frequent use suggests a line-operated supply. Figure 11-15 on page 139 shows such a supply. If you decide to use this circuit, eliminate R_1 and C_2 and power the function generator directly from pin 3 of the IC voltage regulator. The parts descriptions for this supply are listed in the next activity.

ACTIVITY 11-4 CONSTRUCTION PROJECT: PLL SIGNAL GENERATOR

INTRODUCTION AND CONSTRUCTION

What can be done with a highly accurate and stable signal generator? The following list is not complete:

1. Tune musical instruments
2. Test digital timing and counting circuits
3. Calibrate equipment
4. Use with an oscilloscope to increase measurement accuracy
5. Test and align filters
6. Measure revolutions per minute

Figure 11-13 on the next page is a diagram of a phase-locked-loop (PLL) signal generator. The output is a square wave of 3 to 999 kHz in 1-kHz steps. The output frequency is digitally controlled by three binary-coded-decimal (BCD) thumbwheel switches. This generator is very stable and accurate because its output is phase-locked to a quartz crystal.

The heart of the circuit is IC_2, a CD4046A integrated circuit, which contains a voltage-controlled oscillator (VCO) and a phase detector. The phase detector compares the signals applied to pins 14 and 3. If there is any phase difference between these signals, an error voltage is generated which is connected to the VCO at pin 9. The VCO will respond by changing its frequency. The feedback loop is completed in Fig. 11-13 by IC_1, which is a programmable counter. The reference frequency is fixed at 1 kHz and is applied to pin 14 of IC_2. As an example, IC_1 can be programmed to divide by 248 by setting the thumbwheel switches. The frequency coming out of pin 23 will be 1/248 of the frequency going to pin 1. Thus, the VCO must generate 248 kHz so that the signal going to pin 3 of IC_2 will be the same as the reference signal at pin 14.

When a new number is set on the switches, the loop loses lock. The signal fed back is no longer in phase with the reference signal. The error voltage that is developed will drive the VCO in a direction to eliminate the error. Eventually, the error is eliminated as the loop acquires lock.

The reference signal is derived from a 2.56-MHz crystal. IC_4 contains both the oscillator circuitry and a binary divider, which operates at 2^8 ($\div$ 256). The 2.56-MHz signal is divided by 256 for an output of 10 kHz. The 10-kHz signal is fed to pin 14 of IC_3. Since IC_3 is a decade (10) divider, the signal at its output (pin 12) is 1 kHz, which is very stable because it is derived from a crystal oscillator. Hence the output of the PLL generator is phase-locked to a stable reference and is also stable.

The circuit of Fig. 11-13 can generate almost 1000 different frequencies, each nearly as stable and accurate as that produced by a crystal-controlled oscillator. Figure 11-14 on page 139 shows a range-extension circuit that can be used to generate frequencies as low as 10 Hz and decrease step size to as little as 0.1 Hz. It consists of a series of decade dividers. If you decide to add this extension circuit, each decade divider should be wired like IC_3 in Fig. 11-13. Be sure to apply power and ground to each decade divider and don't forget that pin 14 is the input and pin 12 is the output. The extension circuit is *strongly* recommended if you plan to use the signal generator in the audio range. Although the main circuit will go as low as 3 kHz, the step size is too coarse and the VCO noise sensitivity too high. The PLL generator circuit of Fig. 11-13 produces the best signals when it is operating at frequencies above 100 kHz.

All the ICs in Fig. 11-13 are complementary metallic-oxide semiconductors (CMOS). They are static-sensitive and must be handled with care. You should use sockets for these devices. Do not remove the ICs from their protective carriers of foam until the circuit has been completely wired and double-checked. Touch a grounded object immediately before handling the ICs.

Figure 11-15 on page 139 is a power-supply circuit for the signal generator. It provides low-noise regulated 12 V dc. Low-noise supplies are important in PLL circuits because of the sensitivity of the VCO.

Figure 11-16 shows a buffer and transistor-transistor logic (TTL) driver circuit. This circuit should be included in your design to increase the drive capabilities of the signal generator, to protect it, and to make it compatible with the logic levels found in most digital systems. Without the buffer, the more expensive ICs in the signal generator may be

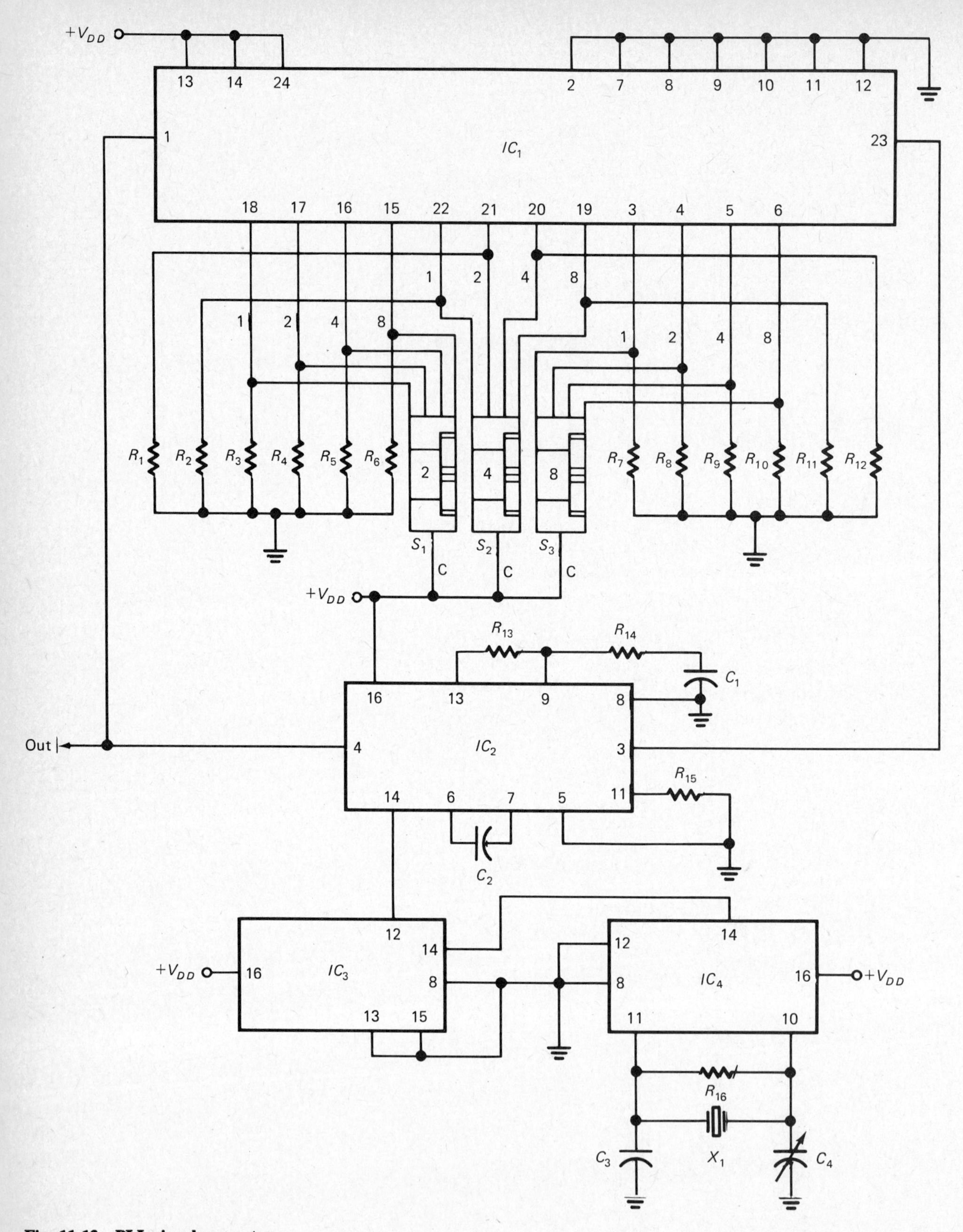

Fig. 11-13 PLL signal generator.

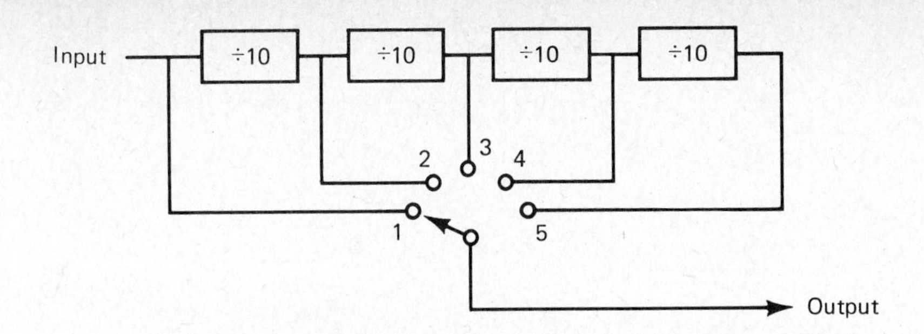

Position	Freq. Range	Step Size
1	100 to 999 kHz	1 kHz
2	10.0 to 99.9 kHz	100 Hz
3	1.00 to 9.99 kHz	10 Hz
4	100 to 999 Hz	1 Hz
5	10.0 to 99.9 Hz	0.1 Hz

Fig. 11-14 Range extension circuit.

damaged if you connect the output to a high-energy portion of a circuit under test. If you use the buffer, it should be connected at the "Out" point in Fig. 11-13. Connect pin 4 of IC_2 to pin 14 of the buffer. If you opt for the range-extension circuit, connect the "Output" of Fig. 11-14 to pin 14 of the buffer IC. The buffer is also a CMOS device, so observe the handling precautions.

Capacitor C_4 in Fig. 11-13 is the only adjustment. Connect the output of the signal generator to a digital frequency counter. Set the switches for an output of 999 kHz. Adjust C_4 until the frequency counter displays 999000 Hz.

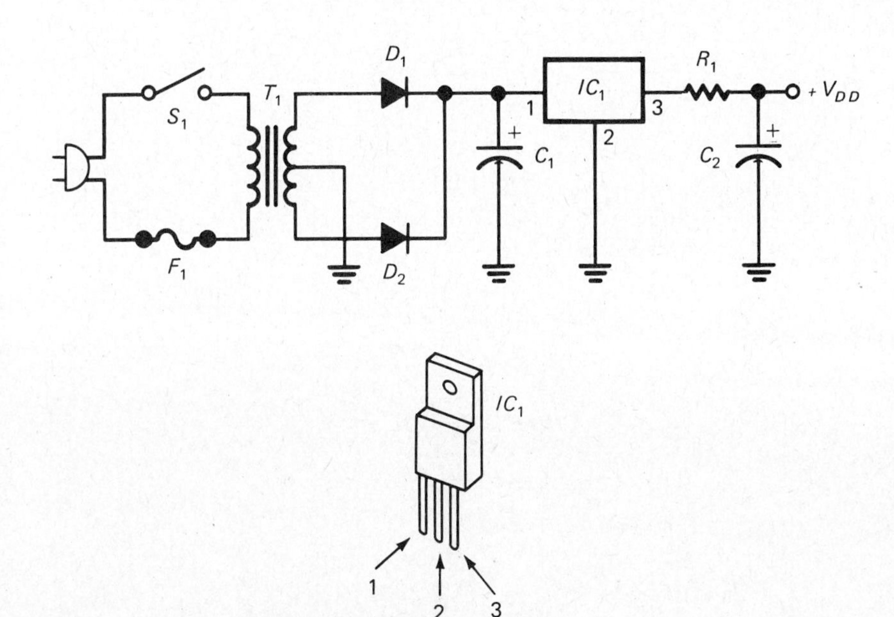

Fig. 11-15 Power supply for PLL signal generator.

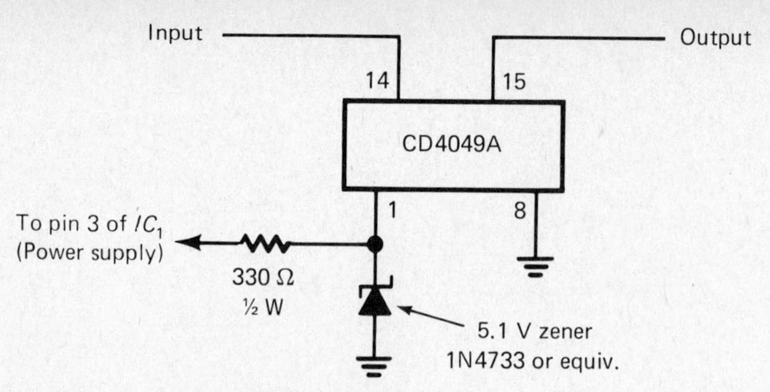

Fig. 11-16 Buffer and TTL driver.

Parts List

Part Numbers	Description
C_1	0.5-μF ceramic or Mylar capacitor
C_2	50-pF ceramic or Mylar capacitor
C_3	15-pF mica or polystyrene capacitor
C_4	25-pF mica or ceramic trimmer capacitor
IC_1	CD4059A IC or equivalent
IC_2	CD4046A IC or equivalent
IC_3	CD4017A IC or equivalent
IC_4	CD4060A IC or equivalent
R_1–R_{12}	33-kΩ ¼-W resistors
R_{13}	10-kΩ ¼-W resistor
R_{14}	560-Ω ¼-W resistor
R_{15}	10-kΩ ¼-W resistor
R_{16}	10-MΩ ¼-W resistor
S_1–S_3	BCD thumbwheel switches
X_1	2.56-MHz parallel resonant crystal, 10-pF load
Misc.	Wire, cabinet, IC sockets, hardware, circuit board, output jack, power cord, etc.
	Range-Extension Option
ICs	CD4017A ICs or equivalent
Switch	Five-position single-pole rotary switch
	Power Supply
C_1, C_2	1-mF 25-V electrolytic capacitors
D_1, D_2	1N4001 rectifiers or equivalent
F_1	¼-W 140-V ac slow-blow fuse
IC_1	7812 voltage-regulator IC or equivalent
R_1	68-Ω ½-W resistor
S_1	120-V ac SPST switch
T_1	28-V 0.3-A center-tap Stancor P-8602 transformer or equivalent
	Buffer-Amplifier Option
IC	CD4049A IC or equivalent
R	330-Ω ½-W resistor
ZD	5.1-V zener diode 1N4733 or equivalent

CHAPTER 12

Radio Receivers

ACTIVITY 12-1
TEST: RADIO RECEIVERS

Choose the letter that best completes the statement or answers the question.

1. Modulation is a process used to
   a. Place intelligence on a radio signal
   b. Develop a high-frequency radio wave
   c. Recover information from a signal
   d. Detect radio signals
2. A continuous-wave transmission involves the use of
   a. Picture information
   b. Audio information
   c. A code, such as Morse
   d. All of the above
3. An AM transmission uses
   a. A code key to turn the carrier on and off
   b. An intelligence signal to control the carrier amplitude
   c. An intelligence signal to control carrier frequency
   d. All of the above
4. A 900-kHz radio signal is amplitude-modulated by a 5-kHz audio sine wave. The frequency or frequencies present in the transmitted signal are
   a. 5 kHz
   b. 20 kHz
   c. 5 and 900 kHz
   d. 895, 900, and 905 kHz
5. A 10-kHz sine wave is used to amplitude-modulate an 800-kHz carrier. The frequency of the upper sideband is
   a. 10 kHz
   b. 800 kHz
   c. 790 kHz
   d. 810 kHz

6. A radio station is assigned a carrier frequency of 1020 kHz. If the station uses AM and limits the highest audio frequency to 10 kHz, the total bandwidth required for transmission is
   a. 10 kHz
   b. 20 kHz
   c. 100 kHz
   d. 102 kHz
7. The most common AM detector is the
   a. Diode detector
   b. Discriminator
   c. Ratio detector
   d. Limiter
8. Detection of an AM signal can be achieved by
   a. Any resistor
   b. Any loudspeaker
   c. Any tuned circuit
   d. Any nonlinear component
9. In a radio receiver, sensitivity is provided by
   a. Several tuned circuits
   b. Several stages of gain
   c. The loudspeaker
   d. The volume control
10. In a radio receiver, selectivity is provided by
    a. Several tuned circuits
    b. Several stages of gain
    c. The loudspeaker
    d. The volume control
11. The tuned RF receiver is not very popular because
    a. It cannot achieve enough sensitivity
    b. It cannot achieve enough selectivity
    c. It cannot be built using transistors
    d. It suffers from tracking and bandwidth variations
12. A superheterodyne receiver achieves adjacent channel selectivity
    a. By a tuned antenna circuit
    b. By a tuned mixer input
    c. By tuned IF circuits
    d. By a tuned detector output
13. Signals are converted to the IF in a superheterodyne receiver by
    a. Mixing with a local oscillator signal
    b. The heterodyne process
    c. A frequency-conversion process
    d. All of the above
14. A superheterodyne receiver has an IF of 455 kHz. It is tuned to a station at 1020 kHz. The frequency of the local oscillator in the receiver is
    a. 455 kHz
    b. 565 kHz
    c. 1275 kHz
    d. 1475 kHz
15. A superheterodyne receiver has an IF of 455 kHz. It is tuned to receive a station at 1200 kHz. Interference is heard from a station transmitting on 2110 kHz. The trouble with the receiver is
    a. Poor adjacent-channel selectivity
    b. Poor image rejection
    c. Poor sensitivity
    d. All of the above

16. What do amplitude modulators, demodulators, detectors, mixers, and heterodyne converters have in common?
a. They are all nonlinear circuits that produce sum and difference frequencies
b. They are all forms of electronic oscillators
c. They are all ICs using digital techniques
d. They are all types of transmitting antennas

17. A superheterodyne receiver has a problem with image interference. The solution is to
a. Add more tuned circuits in the IF stages
b. Realign the IF stages to a new frequency
c. Increase the gain of the RF amplifier
d. Add more tuned circuits before the mixer

18. A block diagram for a receiver shows a stage marked AGC. What is the function of this stage?
a. Amplitude gyrator circuit
b. Automatic gain control
c. Absolute frequency crystal
d. Active gain chassis

19. A superheterodyne receiver uses a dual-tuning capacitor to control the mixer circuit and the local oscillator simultaneously. Small trimmer capacitors are a part of the tuning-capacitor assembly. The purpose of the trimmers is to
a. Help align the IF stages
b. Make fine tuning of weak stations possible
c. Make it possible to track the oscillator- and mixer-tuned circuits properly
d. Set the receiver to the desired band of operation at the factory

20. Compared with AM, FM
a. Requires more bandwidth
b. Produces a constant-amplitude signal
c. Is more noise-immune
d. All of the above

21. What type of receiver uses limiters between the IF stages and the detector?
a. AM
b. FM
c. DSB
d. SSB

22. A receiver block diagram shows a stage marked AFC. What is the purpose of this stage?
a. Automatic frequency control
b. Audio filter circuit
c. Absolute frequency crystal
d. Active fast-compression circuit

23. The advantage of using a ratio detector for FM detection rather than a discriminator is that
a. A ratio detector can drive a zero-center tuning meter
b. The ratio detector requires no alignment
c. The ratio detector needs only a fraction of the components
d. The limiter stage can be eliminated

24. The AM system that eliminates the carrier is
a. SSB
b. DSB
c. USB
d. LSB

25. The carrier is eliminated at the transmitter by using a
    a. Balanced modulator
    b. Filter
    c. Trap
    d. PLL demodulator
26. The advantages of SSB over ordinary AM are
    a. Reduced complexity and cost
    b. Improved fidelity and ease of tuning
    c. Less bandwidth and better power efficiency
    d. All of the above
27. To properly demodulate an SSB signal at the receiver it is necessary to use
    a. A missing-pulse detector
    b. A ratio detector
    c. Sharp filters
    d. A BFO to replace the missing carrier
28. A technician wants to check the local oscillator in an AM receiver by using a second AM receiver. The dial on the second receiver should be set
    a. Exactly like the first receiver dial
    b. All the way at the lowest end of the tuning range
    c. 455 kHz higher than the dial on the first receiver
    d. All the way up at the high end of the band
29. A receiver shows poor sensitivity. The problem could be
    a. An AGC problem
    b. A leaky detector diode
    c. Improper alignment
    d. Any of the above
30. An FM receiver must be retuned every few minutes. The problem could be
    a. Power-supply voltage fluctuation
    b. A defective component in the oscillator
    c. A defective AFC circuit
    d. Any of the above

ACTIVITY 12-2
LAB EXPERIMENT: ELECTRONIC COMMUNICATIONS

PURPOSE

To study several important concepts and circuits used in electronic communications.

MATERIALS

Qty.		*Qty.*	
1	oscilloscope with probe	1	1-MΩ ½-W resistor
1	dc power supply	1	470-kΩ ½-W resistor
2	audio-signal generators*	1	560-Ω ½-W resistor

Materials list continued on the next page.

*Note: Or one signal generator plus the additional materials shown in alternate part 1.

- 1 0.01-μF paper or Mylar capacitor
- 1 365-pF variable capacitor
- 1 0.02-μF paper or Mylar capacitor
- 1 25-μF 25-V electrolytic capacitor
- 1 270-Ω ½-W resistor
- 2 47-pF ceramic or mica capacitors
- 1 220-μH AM antenna coil
- 1 30-mH RF choke
- 1 output transformer, transistor type (audio)
- 1 driver transformer, transistor type (audio)
- 1 1N4001 diode or equivalent
- 1 2N4220 transistor or equivalent
- 1 2N4401 transistor or equivalent
- 1 earphone or headphones, high-impedance type

INTRODUCTION

This activity has been divided into two parts plus an alternate. There is a part 1, an alternate part 1, and a part 2. Alternate part 1 can be used if you do not have access to two signal generators. You may complete the parts in any order.

PROCEDURE

Part 1

1. Build the circuit shown in Fig. 12-1. Note that in this circuit the center-tapped winding is used as the secondary for both transformers. No connection is to be made to the center tap on the driver transformer. Also note that only half the winding is used on the output transformer. Check the frequency settings for both generators. They should be set as shown in Fig. 12-1. Be sure that the generators are set for sinusoidal output.

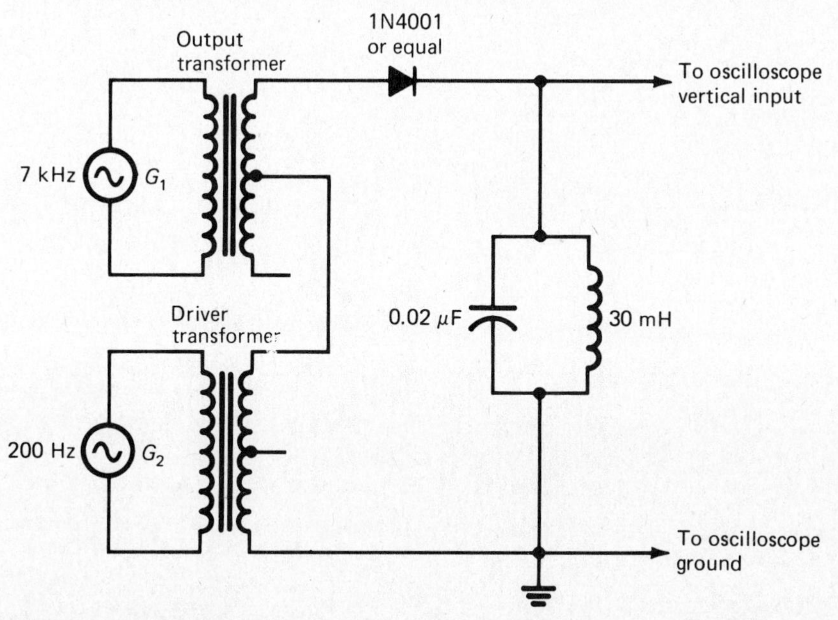

Fig. 12-1 AM circuit.

2. Adjust your oscilloscope for a sweep rate of 1 ms/div. Turn the amplitude of G_2 all the way down to zero. Adjust the amplitude for G_1 until the oscilloscope shows an output signal of 1 V peak-to-peak. Slowly increase the amplitude of G_2 until the output waveform shows amplitude modulation.
3. Compare your oscilloscope waveform with Fig. 12-2(*a*). The appearance should be about the same. It is very difficult for certain oscilloscopes to trigger properly on this type of waveform. If a stable display cannot be obtained, use the external trigger mode and use the signal from G_2 as the source.
4. Short the diode out of the circuit. This can be done by jumping across it with a short lead. Compare your waveform with Fig. 12-2(*b*). They should look about the same.
   a. Which waveform, Fig. 12-2(*a*) or (*b*), shows the simple addition of two sine waves?
   b. Which waveform shows modulation (nonlinear mixing) of two sine waves?
   c. What is the purpose of the diode in Fig. 12-1?
5. Figure 12-2(*a*) is in the time domain. Draw a picture of what would appear in the frequency domain.

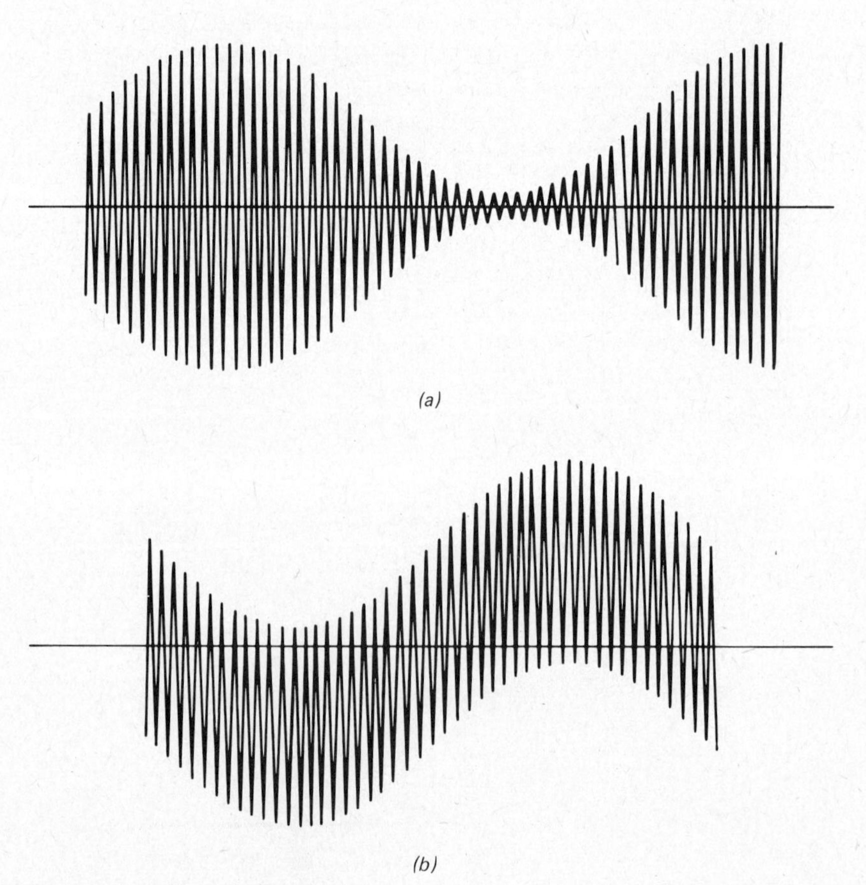

Fig. 12-2 Circuit waveforms.

PROCEDURE

Alternate Part 1

ADDITIONAL MATERIALS

Qty.		*Qty.*	
1	12.6-V center-tapped Stancor P-8130 transformer or equivalent	1	100-Ω resistor
1	10-kΩ ½-W resistor	1	0.5-μF Mylar or paper capacitor
2	1-kΩ ½-W resistors	2	0.1-μF Mylar or paper capacitors

PROCEDURE

1. Figure 12-3 shows an alternate circuit for demonstrating AM. This circuit requires only one signal generator since it uses stepped-down line voltage as the modulating signal. Be very careful when wiring the primary circuit of the transformer. Notice that only half of the secondary winding is used. This connection applies about 7 V ac in series with the dc supply, with the result that the 60-Hz ac amplitude modulates the 1.3-kHz signal applied to the base of the transistor. The modulation occurs in the transistor (it is accomplished by the diode in Fig. 12-1).
2. Build the circuit shown in Fig. 12-3. Set the signal generator for a 1.3-kHz sine-wave output and adjust its amplitude to 6 V peak-to-peak. Set the oscilloscope for 0.2 V/div and a sweep rate of 2 ms/div. Connect the oscilloscope as shown in Fig. 12-3.
3. Compare your waveform with the one shown in Fig. 12-2(*a*). The appearance should be about the same. Some oscilloscopes have difficulty triggering properly on this type of waveform. The ***line-trigger*** function will provide a stable display on oscilloscopes having this feature. Another possibility is to use ***external trigger*** and apply a signal to this oscilloscope input from the junction of the 1-kΩ resistor and the transformer secondary in Fig. 12-3.
4. If necessary, vary the dc supply voltage until your display is similar to that shown in Fig. 12-2(*a*). Draw a picture of what would be displayed in the frequency domain.

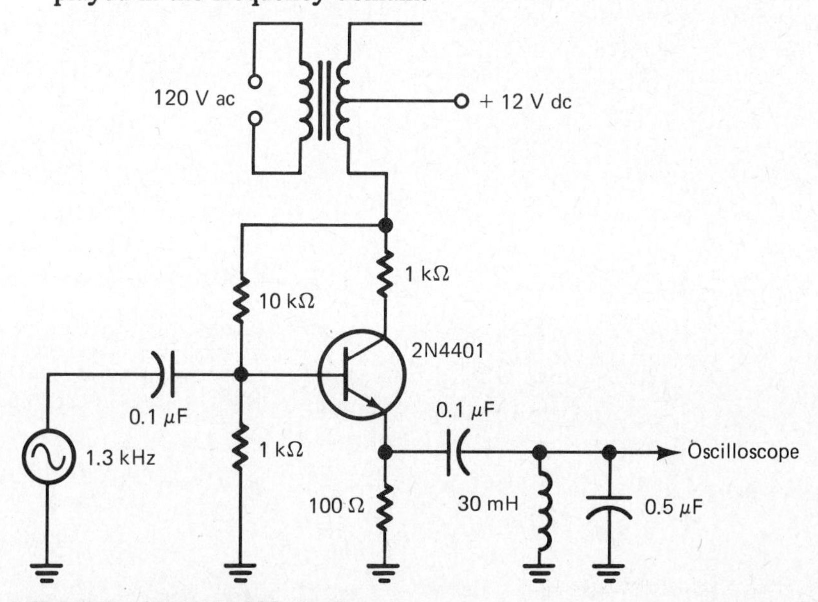

Fig. 12-3 Alternate AM circuit.

PROCEDURE

Part 2

1. Build the circuit shown in Fig. 12-4. The antenna is a length of hookup wire or a few test leads strung together. The antenna length will depend upon the strength of the AM broadcast signals in your area (a longer wire is needed for weak signals). The variable capacitor serves to tune in the signals. It may not be possible to completely separate two strong signals that are close in frequency. This is a limitation of a single-tuned circuit.
2. See how many stations this simple receiver can hear.
   a. Why is a separate diode detector not required in this receiver?
   b. What are some of the ways that the performance of this receiver can be improved?

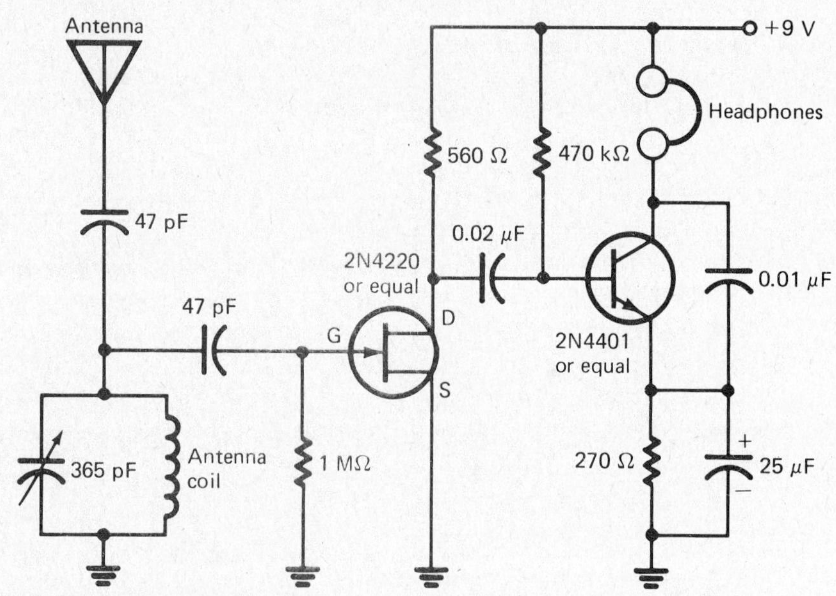

Fig. 12-4 AM radio receiver.

ACTIVITY 12-3 CONSTRUCTION PROJECT: FM WIRELESS MICROPHONE

INTRODUCTION AND CONSTRUCTION

Figure 12-5 on the next page shows the schematic for a small FM transmitter that operates in the commercial broadcast band. It is battery-operated and can be built on a small circuit board (about 1 × 2 in.).

Q_1 is the audio amplifier. It has a high input impedance to match the output of a ceramic microphone. Q_2 is a common-base RF oscillator. The audio signal from Q_1 varies the base voltage of Q_2, and frequency modulation of the oscillator signal results. Q_3 is a buffer amplifier, included to minimize the effects of the antenna on the oscillator. The antenna is a length of small-gauge insulated hook-up wire.

L_1 in Fig. 12-5 is a slug-tuned RF coil with six turns of no. 20 solid wire wound on a form with a diameter of 3/16 in. The coil is tapped one turn from the C_9 end. The coil form and tuning slug can be salvaged from old equipment (such as a television receiver), or L_1 can be an air-core coil if C_8 is replaced with a miniature 50-pF trimmer capacitor.

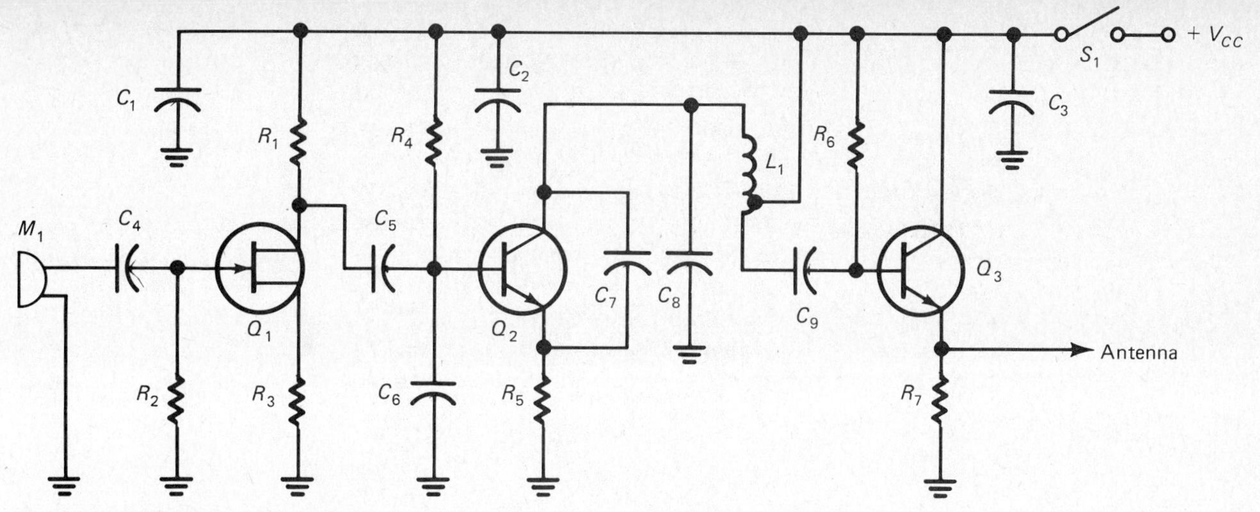

Fig. 12-5 FM wireless microphone.

RF circuits should be built with a good ground plane and with short leads. Figure 12-6 shows a suggested layout and construction method for this project. The board is ordinary single-sided copper-clad material. A V_{CC} bus is produced by removing a thin strip of foil from the top of the board with a knife and needle-nose pliers. Score the copper with the knife and use the pliers to pull a thin strip of copper from the board. The foil can also be removed with a hacksaw or with a miniature grinding tool.

Another thing that should be done to the board shown in Fig. 12-6 is to isolate two copper pads for mounting and supporting the coil. This can be accomplished with a special pad-cutting tool, with a knife, or with a grinding tool. The other leads are self-supporting. Note that the

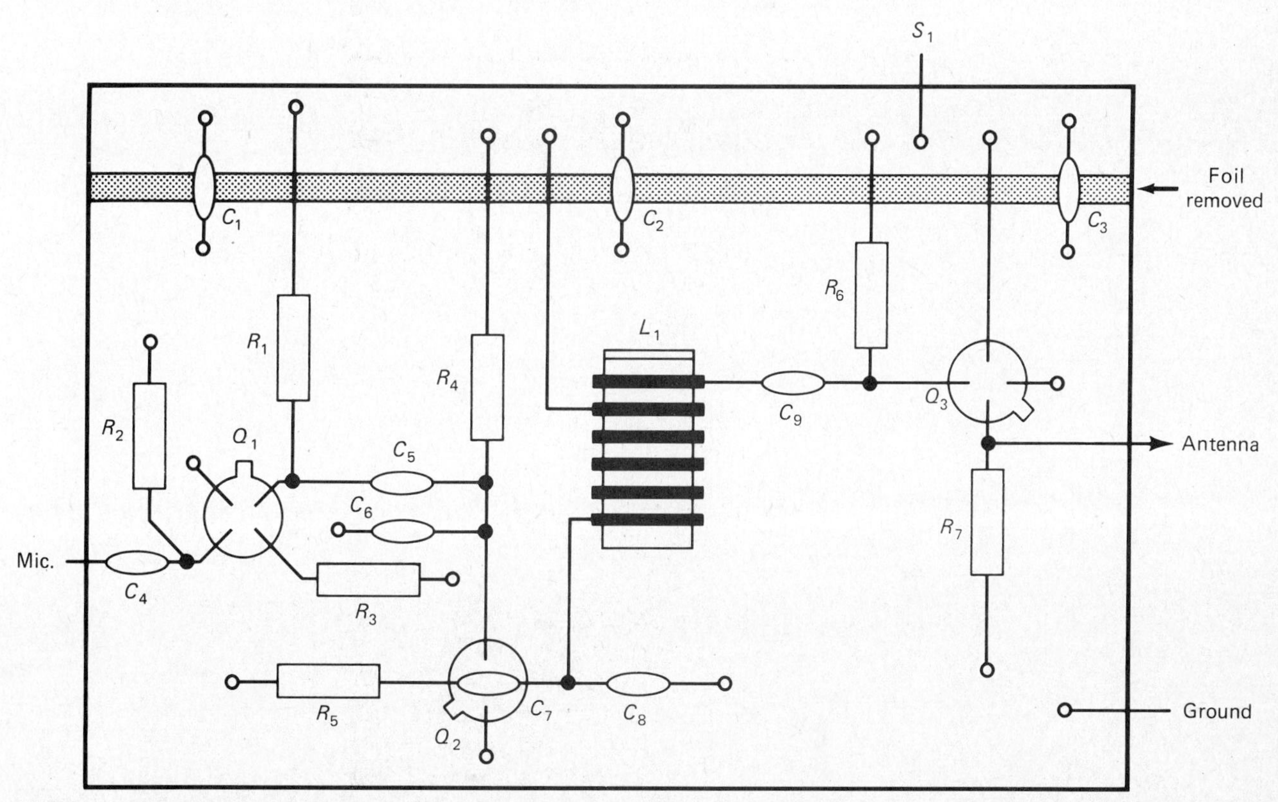

Fig. 12-6 Suggested circuit layout for an FM wireless microphone.

open dots are places where leads are soldered to the foil of the board. The black dots are places where the leads are soldered to other leads, and these points must not touch the foil. Be sure to clean the foil side of the board with fine steelwool before doing any soldering.

The transistors in Fig. 12-6 *are mounted upside down.* The transistor cases are grounded and therefore can touch the copper foil. Note the orientation of the tabs on the transistor cases. If you use a careful layout and small components, you can build the circuit on a circuit board the size of an ordinary 9-V battery (NEDA 1604A). The transmitter is designed to be powered by such a battery and the resulting total package is just a little bigger than the battery itself.

Use a 1-ft length of wire as an antenna for testing and adjustment. After you have checked your wiring, turn the transmitter on. You should be able to adjust L_1 to place a carrier on the FM broadcast band (88 to 108 MHz). Tune the coil and the FM receiver until you find a spot where the interference with commercial stations is minimum. You should be able to hear your voice from the FM receiver when you talk into the microphone.

The length of the antenna will determine the range of the transmitter. Experiment with different lengths to achieve *only* the range you need. The Federal Communications Commission does not permit transmitters of this type to interfere with the reception of others.

Parts List

Part Numbers	Description
C_1–C_3, C_6, C_9	470-pF miniature Mylar or ceramic capacitors
C_4, C_5	0.1-μF miniature Mylar or ceramic capacitors
C_7, C_8	10-pF miniature silver mica or polystyrene capacitors
L_1	3/16-in.-diameter slug-tuned coil, six turns, no. 20 solid wire, tapped at one turn
M_1	High-impedance crystal microphone
Q_1	2N4220 N-channel JFET or equivalent
Q_2, Q_3	2N5179 transistors or equivalent
R_1	10-kΩ ¼-W resistor
R_2	1-MΩ ¼-W resistor
R_3	1-kΩ ¼-W resistor
R_4, R_6	33-kΩ ¼-W resistors
R_5, R_7	100-Ω ¼-W resistors
S_1	SPST switch
Misc.	Wire, circuit board, 9-V Eveready 522 alkaline battery or equivalent, battery clip

CHAPTER 13

Linear Integrated Circuits

ACTIVITY 13-1
TEST: LINEAR INTEGRATED CIRCUITS

Choose the letter that best completes the statement or answers the question.

1. Early development of ICs was mostly in what area?
   a. Radio devices
   b. Television devices
   c. Digital devices
   d. Voltage regulators
2. A circuit will use individual resistors, capacitors, diodes, and transistors to achieve its function. What is such a circuit said to be?
   a. Printed
   b. Hybrid
   c. Hand-crafted
   d. Discrete
3. What advantages are there in using ICs in electronic design?
   a. They decrease size and cost
   b. They make the design easier to align and test
   c. They increase reliability and performance
   d. All of the above
4. How is the reliability of electronic equipment related to the number of parts in the equipment?
   a. Directly
   b. Indirectly
   c. Not at all
   d. None of the above
5. What is the most positive way of identifying a device as an IC in a particular piece of electronic equipment?
   a. Use the schematic and/or service notes
   b. By visual inspection of the package
   c. By counting the pins
   d. By checking the color code

6. What is needed when troubleshooting an IC?
   a. The internal schematic for the IC
   b. An understanding of the internal workings of the IC
   c. Knowing how the IC is supposed to perform in the circuit
   d. A high-quality oscilloscope

7. What is the major process used in manufacturing ICs?
   a. Anodization
   b. Photolithography
   c. Germanium migration
   d. Wafer bonding

8. What is the next step after the wafer has been oxidized and coated with photoresist?
   a. Expose through a photomask
   b. Develop the photoresist
   c. Etch
   d. Diffusion

9. What does batch processing refer to?
   a. Hybrid ICs
   b. Each wafer yields a batch of ICs
   c. Bonding the ICs
   d. All of the above

10. What process does the wafer undergo after it receives a probe test?
    a. It is processed in an aluminum-diffusion furnace
    b. It is mounted in a package and sealed
    c. It is scribed and broken apart
    d. None of the above

11. How are the pads on the chip wired to the tabs on the metal headers?
    a. Using miniature printed circuitry
    b. Using copper-bronze leaf contacts
    c. By wire-wrap techniques
    d. By the ball-bonding process

12. What is the function of the isolation diffusion in manufacturing ICs?
    a. It isolates the various component functions electrically
    b. It isolates the transistors from the oxide layer
    c. It isolates the collector of the transistor from the substrate
    d. It isolates the emitter and collector of the transistors

13. How are the various circuit functions interconnected in a monolithic IC?
    a. Jumper wires
    b. Evaporated aluminum
    c. Gold bonds
    d. Screen-printed conductors

14. A monolithic IC uses MOS capacitors. What forms the dielectric for these capacitors?
    a. A depletion region in a PN junction
    b. Silicon dioxide
    c. A depleted P zone
    d. Air

15. An IC uses several types of components mounted on a ceramic substrate. What is this type of IC called?
    a. Monolithic
    b. Dual-in-line
    c. Hybrid
    d. Ceramic

Questions 16 to 18 refer to Fig. 13-1.

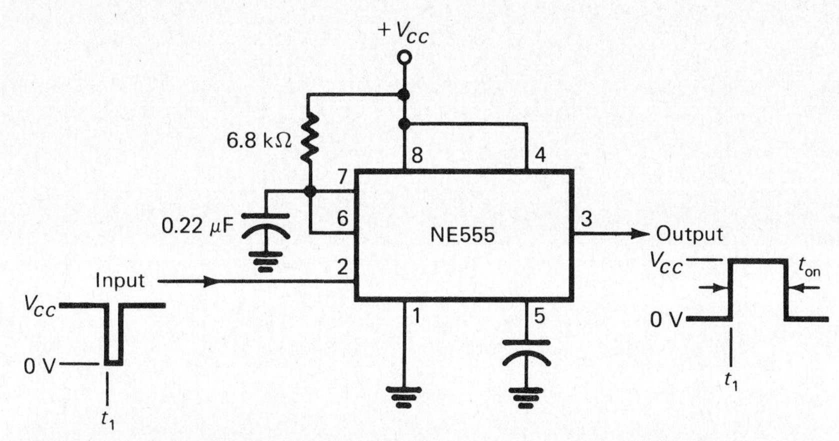

Fig. 13-1 Circuit for Questions 16 to 18.

16. As shown in the figure, a negative-going pulse applied to the input causes the output of the timer to pulse high for a period of time. The timer IC is set up to operate in what mode?
    a. One-shot (monostable)
    b. Free-running (astable)
    c. Time-delay
    d. None of the above
17. The input pulse is 0.05 ms long. How long is the output pulse t_{on}?
    a. 0.01 ms
    b. 0.05 ms
    c. 1.65 ms
    d. 238 ms
18. The 0.22-μF capacitor is replaced with a 1.5-μF capacitor. What happens to the output pulse length?
    a. Depends on the input pulse length
    b. Increases
    c. Decreases
    d. Remains the same
19. An NE555 timer IC is set up as a free-running oscillator. How can the output frequency be increased?
    a. Decrease the size of the timing capacitor
    b. Increase the size of the timing resistors
    c. Increase the size of the timing capacitor
    d. Decrease the input-signal frequency
20. An NE555 timer IC is set up so that the output changes state at some fixed time after a trigger signal is received. What is this mode called?
    a. One-shot
    b. Free-running
    c. Time-delay
    d. Lag-lead
21. Which of the following linear ICs would be used to detect an FM signal?
    a. IF amplifier
    b. Audio power amplifier
    c. Timer
    d. Phase-locked loop

22. What should you know when troubleshooting equipment that uses ICs?
  a. The inner details for each IC
  b. Complete specifications for each IC
  c. Voltage and temperature characteristics for each IC
  d. The block diagram and how each stage should function

Questions 23 to 26 refer to Fig. 13-2.

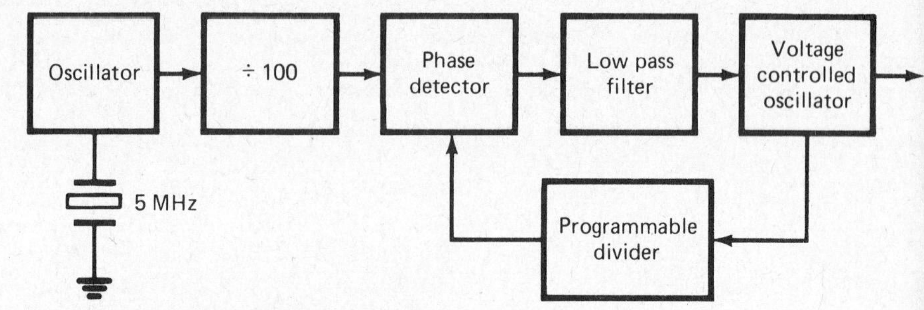

Fig. 13-2 Circuit for Questions 23 to 26.

23. What is the circuit shown?
  a. A tone decoder
  b. An FM detector
  c. A television IF amplifier
  d. A frequency synthesizer

24 Assume that the loop is locked. The input frequencies to the phase detector will be
  a. 50 kHz at the left and 5 MHz at the bottom
  b. 50 kHz at the left and 50 kHz at the bottom
  c. 50 kHz at the left and 50 kHz × divider setting at the bottom
  d. None of the above

25. Assume that the divider is programmed to divide by 10. What is the output frequency?
  a. 50 MHz
  b. 5 MHz
  c. 0.5 MHz
  d. None of the above

26. Assuming proper operation, the frequency stability of the output is determined by
  a. The stability of the crystal oscillator
  b. The fixed 100-divide circuit
  c. The phase detector
  d. The stability of the VCO

ACTIVITY 13-2
LAB EXPERIMENT: INTEGRATED CIRCUITS

PURPOSE

To investigate a few common applications for two linear ICs.

MATERIALS

Qty.		Qty.	
1	multimeter	1	50-μF 15-V electrolytic capacitor
1	oscilloscope with probe	1	0.5-μF paper or Mylar capacitor
1	dc power supply	3	0.1-μF paper or Mylar capacitors
1	audio-signal generator	1	0.05-μF paper or Mylar capacitor
1	frequency counter (optional)	1	1N4001 diode or equivalent
2	10-kΩ ½-W resistors	1	NE555 IC or equivalent
1	2.2-kΩ ½-W resistor	1	NE567 IC or equivalent
1	680-Ω ½-W resistor	1	push-button normally open switch, momentary contact
1	330-Ω ½-W resistor		
1	10-kΩ linear potentiometer		
1	1-kΩ linear potentiometer		

PROCEDURE

1. Build the circuit shown in Fig. 13-3. Set up your oscilloscope for 200 ms/div and dc-couple the vertical amplifier. Connect the oscilloscope to the output of the timer IC.
2. Trigger the timer by using the push-button switch connected to pin 2 of the IC.
   a. What happens to the output of the IC?
   b. Does the output stay this way?
3. Retrigger the circuit several times and measure how long the output remains high each time.
   a. How long does the output stay high?
   b. Calculate the output pulse width. For the one-shot mode

$$t = 1.1 \times R \times C$$

4. Compare the measured pulse width with the calculated pulse width. (Electrolytic capacitors are not known for their precision; considerable error is typical.)
   a. What would happen to the output pulse width if a lower-value capacitor were substituted for the 50-μF unit?
   b. What would happen to the pulse width if a lower-value resistor were substituted for the 10-kΩ unit?

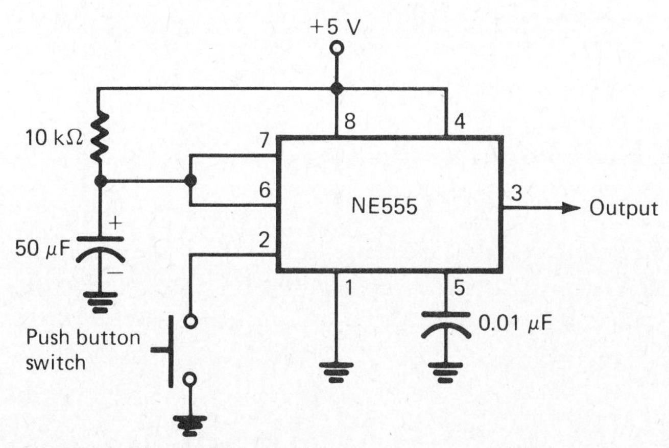

Fig. 13-3 Monostable circuit.

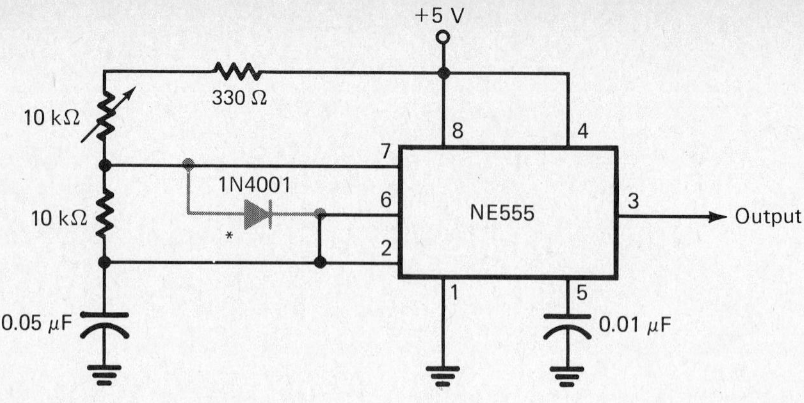

Fig. 13-4 Astable circuit.

5. Turn off the power. Rewire the circuit so that it appears as shown in Fig. 13-4. Again connect the output of the timer IC to the oscilloscope. Adjust the potentiometer for maximum resistance (10 kΩ). Turn on the power. Adjust the oscilloscope for a good, stable display of the output waveform.
   a. What type of waveform is seen on the oscilloscope?
   b. Is it symmetrical?
   c. Is the width of the positive-going pulse the same as the width of the negative-going pulse?
6. Slowly reduce the resistance of the potentiometer while watching the waveform on the scope. What happens?
7. Measure the duty-cycle range of the circuit. Adjust the potentiometer for minimum resistance. Measure the duty cycle of the output waveform. Adjust the potentiometer for maximum resistance and remeasure the duty cycle.
8. Calculate the minimum and maximum duty cycles for the circuit:

$$D = \frac{R_A + R_B}{R_A + 2R_B} \times 100\%$$

$$D_{\text{min}} = \frac{330\ \Omega + 10\ \text{k}\Omega}{330\ \Omega + 20\ \text{k}\Omega} \times 100\% = ?$$

$$D_{\text{max}} = \frac{10.3\ \text{k}\Omega + 10\ \text{k}\Omega}{10.3\ \text{k}\Omega + 20\ \text{k}\Omega} \times 100\% = ?$$

Note: The measured values from step 7 should agree reasonably well with the calculated values.

9. Turn off the power. Add the diode as shown in Fig. 13-4; it will be on when the 0.05-μF timing capacitor is charging. The fixed 10-kΩ resistor is thus bypassed, and the charging time can be made very short by adjusting the 10-kΩ potentiometer for minimum resistance. It should now be possible to achieve duty cycles below 50 percent. Turn the power back on. Can very narrow positive-going output pulses be achieved by adjusting the potentiometer for minimum resistance?
10. Measure the duty cycle range for the astable circuit with the diode added.

11. Calculate the duty cycle range for the circuit:

$$D = \frac{R_A}{R_A + R_B} \times 100\%$$

$$D_{min} = \frac{330\ \Omega}{330\ \Omega + 10k\ \Omega} \times 100\% = ?$$

$$D_{max} = \frac{10.3\ k\Omega}{10.3\ k\Omega + 10\ k\Omega} \times 100\% = ?$$

Note: There should be reasonable agreement between step 10 and your calculations.

12. If you have access to a frequency counter, connect it to the output of the astable circuit (Fig. 13-4). If not, use the oscilloscope to measure the period of the output waveform and convert this to frequency by taking the reciprocal. Measure the frequency range of the astable circuit. The diode should still be connected.
13. Calculate the frequency range of the astable circuit:

$$fo = \frac{1.45}{(R_A + R_B)\ C}$$

$$fo_{min} = \frac{1.45}{(10.3\ k\Omega + 10\ k\Omega)\ 0.05\ \mu F} = ?$$

$$fo_{max} = \frac{1.45}{(330\ \Omega + 10\ k\Omega)\ 0.05\ \mu F} = ?$$

Note: There should be reasonable agreement between the measured values in step 12 and the calculations.

14. Pin 5 of the NE555 timer IC provides access to one input of the threshold comparator. If the voltage at this pin is changed, the trip point will change and so will the output frequency of the astable circuit. Set the 10-kΩ potentiometer for an output duty cycle of 50 percent (square wave). Turn off the power and add a 1-kΩ potentiometer and a fixed 2.2-kΩ resistor as shown in Fig. 13-5. This

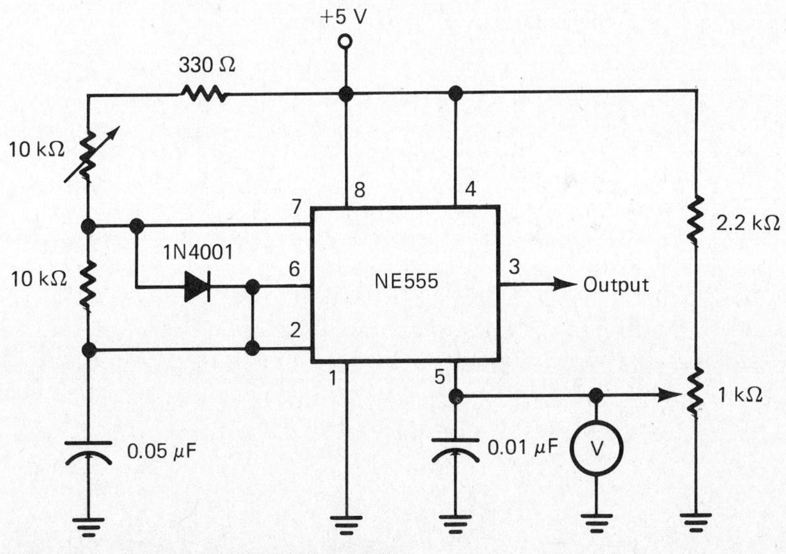

Fig. 13-5 Voltage controlled oscillator.

modification allows the astable circuit to act as a VCO. The diode should still be connected. Turn the power back on. If you have access to a frequency counter, connect it to the output of the 555 timer IC. If not, use your oscilloscope to measure the period of the output waveform and convert it into frequency by taking the reciprocal. Monitor the voltage at pin 5 of the IC with a multimeter. Prepare a graph, like that in Fig. 13-6 and plot the voltage versus frequency response for the VCO. Take enough readings to produce an accurate plot.

15. Turn off the power. Modify the wiring to duplicate the time-delay circuit shown in Fig. 13-7 on the next page. Connect the output to the oscilloscope. Set the oscilloscope for a sweep speed of 200 ms/div and dc-couple the vertical amplifier. Turn on the power. Remove the jumper wire across the capacitor while watching the oscilloscope.

a. What happens at the output when the jumper wire is removed?

b. Calculate the time delay for the circuit. Remember that electrolytic capacitors are not noted for accuracy. Turn off the power and tear the circuit down.

16. Build the tone-decoder circuit shown in Fig. 13-8 on the next page using an NE567 IC. Adjust the signal generator for a 5-V peak-to-peak sine-waveoutput. Adjust the frequency of the generator to 1 kHz. Connect the oscilloscope to the output (pin 8). Turn on the power. Vary the frequency of the generator from around 700 to 1400 Hz.

a. What happens at the output?

b. Why is this circuit called a tone decoder?

c. Measure the bandwidth of the tone decoder by carefully adjusting the frequency of the signal generator while watching the output on the oscilloscope. The bandwidth is the lowest frequency that keeps the output low subtracted from the highest frequency that also keeps the output low.

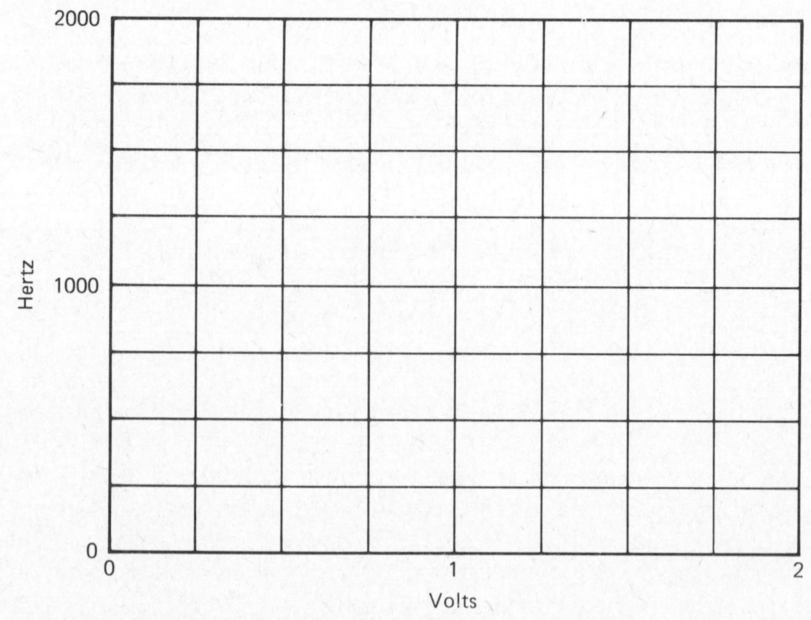

Fig. 13-6 Example of graph paper to plot VCO performance.

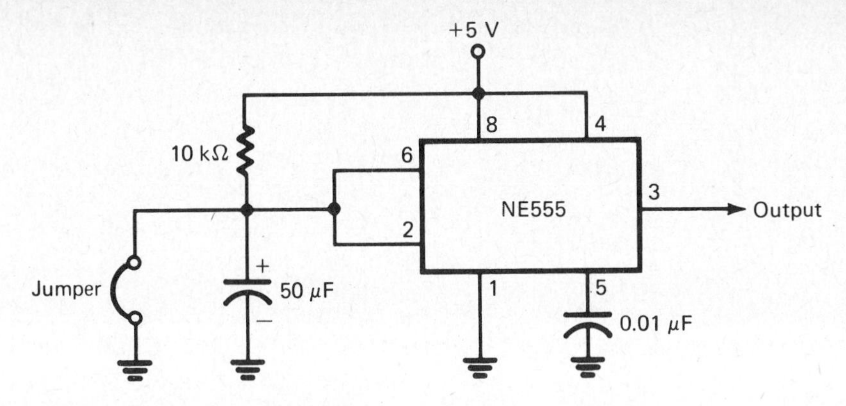

Fig. 13-7 Time-delay circuit.

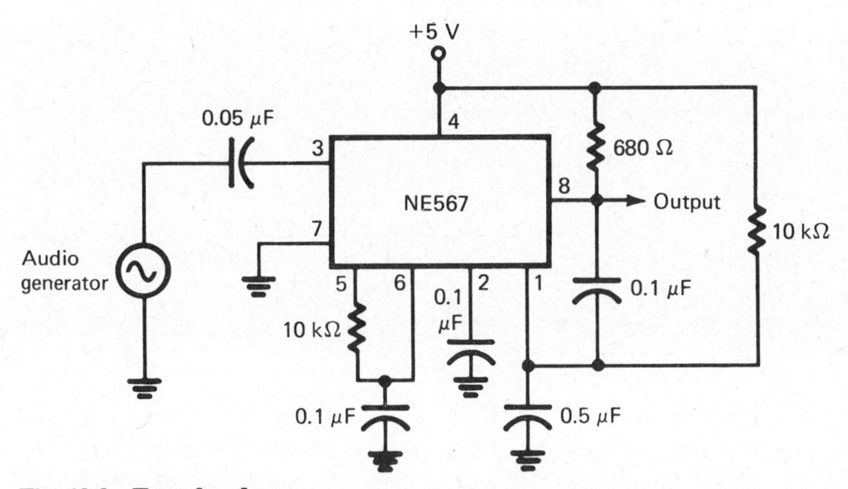

Fig. 13-8 Tone decoder.

ACTIVITY 13-3
CONSTRUCTION PROJECT: LINE VOLTMETER

INTRODUCTION AND CONSTRUCTION

The ac power line varies from location to location, building to building, room to room, and in some cases outlet to outlet. A circuit may be heavily loaded, which tends to produce low line voltage; or it may show a momentary dip in voltage when a heavy load is activated. Other circuits may support inductive loads such as motors, which can induce a momentary surge in line voltage when they are shut down.

Some equipment, for example, a computer, is sensitive to line voltage and its fluctuations. The voltmeter shown in Fig. 13-9 is designed to monitor line voltage and is especially valuable for evaluating ac circuits for their suitability to power critical equipment.

It can be frustrating and time-consuming to investigate a power circuit for possible problems using an ordinary analog or digital voltmeter. The voltmeter in Fig. 13-9 on the next page features a dot type display with *memory* for overvoltage and undervoltage conditions. This design provides an easy way to monitor a power circuit and determine whether it is suitable for a computer or other sensitive equipment.

The voltmeter circuit is greatly simplified by the LM3914 IC. This device has a stack of 10 voltage comparators biased by an internal voltage divider. The ends of the divider are connected to pins 4 and 6 of

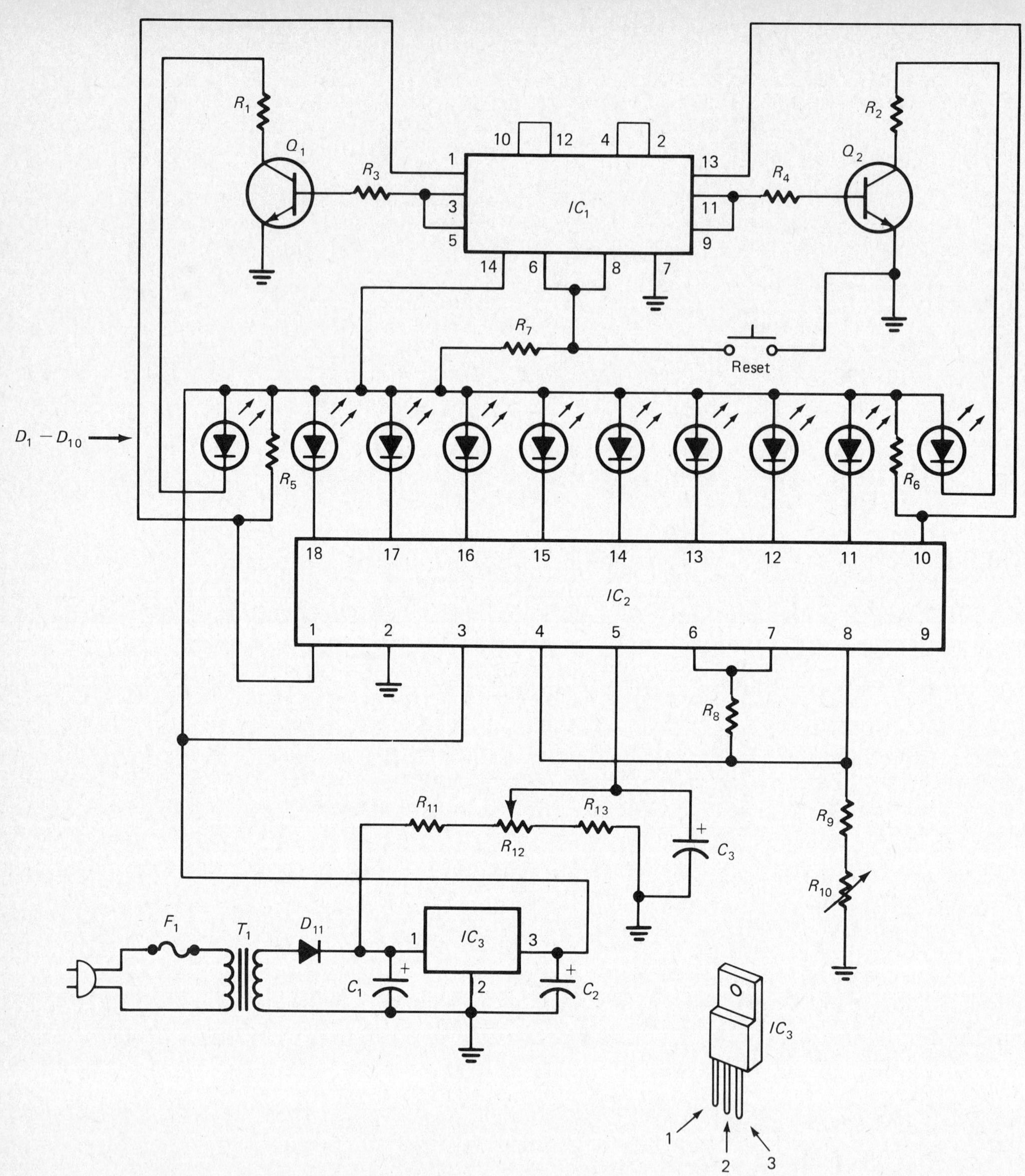

Fig. 13-9 Line voltmeter with expanded scale and memory.

the IC. When a signal is applied to pin 5, it is compared with an internally developed reference voltage. Depending on the signal voltage, the reference voltage, and the mode of operation, one or more of the comparators may switch states and activate the appropriate LEDs. This project uses the dot mode and normally only one LED lights at a time. The graph mode can be selected by connecting pins 9 and 3 of the IC together. However, the graph mode is *not* appropriate for this particular design due to the loading effects of the LED currents on the measured voltage.

The design of Fig. 13-9 is straightforward. The transformer steps the ac line down to about 12 V. This ac voltage is rectified and filtered and then voltage-regulated by IC_3. R_{11}, R_{12}, and R_{13}, form a voltage divider for the rectified and filtered line voltage. The divider supplies pin 5 of IC_2, the LM3914. R_9 and R_{10} set the LED current and bias the voltage divider so as to expand the voltmeter for an effective line range of 95 to 140 V ac. In applications where scale expansion is not required, pins 8 and 4 may be grounded.

The memory function in Fig. 13-9 is provided by IC_1, which is connected to form two latches. If the ac line voltage ever drops below about 97.5 V, pin 1 of IC_2 goes low. This sets one of the latches and Q_1 and the left-hand LED are turned on and stay on until the latch is reset. Likewise, if the ac line ever exceeds about 137.5 V, the other latch is turned on and Q_2 and the right-hand LED come on and stay on. A RESET switch is provided to turn the latches off. Thus, the circuit "remembers" if there was a low or a high voltage (or both) until it is reset.

The LEDs can be almost any style, shape, or color. They also can be purchased in a single package intended for dot/bar displays. The circuit can be constructed with point-to-point wiring on prototype perfboard. Sockets for IC_1 and IC_2 are recommended. Pay attention to the circuit grounds. The manufacturer of the LM3914 (IC_2) recommends a single-point ground near pin 2 for the best stability. Since the voltmeter draws little current, a heat sink is not needed for IC_3, the voltage regulator.

Calibration and verification of the voltmeter can be accomplished with a variable ac supply (such as a variac). An accurate multimeter should be used to monitor the variable line voltage. Preset R_{10} and R_{12} in Fig. 13-9 to midrange and adjust the ac line to 97.5 V. Adjust R_{10} so that the lowest two LEDs are on. Then, adjust the ac line for 137.5 V and reset the voltmeter. Adjust R_{12} so that the highest two LEDs are on. To take care of interaction, repeat the procedure until no further changes are noted. The display should now track the ac line voltage. Each LED represents a 5-V step, the lowest LED indicating 95 V and the highest indicating 140 V. A typical line voltage of 117 V will cause the two middle LEDs to light.

If an adjustable ac supply is not available, use a DMM and adjust R_{10} so that pin 8 of IC_2 is at 1.783 V dc referenced to ground. Then monitor the ac line with the DMM and adjust R_{12} to light the appropriate LED. For example, the sixth LED should be on for an ac line voltage of 120 V.

The circuit can be used to monitor other systems as well. For example, the transformer can be eliminated for use in 12-V automotive applications. Retain the fuse for overcurrent protection and also retain D_{11} to protect the voltmeter against damage from reverse polarity. The circuit can be calibrated for a range of 9.5 to 14 V dc and will have 0.5 V resolution.

Parts List

Part Numbers	Description
C_1	220-μF 25-V electrolytic capacitor
C_2, C_3	4.7-μF 15-V electrolytic capacitors
D_1–D_{10}	LEDs, almost any type suitable (or a single package of 10 such as General Instrument CMD57164)

Parts List (*Continued*)

Part Numbers	Description
D_{11}	1N4001 diode or equivalent
F_1	¼-A slow-blow fuse
IC_1	CD4011B IC or equivalent
IC_2	LM3914 IC or equivalent
IC_3	7805 IC or equivalent
R_1, R_2	330-Ω ¼-W resistors
R_3, R_4, R_7	10-kΩ ¼-W resistors
R_5, R_6	1-kΩ ¼-W resistors
R_8, R_9	1.2-kΩ ¼-W resistors
R_{10}	500-Ω linear miniature potentiometer
R_{11}	22-kΩ ¼-W resistor
R_{12}	1-kΩ linear miniature potentiometer
R_{13}	4.7-kΩ ¼-W resistor
T_1	12-V ac 0.15-A Stancor P-8390 transformer or equivalent
Misc.	Wire, line cord, cabinet, hardware, circuit board, normally open momentary-contact push-button switch, sockets

CHAPTER 14

Electronic Control Devices and Circuits

ACTIVITY 14-1
TEST: ELECTRONIC CONTROL DEVICES AND CIRCUITS

Choose the letter that best completes the statement or answers the question.

Questions 1 to 4 refer to Fig. 14-1.

1. Switch S_1 has just been closed. What is the condition of L_1?
   a. Off
   b. Dim
   c. Bright
   d. Flickering
2. Switch S_1 has just been closed, and then S_2 has been pushed (closed) once. What is the condition of L_1?
   a. Off
   b. Dim
   c. Bright
   d. Flickering
3. The lamp is on. How can it be turned off so it stays off?
   a. Close S_2
   b. Open S_2
   c. Short across the lamp momentarily
   d. None of the above
4. Which of the following terms best describes this circuit?
   a. Amplifier
   b. Latch
   c. Push-pull
   d. Complementary symmetry
5. A rheostat is used to control the brightness of a lamp. The lamp's resistance is 100 Ω. The rheostat is adjusted for 200 Ω. The line is 120 V. What percentage of the total power is dissipated in the lamp?
   a. 21 percent
   b. 33 percent
   c. 43 percent
   d. 68 percent

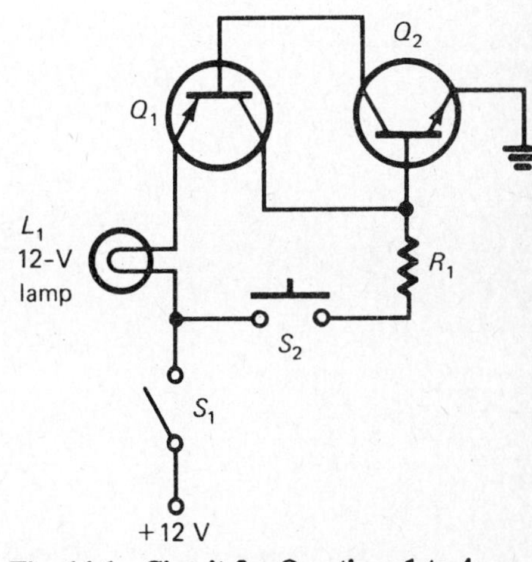

Fig. 14-1 Circuit for Questions 1 to 4.

6. What is the name usually given to the four-layer diode (PNPN) structure?
   a. Silicon-controlled rectifier
   b. Controlled avalanche rectifier
   c. Back-bias rectifier
   d. Diac rectifier

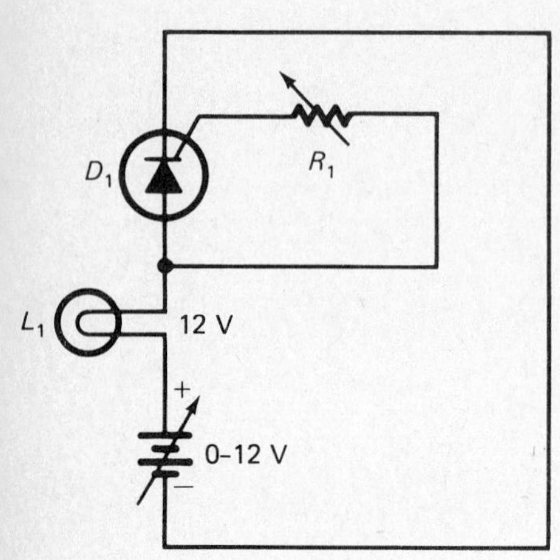

Fig. 14-2 Circuit for Questions 7 to 9.

Questions 7 to 9 refer to Fig. 14-2.

7. The lamp is on. What happens when R_1 is adjusted?
   a. The lamp gets brighter
   b. The lamp gets dimmer
   c. The lamp goes off
   d. The lamp is unchanged
8. The lamp is off. What happens when R_1 is adjusted to increase the gate current?
   a. The firing voltage for D_1 decreases
   b. The firing voltage for D_1 increases
   c. It has no effect on the firing voltage of D_1
   d. The D_1 runs very hot
9. The lamp is on. To shut D_1 off, the adjustable power supply will have to be
   a. Set where the current drops below the holding current value
   b. Turned full on
   c. Turned half off
   d. Set where R_1 is at minimum resistance
10. In actual operation, how are SCRs usually turned on?
    a. With a high reverse bias
    b. By applying a high forward bias
    c. By applying a high gate current
    d. By applying a high line transient
11. An SCR is used to control power in an ac circuit. How is commutation achieved?
    a. With a snubber network
    b. It is automatic when the line voltage drops to zero
    c. By controlling conduction angle
    d. By controlling circuit resistance
12. An SCR is used to control power in an ac circuit. The conduction angle is as large as possible. What will the load be receiving?
    a. Half-wave, pulsating dc
    b. Zero power
    c. Very low power
    d. Too much power
13. How does a thyristor control the load power dissipation in an ac circuit?
    a. By varying circuit resistance as a rheostat
    b. By controlling circuit voltage
    c. By diverting circuit energy from the load to itself
    d. None of the above
14. It is possible to provide full-wave control in an ac circuit by using an SCR and what other device?
    a. A diac
    b. A bridge rectifier
    c. Two balanced loads
    d. A transformer

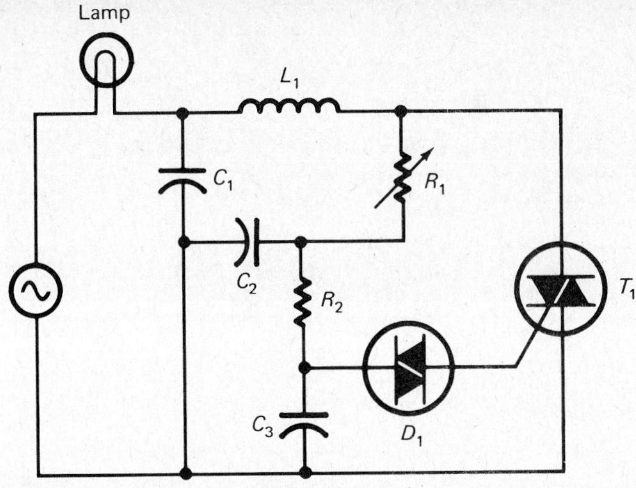

Fig. 14-3 Circuit for Questions 15 to 23.

Questions 15 to 23 refer to Fig. 14-3.

15. The lamp is at about half brightness. What waveform should appear across the lamp?
   a. Half-wave, pulsating dc
   b. Sinusoidal ac
   c. Square-wave ac
   d. None of the above

16. Resistor R_1 is adjusted for less resistance. What effect should this have on the triac?
   a. None at all
   b. It will gate on later and dim the lamp
   c. It will gate on sooner
   d. The triac will turn off and stay off

17. Which component is a bilateral triggering device for gating on the triac?
   a. The R_2
   b. The C_3
   c. The D_1
   d. None of the above

18. The triac is defective. It is shorted in both directions. What is the symptom?
   a. Line fuse blows
   b. Lamp at full brightness, no control
   c. Lamp off, no control
   d. None of the above

19. Resistor R_2 is open. What is the symptom?
   a. The R_1 runs too hot
   b. Lamp at full brightness, no control
   c. Lamp off, no control
   d. Excessive radio interference

20. The inductor L_1 is open. What is the symptom?
   a. The lamp is full on with no control
   b. The triac will be damaged
   c. The lamp is off
   d. RF interference

Questions 21 to 23 refer to Fig. 14-3 on page 165.

21. The control works normally, but there is excessive RF interference. What is the most likely cause?
 a. The L_1 is open
 b. The C_3 is open
 c. The D_1 is open
 d. The C_1 is open

22. The lamp is at full brightness. What is the conduction angle?
 a. 0°
 b. 90°
 c. 180°
 d. 360°

23. What components make up the snubber network?
 a. The R_1 and C_2
 b. The R_2 and C_3
 c. The C_3 and D_1
 d. There is no snubber network

24. What is a diac considered?
 a. A linear device
 b. A negative-resistance device
 c. A unidirectional latch
 d. A commutating device

25. Why is feedback often added to electronic control circuits?
 a. To obtain automatic regulation
 b. To provide circuit simplicity
 c. To provide overcurrent protection
 d. To obtain better electrical efficiency

Questions 26 to 28 refer to Fig. 14-4.

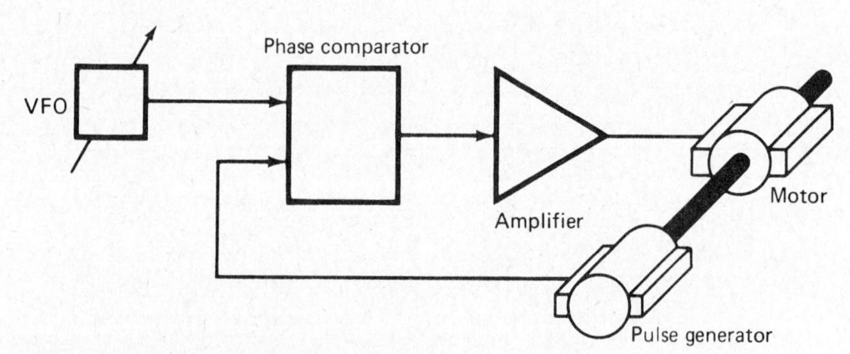

Fig. 14-4 Diagram for Questions 26 to 28.

26. What term is often used to describe a system like this?
 a. Servomechanism
 b. Automatic gain control
 c. Voltage regulator
 d. None of the above

27. Assume the VFO is defective and develops an output frequency that is too high. What is the likely symptom?
 a. Motor runs too slow
 b. Motor runs too fast
 c. Motor will stop
 d. The pulse generator will stop working

28. Assume that the pulse generator is defective and is not sending enough pulses to the phase comparator. What is the likely symptom?
 a. The motor will stop
 b. The motor will run too fast
 c. The motor will run very slow
 d. None of the above

29. Suppose you are working on a circuit that samples the output signal of an amplifier and adjusts the amplifier gain to keep the signal constant. Why is this *not* a servomechanism?
   a. No feedback is used
   b. The circuit is not automatic
   c. No mechanical action is involved
   d. No speed sensor is involved
30. Which of the following loads is safe for use with a triac power controller?
   a. A washing machine
   b. A television receiver
   c. A CB transceiver
   d. An incandescent lamp
31. Why is it usually *not* safe to connect an oscilloscope into a line-operated triac control circuit?
   a. Triacs are too sensitive
   b. A ground loop is likely
   c. Because diacs are often used to gate the triac
   d. The snubber circuit would not work properly
32. You are troubleshooting a triac control circuit. You notice that the load always runs at full power. Then you disconnect the gate lead and note that the load goes completely off. What can you conclude about the triac?
   a. It is shorted
   b. It is open
   c. It is probably good
   d. None of the above
33. Too much loop gain in a servomechanism will produce
   a. An underdamped response
   b. An overdamped response
   c. A critically damped response
   d. None of the above

ACTIVITY 14-2 LAB EXPERIMENT: CONTROL DEVICES AND CIRCUITS

PURPOSE

To study common thyristors and their application as control devices.

MATERIALS

Qty.	
1	oscilloscope with probe
1	VOM
1	12.6-V ac power supply, *line-isolated* (Stancor filament transformer P-8130 or equivalent)
1	0.1-μF paper or Mylar capacitor
1	25-μF 6-V electrolytic capacitor
1	50-μF 25-V electrolytic capacitor
1	820-Ω ½-W resistor
1	220-Ω ½-W resistor
1	100-Ω ½-W resistor
1	100-Ω 2-W resistor
1	500-Ω 2-W potentiometer, linear taper
2	MR504 diodes or equivalent
1	GE-C15B silicon controlled rectifier (SCR) or equivalent
1	GE-SC1428B triac or equivalent

INTRODUCTION

This activity has been divided into three parts. It is not necessary to complete the parts in order. Be sure to record all results and answer the questions before moving to another part. Work carefully for the best understanding of the concepts involved.

Part 1

PROCEDURE

Note: A DMM *cannot* be used in this procedure.

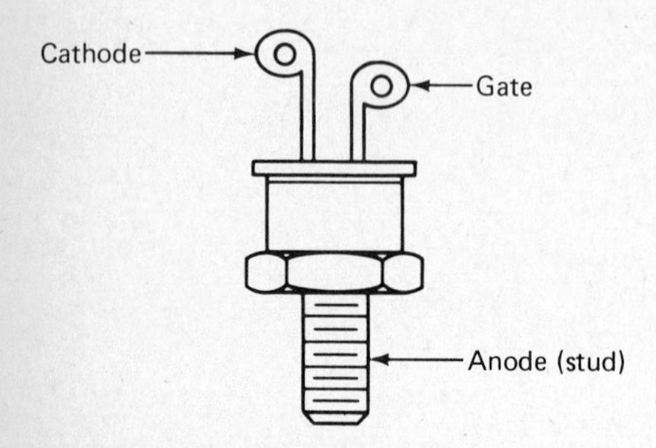

Fig. 14-5 SCR connections.

1. It is often possible to test thyristors with an ohmmeter, but the results will vary according to the device characteristics and the ohmmeter characteristics. For example, if the device is to be tested for its latching ability, the ohmmeter will need to supply at least the minimum holding current. If the ohmmeter cannot do this, it will not be possible to make the device latch on. Obtain the SCR and VOM. Set the VOM to its $R \times 1$ resistance range. Refer to Fig. 14-5 for the proper device connections. Connect the positive lead of the ohmmeter to the anode of the SCR. Connect the negative lead to the cathode of the SCR.
   a. Does this forward-bias the SCR?
   b. Does the SCR turn on? Why?

2. Momentarily short the cathode lead to the anode lead. The ohmmeter should still be connected as described before. Does the SCR latch on? Why?

3. Momentarily short the gate lead to the cathode lead. The ohmmeter is still connected as before. Does the SCR latch on? Why?

4. Momentarily short the gate lead to the anode lead. The ohmmeter is still connected as before.
   a. Does the SCR latch on? Why?
   b. Why is the $R \times 1$ resistance range the best for testing the latching ability of an SCR?

5. Reverse the ohmmeter connections (positive lead to the cathode and negative lead to the anode). Verify that it is not possible to latch an SCR when it is reverse-biased.

6. Obtain the triac. The ohmmeter should still be on the $R \times 1$ range. Refer to Fig. 14-6 for the proper connections. Connect the positive lead to main terminal 2 and the negative lead to main terminal 1. Momentarily short from the gate to main terminal 2. Does the triac latch on? Why?

7. Reverse the ohmmeter connections. Connect the positive lead to main terminal 1 and the negative lead to main terminal 2. Momentarily short the gate to one main terminal and then the other. The triac will probably *not* latch on. The gate sensitivity is reduced in this mode. It may be possible to gate the triac on in this mode by using a small 1.5-V dry cell in addition to the bias supplied by the ohmmeter. Do not disturb the ohmmeter connections. Connect the positive lead from the dry cell to main terminal 1. Momentarily touch the negative dry-cell lead to the gate terminal. The triac should latch on.
   a. Is it possible to latch a triac on in two directions?
   b. Is this an advantage over the SCR when power is to be controlled in an ac circuit?

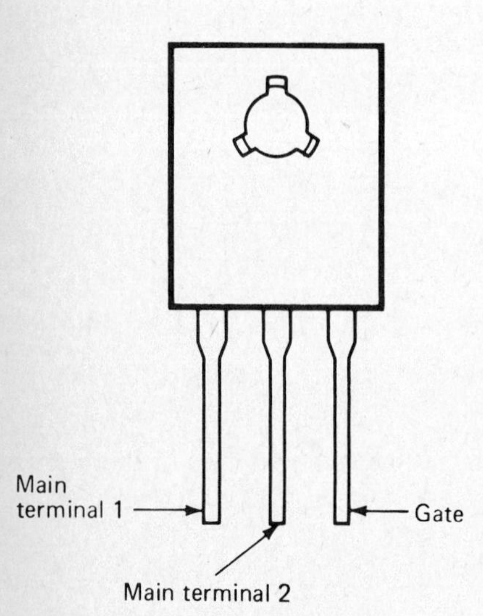

Fig. 14-6 Triac connections.

Part 2

PROCEDURE

Build the circuit shown in Fig. 14-7 (refer to Fig. 14-5 for the proper SCR connections). Be very careful to build the circuit exactly as shown. Connect your oscilloscope. Adjust the 500-Ω potentiometer to the center of rotation. Turn the power on and adjust your oscilloscope for a stable pattern. Note the effect of the 500-Ω potentiometer on the waveform.

1. What does the potentiometer control?
2. Does this circuit achieve full-wave control?
3. Define conduction angle as it applies to this circuit.
4. Predict the waveform across the 100-Ω 2-W resistor if the SCR were to short from cathode to anode.

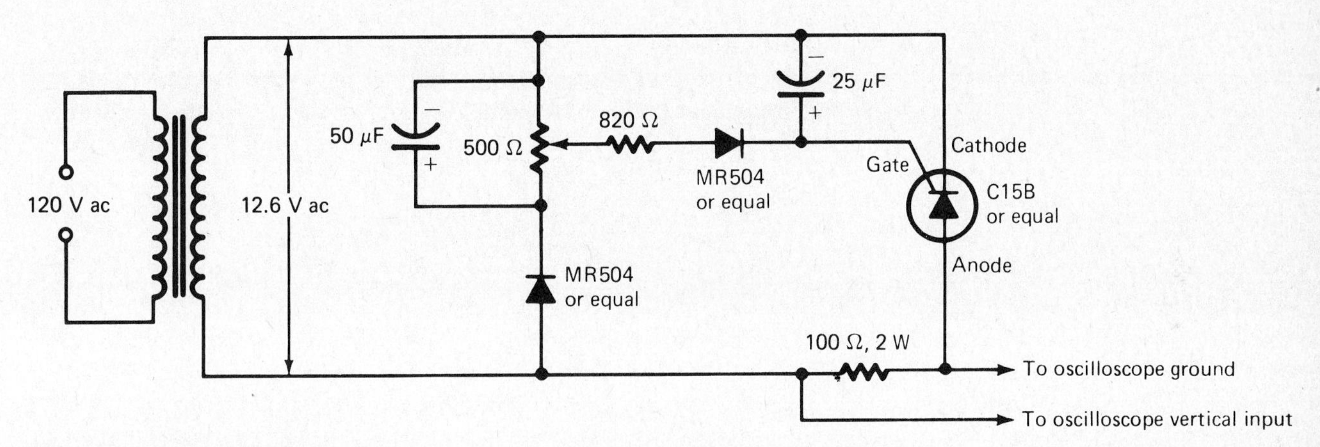

Fig. 14-7 SCR control circuit.

Part 3

PROCEDURE

Build the circuit shown in Fig. 14-8. Refer to Fig. 14-6 for the proper triac connections. Be very careful to build the circuit exactly as shown. Connect your oscilloscope. Adjust the 500-Ω potentiometer to the center of rotation. Turn the power on and adjust your oscilloscope for a stable pattern. Note the effect of the potentiometer on the waveform.

1. What does the potentiometer control?

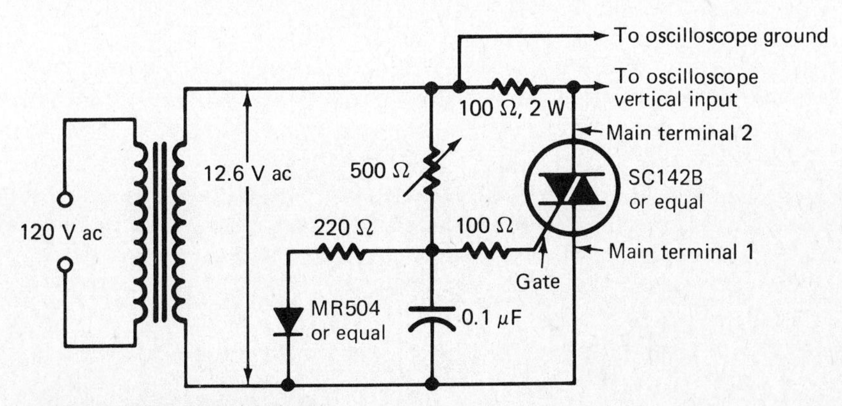

Fig. 14-8 Triac control circuit.

2. Does the triac circuit achieve full-wave control?
3. Define conduction angle as it applies to this circuit.
4. Predict the waveform across the 100-Ω 2-W resistor if the triac gate lead were to open.

ACTIVITY 14-3 CONSTRUCTION PROJECT: REGULATED MOTOR-SPEED CONTROL

INTRODUCTION

Figure 14-9 shows the schematic for a regulated motor-speed control. This device will increase the usefulness of older electric drills that lack the variable-speed feature.

The circuit of Fig. 14-9 uses feedback to regulate the motor speed. Once the correct speed has been set by the potentiometer, the motor will remain at that speed over quite a range of load variation. The feedback is accomplished by the 2-μF capacitor and 220-Ω resistor in the gate circuit of the SCR. As the load on the motor increases, the speed tends to drop. This will cause a reduction in the induced voltage across the motor. This induced voltage acts to delay the firing of the SCR. Thus, as the feedback drops because the motor slows down, the SCR gates on sooner and tends to speed the motor up. The overall result is a fairly constant motor speed.

CAUTION! ***This speed-control circuit is not intended for use with induction motors. It is to be used only with*** **universal (ac/dc) motors** ***such as those found on portable power tools. Any attempt to use a speed-control circuit with the wrong motor will damage the motor or the control or both. If there is any doubt, check the manufacturer's specifications. Universal motors have a wound armature, a commutator, and brushes.***

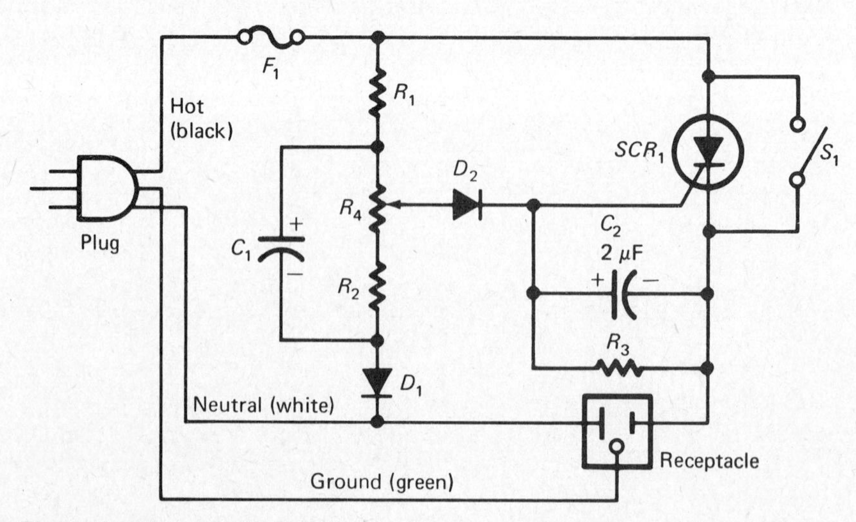

Fig. 14-9 Motor-speed control.

Parts List

Part Numbers	Description
C_1	50-μF 25-V electrolytic capacitor
C_2	2-μF 25-V electrolytic capacitor
R_1	2.5-kΩ 5-W wirewound resistor
R_2	100-Ω ½-W resistor
R_3	220-Ω ½-W resistor
R_4	500-Ω 2-W linear-taper potentiometer
D_1, D_2	1N4004 diodes or equivalent
SCR_1	GE-C15C SCR or equivalent
F_1	120-V 5-A fuse
S_1	120-V 5-A SPST switch
Power plug	three-prong grounding type
Power receptacle	three-wire grounding type
Misc.	Wire, cabinet, fuse holder, knob, hardware, heat sink

CONSTRUCTION

You must use correct wiring practices to make the speed control safe. Figure 14-9 shows the proper color code for the wiring. When connecting the power plug, connect the black wire to the gold screw, the white wire to the silver screw, and the green wire to the green, or ground, screw. Doublecheck these connections.

The SCR can run hot under heavy loads. It is best to provide it with a heat sink. You *must* be very careful to insulate the SCR from its heat sink. Use insulating washers, a bushing, and silicon grease. Do this carefully. Check after assembly by using an ohmmeter on a high resistance range. The meter should read infinity from the anode (stud) to the heat sink.

This speed control is a half-wave circuit and is why a switch is included in the schematic of Fig. 14-9. If full speed is desired, the switch can be closed. This bypasses the SCR, and the motor will run at full speed. Of course, no speed control is possible with the switch closed. The potentiometer will have no effect.

Universal motors can become hot after extended use. They usually include a built-in cooling fan. At reduced speed the cooling fan is not as effective. When using a speed control, it is a good idea occasionally to run the motor at full speed with no load on it. This cools the motor more rapidly than simply shutting it off.

ACTIVITY 14-4
CONSTRUCTION PROJECT: TIMER

INTRODUCTION

Figure 14-10 on page 173 shows the schematic diagram for an industrial-quality timer that provides precise intervals of 1 s to over 27 h in programmable 1- or 10-s steps. The timer can be used to control photographic lights, battery charging, or almost any other application where an accurately timed event is important.

The timer is programmed by four binary-coded decimal (BCD) thumbwheel switches. For example, if a 2-min interval is required, the BCD switches would be set to 0120, since 120 s is equal to 2 min. The multiplier switch would be set to ×1. The LED displays show the programmed information, 0120 in this case. When the start button is pressed, relay K_1 is energized and the timing cycle begins. As every second passes, the LEDs show the count decrementing toward 0000. When the interval is over, the relay releases. You can wire the relay contacts to suit your needs: both normally closed (NC) and normally open (NO) contacts are supplied to allow a load to be energized or deenergized for the programmed interval. At the end of the interval, the LEDs return to the setting of the BCD switches. Then, you may run a second timed interval or change the BCD switches and run a different timed interval. If a timed interval is in progress, it may be aborted by pressing the reset switch. This will allow the interval to be restarted or a new time value to be programmed.

Parts List

Part Numbers	Description
C_1	500 μF 25-V electrolytic capacitor
C_2	4.7-μF 15-V electrolytic capacitor
C_3–C_5	0.1-μF 50-V ceramic capacitors
C_6	100-pF ceramic capacitor
C_7	1-nF ceramic capacitor
D_1–D_3	1N4005 silicon diodes or equivalent
D_4–D_{19}	1N914 silicon diodes or equivalent
D_{20}–D_{23}	MAN74A common-cathode LEDs
F_1	3/8-A 120-V 3AG slow-blow fuse
IC_1	ICM7217 AIPI IC or equivalent
IC_2	CD4011 IC or equivalent
IC_3, IC_4	MC14566 ICs or equivalent
IC_5	7805 IC or equivalent
K_1	12-V dc SPDT relay, contacts rated at 5 A, 120 V ac
Q_1	2N4401 transistor or equivalent
Q_2	2N2222 transistor or equivalent
R_1	47-kΩ 1/4-W resistor
R_2	18-kΩ 1/4-W resistor
R_3	1-MΩ 1/4-W resistor
R_4	3.3-kΩ 1/4-W resistor
R_5	47-Ω 1/4-W resistor
R_6	10-kΩ 1/4-W resistor
R_7, R_8	1-kΩ 1/4-W resistors
R_9	4.7-kΩ 1/4-W resistor
S_1	2-A 120-V SPST switch
S_2	1-A 50-V SPDT switch
S_3, S_4	normally open momentary-contact switches
S_5–S_8	10-position BCD thumbwheel type switches
T_1	20-V 1-A center-tapped Stancor P-8606 power transformer or equivalent
Misc.	Chassis, cabinet, hardware, fuse holder, line cord, outlet, circuit board, IC sockets, wire terminals, endplates for BCD

Most of the work is done by IC_1 in Fig. 14-10. It reads in the programmed value from the BCD switches and also provides the multiplexed information to the LED displays. Multiplexing means that the displays are only on one digit at a time. This happens so rapidly that they all appear to be glowing constantly. IC_1 also contains counting circuits, and IC_2 contains some logic circuits to assist IC_1 in controlling the relay and the pulses that are counted. The pulses come from IC_3 or IC_4. These ICs contain counters that derive accurate 1- or

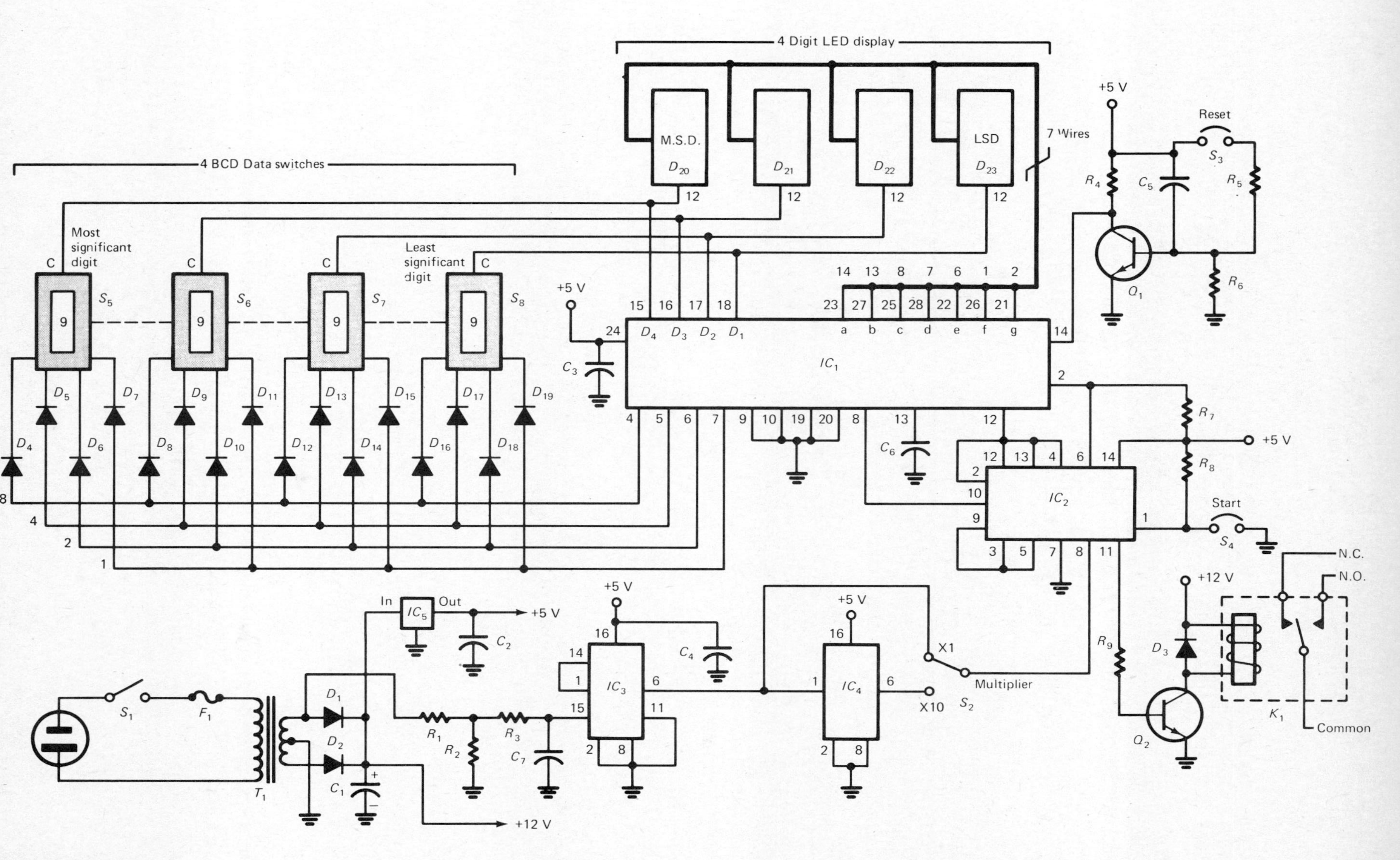

Fig. 14-10 Timer.

0.1-Hz pulses from the 60-Hz ac line. When the multiplier switch is in the $\times 1$ position, the pulse frequency is 1 Hz and the timer is programmable up to 9999 (almost 167 min). When the multiplier switch is in the $\times 10$ position, the pulse frequency is 0.1 Hz and the timer is programmable in 10-s steps up to 99990 s (1666.5 min). IC_5 is a 5-V regulator.

CONSTRUCTION

You can wire the timer using a circuit board. Sockets are strongly recommended for IC_1 through IC_4. The LEDs should also be socketed. Pay close attention to the wiring of the multiplexed display. All display segments are wired in parallel. Only the cathodes (pin 12) of the displays are wired individually. The schematic diagram shown in Fig. 14-10 shows that segment A of all displays is to be driven by pin 23 of IC_1. The schematic also shows that segment A happens to be pin 14 on the LED package.

Be very careful with the line wiring and with the relay wiring. You may choose to have the timer energize a circuit during the timed interval. In this case, you would use the common and the normally open relay contacts to switch the hot side of the ac line going to the controlled load. If you wish the load switched off for the timed interval, use the common and the normally closed relay contacts.

Do not handle the ICs until it is time to plug them into their sockets. Check the wiring very carefully before energizing the timer. The timer will work without the LED displays if the intended application is in a photographic darkroom.

CHAPTER 15

Regulated Power Supplies

ACTIVITY 15-1
TEST: REGULATED POWER SUPPLIES

Choose the letter that best completes the statement or answers the question.

1. Why is the secondary waveform clipped in a ferroresonant transformer?
   a. This is caused by the rectifiers
   b. The zener regulator is clipping
   c. The core is being driven into saturation
   d. There is a defect in the resonating capacitor

Questions 2 to 7 refer to Fig. 15-1.

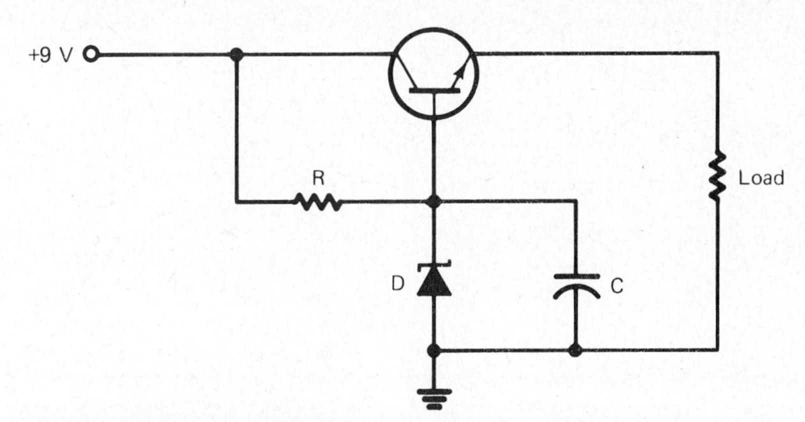

Fig. 15-1 Circuit for Questions 2 to 7.

2. What is the circuit shown?
   a. An amplified zener regulator
   b. A foldback current limiter
   c. A switch-mode regulator
   d. A closed-loop voltage regulator

Questions 3 to 7 refer to Fig. 15-1 on page 175.

3. With a 5.7-V zener, the load voltage should be
   a. 14.7 V
   b. 9.0 V
   c. 5.7 V
   d. 5.0 V

4. If the transistor develops a collector-to-emitter short, the load voltage will
   a. Drop to 0
   b. Drop to 0.7 V
   c. Drop to 5.7 V
   d. None of the above

5. Which load situation will produce the most dissipation in the transistor?
   a. Zero-load current
   b. Light-load current
   c. Normal-load current
   d. A shorted load

6. Which load situation will produce the most dissipation in the diode?
   a. Zero-load current
   b. Light-load current
   c. Normal-load current
   d. A shorted load

7. If the diode shorts, the load voltage will be
   a. 9.7 V
   b. 9.0 V
   c. 0 V
   d. None of the above

Questions 8 to 13 refer to Fig. 15-2.

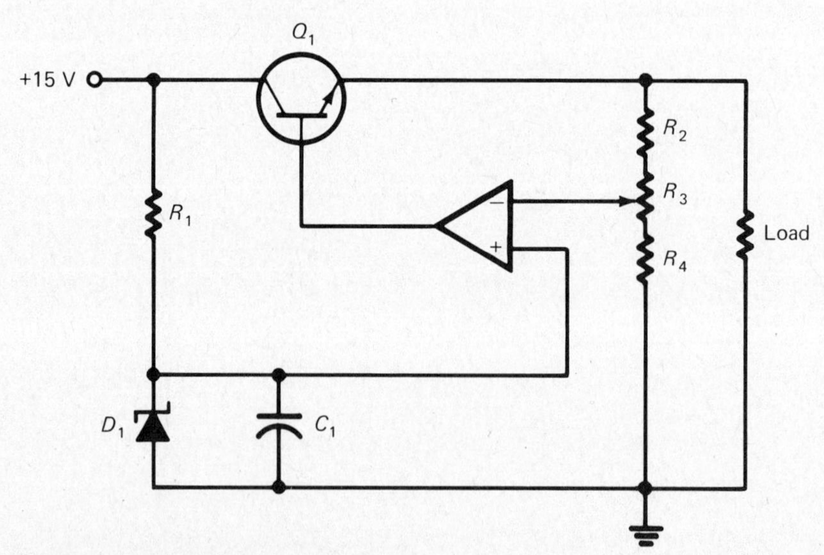

Fig. 15-2 Circuit for Questions 8 to 13.

8. What is the circuit shown?
   a. A zener shunt regulator
   b. A feedback voltage regulator
   c. A current limiter
   d. A step-down switch-mode regulator

9. Assume a 6-V zener diode and also assume that the wiper arm of R_3 is at the electrical center of the voltage divider. The load voltage should be
   a. 21 V
   b. 15 V
   c. 12 V
   d. 6 V
10. If the load current increases, the output of the op amp will
   a. Go in a positive direction
   b. Go in a negative direction
   c. Go to zero
   d. None of the above
11. If the wiper arm of R_3 is moved down toward R_4, the load voltage will
   a. Go to zero
   b. Decrease
   c. Increase
   d. Stay the same
12. The load voltage is zero. The problem could be
   a. A shorted zener
   b. A defective op amp
   c. An open transistor
   d. Any of the above
13. Transistor Q_1 is called
   a. A current-regulator transistor
   b. A series-pass transistor
   c. An error-amplifier transistor
   d. A common-emitter transistor

Questions 14 and 15 refer to Fig. 15-3.

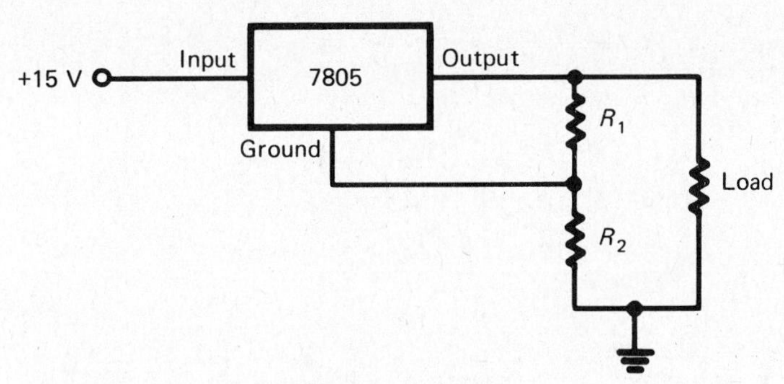

Fig. 15-3 Circuit for Questions 14 and 15.

14. Resistors R_1 and R_2 are 100-Ω resistors. The quiescent current of the IC is 6 mA. The load voltage should be
   a. 10.6 V
   b. 8.4 V
   c. 5.0 V
   d. 2.5 V
15. What is the disadvantage in making R_2 too large in value?
   a. The R_1 may be damaged
   b. The R_2 may be damaged
   c. The voltage regulation will be degraded
   d. The internal current limiting will not work

16. Why is an isolation transformer advisable when troubleshooting power supplies?
    a. To eliminate ground loops
    b. To block line transients
    c. Both of the above
    d. None of the above
17. Low output in a regulated power supply is often caused by
    a. A shorted pass transistor
    b. An open pass transistor
    c. A shorted reference diode
    d. A current overload

Questions 18 to 20 refer to Fig. 15-4.

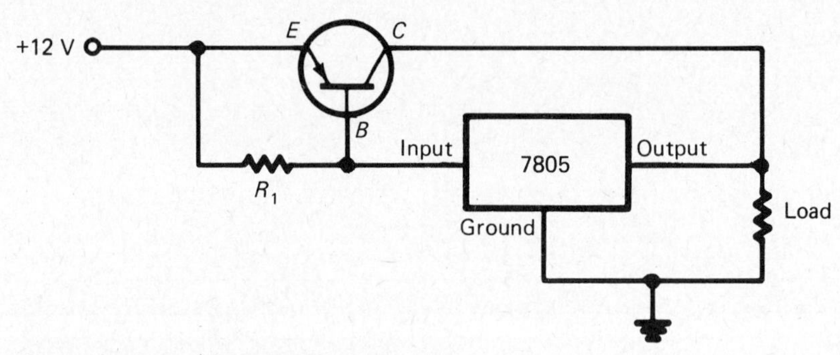

Fig. 15-4 Circuit for Questions 18 to 20.

18. The load voltage should be
    a. 12 V
    b. 5 V
    c. 4.3 V
    d. Depends on the value of R_1
19. If the transistor is silicon, at what value of load current will it begin to conduct if R_1 is a 2.8-Ω resistor?
    a. 50 mA
    b. 250 mA
    c. 1000 mA
    d. None of the above
20. Which component provides overcurrent protection for the transistor?
    a. The R_1
    b. The transistor itself
    c. The IC
    d. It has no overcurrent protection
21. Which type of power supply uses pulse-width modulation to control output voltage?
    a. Switch-mode
    b. Linear
    c. Power supplies based on the 78XX series of ICs
    d. All of the above
22. What is the disadvantage of linear power supplies?
    a. Size
    b. Weight
    c. Heat
    d. All of the above

23. Which of the following problems is associated with switch-mode power supplies?
  a. Noise and electromagnetic interference (EMI)
  b. Poor efficiency
  c. Poor regulation
  d. All of the above
24. What are dc converters used for?
  a. To change low-voltage direct current into high-voltage direct current
  b. To change high-voltage direct current into low-voltage direct current
  c. To provide line isolation
  d. All of the above

Questions 25 to 27 refer to Fig. 15-5.

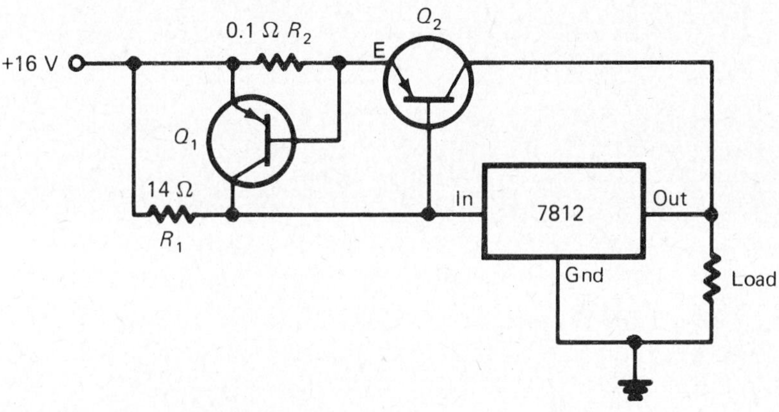

Fig. 15-5 Circuit for Questions 25 to 27.

25. The output voltage should be
  a. 16 V
  b. 12 V
  c. 9 V
  d. 5 V
26. The transistors are silicon. Transistor Q_2 should begin to conduct at a current of
  a. 50 mA
  b. 500 mA
  c. 5 A
  d. 7 A
27. The transistors are silicon. At what current does limiting begin?
  a. About 1 A
  b. About 4 A
  c. About 7 A
  d. About 12 A
28. What is the advantage of foldback current limiting over conventional current limiting?
  a. The circuitry is much simpler
  b. The pass device operates in the constant-current mode
  c. It provides better protection for a long-term short circuit
  d. All of the above

29. What happens to the slave output in a dual-tracking power supply if the master output voltage is increased?
   a. It remains constant
   b. It decreases
   c. It increases
   d. Any of the above, depending on the IC used
30. What kind of protection is offered by a crowbar circuit?
   a. Overcurrent
   b. Overvoltage
   c. Overtemperature
   d. All of the above
31. What kind of protection is offered by an MOV device?
   a. Short-term short circuit
   b. Long-term short circuit
   c. Secondary breakdown
   d. Line transient

Questions 32 to 36 refer to Fig. 15-6.

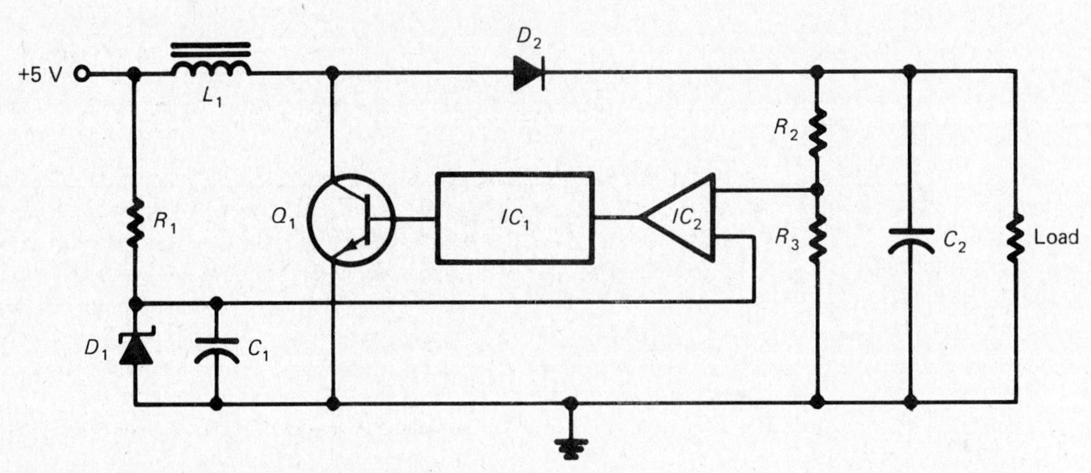

Fig. 15-6 Circuit for Questions 32 to 36.

32. Which switch-mode configuration is shown?
   a. Step-down
   b. Inverting
   c. Step-up
   d. Sine-wave converter
33. Which component provides a rectangular waveform of varying duty cycle?
   a. The Q_1
   b. The IC_1
   c. The L_1
   d. The D_2
34. What will happen to the duty cycle at the base of Q_1 if the load current is increased?
   a. It will increase
   b. It will decrease
   c. It will remain constant
   d. It will remain constant, but the frequency will go up

35. Which component makes possible a load voltage in excess of 5 V when it discharges?
  a. The C_1
  b. The L_1
  c. The C_2
  d. The Q_1
36. Why may C_2 have fewer microfarads than it would in a linear power supply?
  a. Rectangular waves are easy to filter
  b. The integrated circuits are not ripple-sensitive
  c. The C_1 eliminates much of the ripple
  d. The ripple frequency is much higher than 60 Hz
37. What is the advantage of using a frequency-controlled sine-wave converter in place of pulse-width-modulated rectangular waves?
  a. Fast recovery rectifiers are not needed
  b. Slower transistors may be used
  c. Reduced EMI
  d. Circuit complexity and cost are reduced
38. A pass transistor with a collector-to-emitter short will cause the output voltage to
  a. Drop to zero
  b. Be abnormally high
  c. Be abnormally low
  d. Be nearly normal but have excessive ripple
39. A switch-mode power supply is making a chirping sound. The difficulty could be
  a. An open load circuit
  b. A shorted load circuit
  c. The line fuse is blown
  d. An open diode
40. An open reference diode would most likely cause the symptom of
  a. High output voltage
  b. Low output voltage
  c. No output voltage
  d. Decreased EMI

ACTIVITY 15-2
LAB EXPERIMENT: REGULATED POWER SUPPLIES

PURPOSE

To construct and measure the performance of several regulated power-supply circuits.

MATERIALS

Qty.		*Qty.*	
1	multimeter	1	5.6-kΩ ½-W resistor
1	oscilloscope with probe	2	10-kΩ ½-W resistors
1	0- to 15-V dc power supply	1	56-kΩ ½-W resistor
1	100-Ω ½-W resistor	1	100-Ω potentiometer, linear taper
2	1-kΩ ½-W resistors	1	1-kΩ potentiometer, linear taper
1	2.2-kΩ ½-W resistor		
2	4.7-kΩ ½-W resistors		

Materials list continued on the next page.

Qty.		*Qty.*	
1	0.001-μF paper or Mylar capacitor	1	2N4401 transistor or equivalent
1	0.002-μF paper or Mylar capacitor	1	μA741CP IC op amp or equivalent
1	25-μF 15-V electrolytic capacitor	2	NE555 integrated timers or equivalent
1	25-μF 50-V electrolytic capacitor	1	MC7805CT IC regulator or equivalent
1	1N4001 diode or equivalent	1	8-Ω dc resistance 470-μH molded air-core coil or equivalent
1	1N914 diode or equivalent		
1	1N4733 diode or equivalent		

PROCEDURE

1. Build the circuit shown in Fig. 15-7. Be careful to observe polarity for the solid-state devices and the electrolytic capacitors. Make the following measurements:
   a. V_B
   b. V_E
2. Note: Make your measurements *quickly* in this part of the experiment. The load current is high enough to heat the transistor. Turn the power supply off as soon as your readings are completed. Add a 100-Ω resistor in *parallel* with the 4.7-kΩ resistor shown in Fig. 15-7. Make the following measurements:
   a. V_B
   b. V_E
3. Calculate the voltage regulation for the circuit shown in Fig. 15-7. Use the V_E readings taken in steps 1 and 2.

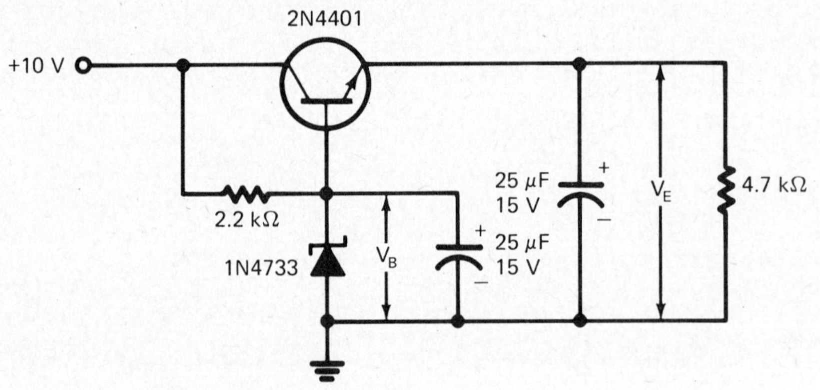

Fig. 15-7 Amplified zener circuit.

4. Build the circuit shown in Fig. 15-8. Make the following measurements:
   a. V_B
   b. V_E
5. Note: Make your measurements *quickly* in this part of the experiment. The load current is high enough to heat the transistor. Turn the power supply off as soon as your readings are completed. Add a 100-Ω resistor in *parallel* with the 4.7 kΩ resistor shown in Fig. 15-8. Make the following measurements:
   a. V_B
   b. V_E

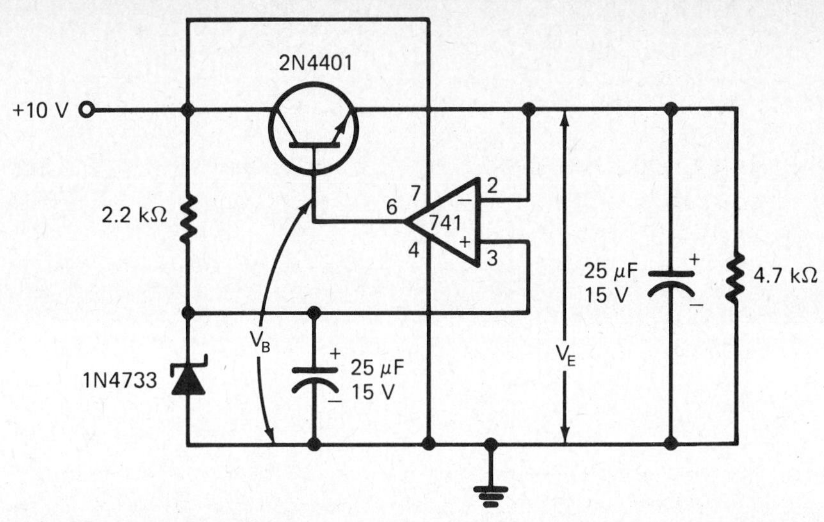

Fig. 15-8 Feedback regulator.

6. Calculate the voltage regulation for the circuit shown in Fig. 15-8. Use the V_E readings taken in steps 5 and 6.
7. Build the circuit shown in Fig. 15-9. Adjust V_{in} for 15 V. Adjust the 100-Ω variable resistor for minimum and maximum values of V_{out}. Record these readings:
   a. $V_{out\,(min)}$
   b. $V_{out\,(max)}$
8. Measure the quiescent current I_q in the IC regulator. You will have to open the IC ground lead and insert a milliammeter.
9. Calculate the maximum output voltage $V_{out\,(max)}$ from the regulator. Use the two 100-Ω resistors and the quiescent current measured in step 8.
10. Set V_{out} to its minimum value by adjusting the 100-Ω variable resistor. Monitor V_{out} while *slowly* decreasing V_{in}. Stop decreasing

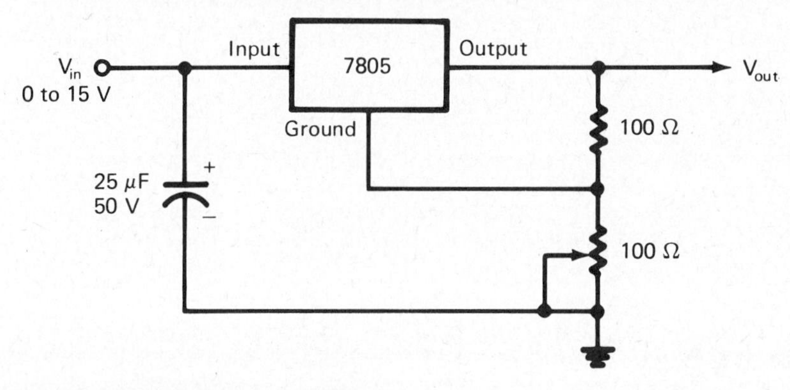

Fig. 15-9 Integrated circuit regulator.

V_{in} at the moment V_{out} shows any drop. Record the minimum value of V_{in} that can be used to supply the IC regulator.

11. Build the circuit shown in Fig. 15-10 on the next page. Carefully check all connections and polarities before applying 5 V. The 555 IC timer on the left is wired in the astable configuration. You should verify its operation by probing with your oscilloscope on pin 3.

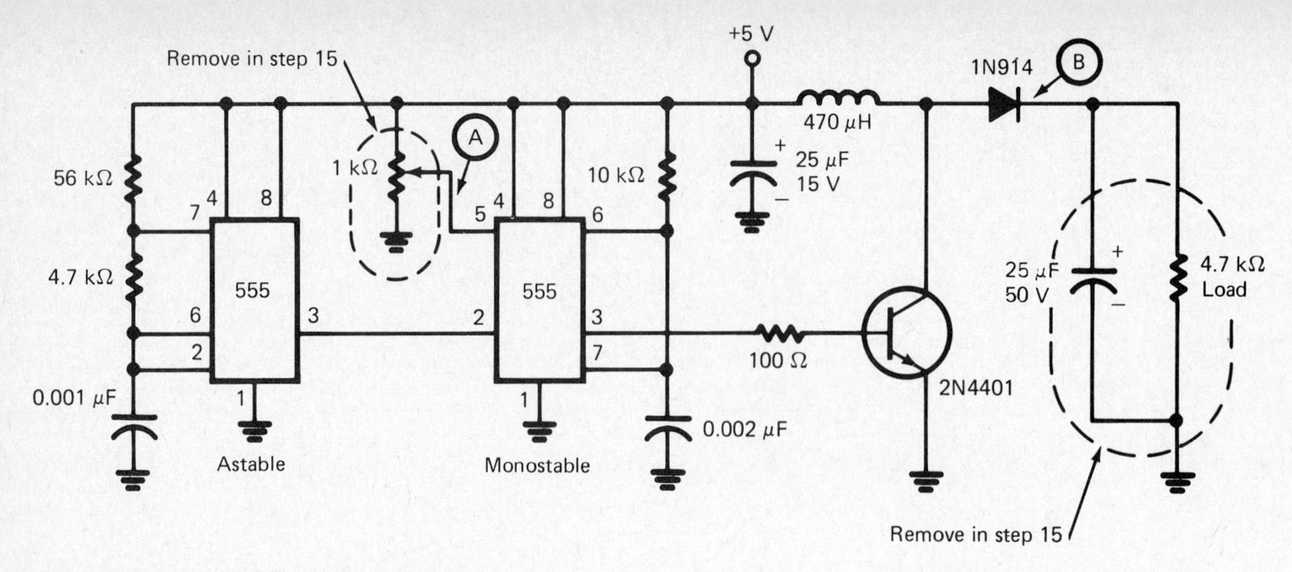

Fig. 15-10 Switch-mode step-up configuration.

A rectangular waveform should appear at this point. The second 555 timer is wired in the monostable mode. Verify its operation by probing pin 3 with the oscilloscope. A rectangular wave should appear, and the duty cycle should be adjustable over a wide range by changing the 1-kΩ potentiometer setting. The switch transistor, coil, and diode are arranged in the step-up configuration. The load voltage should be greater than 5 V.

12. Measure the duty cycle at pin 3 of the monostable IC. Then adjust the 1-kΩ potentiometer for a duty cycle of 50 percent (the width of the high pulse will equal the width of the low pulse).
13. Make a copy of the sample graph shown in Fig. 15-11. Plot the output voltage versus the load current. Do *not* change the duty cycle. Use enough combinations of load resistors to produce various load currents for an *accurate* graph.
14. Put a 1-kΩ load resistor into the circuit shown in Fig. 15-10. Eliminate any other load resistors. Make a copy of the sample graph shown in Fig. 15-12. Plot output versus duty cycle for the switch-mode power supply. Use your oscilloscope to measure the duty cycle at pin 3 of the monostable IC:

$$\%\ \text{Duty cycle} = \frac{t_{\text{high}}}{t_{\text{high}} + t_{\text{low}}} \times 100$$

Take enough readings for an accurate graph.

15. *Modify* the switch-mode circuit by *adding* the error amplifier shown in Fig 15-13. The potentiometer in Fig. 15-10 is *eliminated* and the output of the op amp now feeds point *A*. The load circuit now includes a voltage divider and connects at point *B*. The modified circuit uses an op amp to compare the output voltage with a reference voltage (2.5 V at pin 3 of the op amp). Any error is amplified, and the duty cycle of the monostable IC is adjusted accordingly.
16. Make a copy of the sample graph shown in Fig. 15-14 on page 186. Plot output versus load. Use enough combinations of load resistors to produce various load currents for an *accurate* graph.

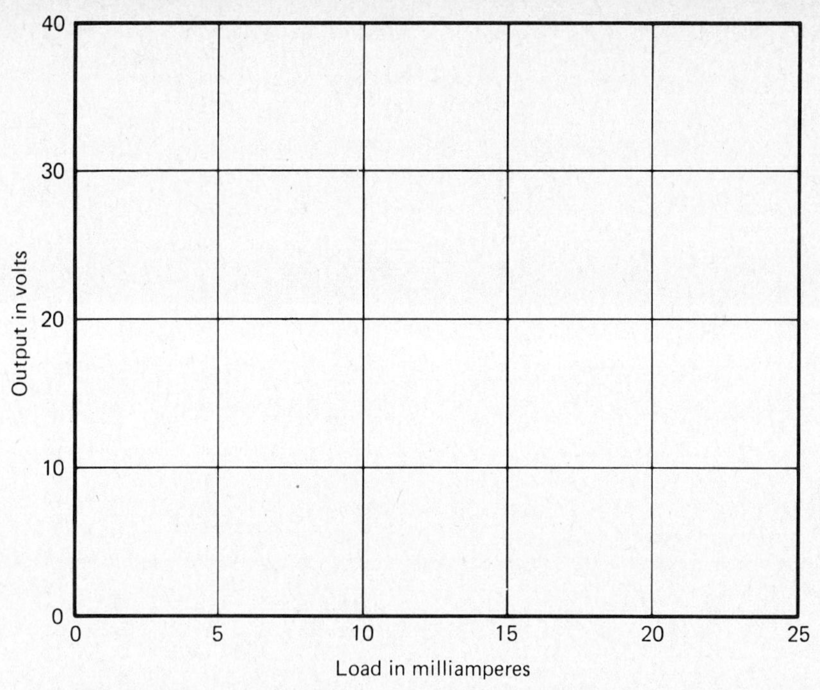

Fig. 15-11 An example of graph paper used to plot output vs. load for a fixed 50% duty cycle.

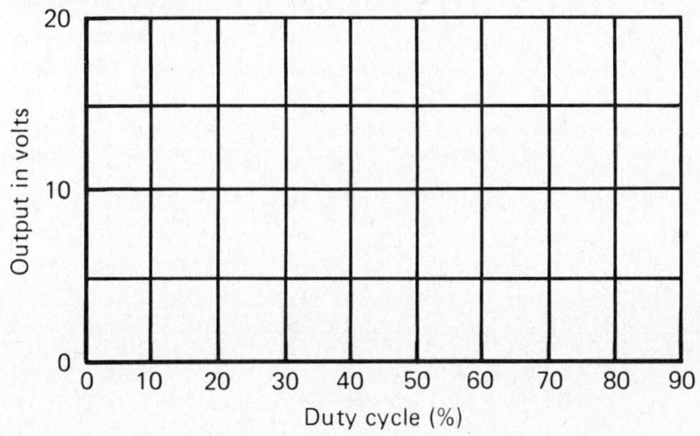

Fig. 15-12 An example of graph paper used to plot output vs. duty cycle for a 1-kΩ load.

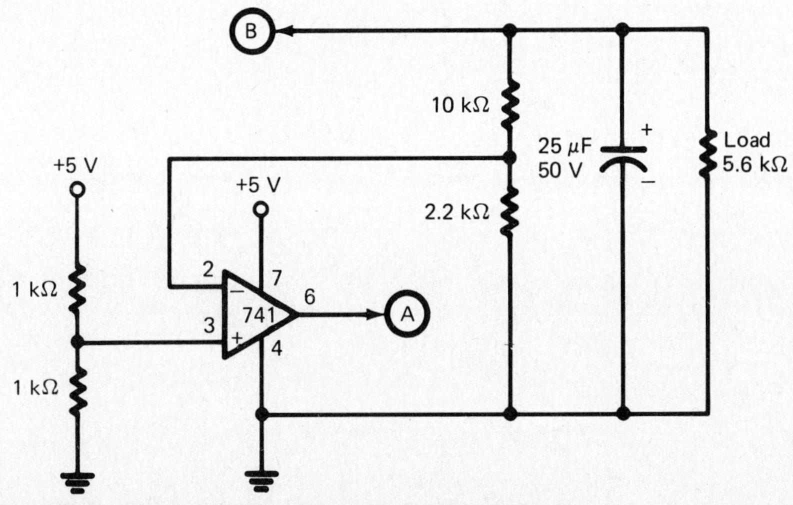

Fig. 15-13 Error amplifier for switch-mode circuit.

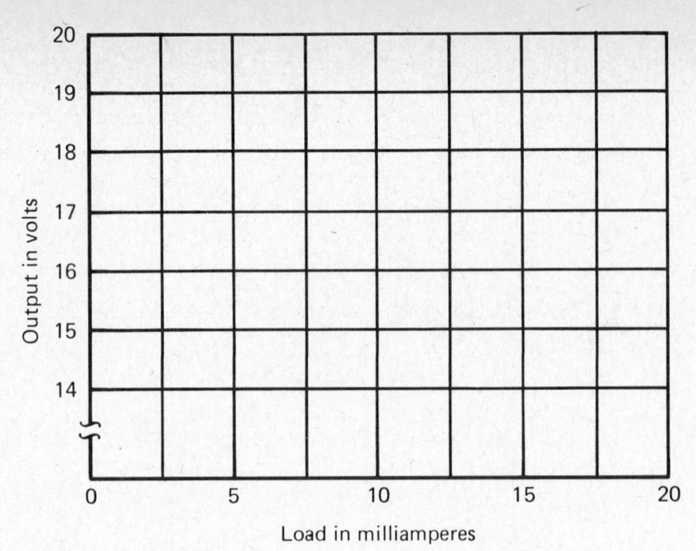

Fig. 15-14 An example of graph paper used to plot output vs. load.

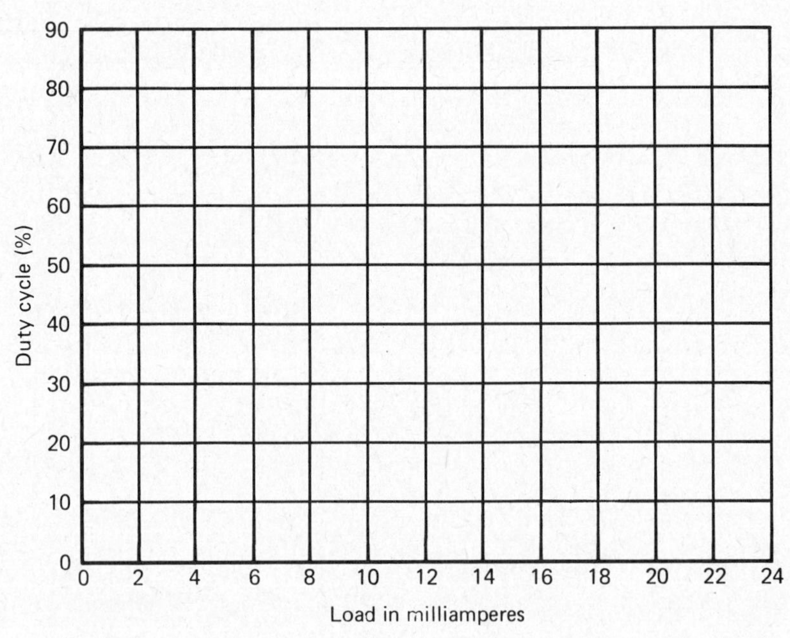

Fig. 15-15 An example of graph paper used to plot duty cycle vs. load.

18. Turn off the 5-V power supply. Replace the 1N914 diode with a 1N4001 rectifier diode. Turn the power supply back on. Take a few readings at the higher load currents and larger duty cycles. How does the performance of the switch-mode power supply compare with the way it was working with the 1N914 diode?

DISCUSSION TOPICS

1. What happens to V_{BE} in Fig. 15-7 when the load current increases? Does this increase in V_{BE} affect the voltage regulation of the circuit?

2. Why is the load voltage higher for the circuit of Fig. 15-8 than it is for the one in Fig. 15-7?
3. Explain the change in V_B in Fig. 15-8 when the load is increased.
4. Why is the voltage regulation better in Fig. 15-8 than it is in Fig. 15-7?
5. What would happen to the output voltage in Fig. 15-8 if the inverting input of the op amp were connected to a voltage divider across V_{out}?
6. How does the setting of the variable 100-Ω resistor in Fig. 15-9 affect V_{out}?
7. Can the circuit of Fig. 15-9 provide a regulated 5-V output with a V_{in} of less than 6.6 V? Why?
8. Why does the performance of the switch-mode power supply deteriorate with the 1N4001 rectifier diode?

ACTIVITY 15-3
CONSTRUCTION PROJECT:
TRIPLE OUTPUT, DUAL-TRACKING POWER SUPPLY

INTRODUCTION

Today's circuits often require more than one voltage for operation. Technicians who are involved with circuit development or repair must have several adjustable and regulated power supplies on their benches. This type of power supply will meet the needs of almost all modern circuits. It provides three outputs: 5 V at 3 A, 0 to 20 V positive at 1 A, and 5 to 20 V negative at 1 A. The power supply is designed so that the two adjustable outputs can be operated in two modes, tracking and independent. The tracking mode is especially helpful for experimenting with op-amp circuits. The 5-V power supply is fixed and is useful for logic circuits. All three power-supply outputs are current-limited for short-circuit protection.

Figure 15-16 on the next page shows the schematic for the unit. The fixed 5-V section is at the bottom. Transformer T_3 and BR_3 develop about 10 V of unregulated direct current. Capacitor C_3 is the filter capacitor. Integrated circuit IC_4 is a fixed 5-V regulator. It is a power device and can deliver over 1 A of load current. Since 1 A is not enough for some logic circuits, transistor Q_1 has been added to boost the current capacity to 3 A. The current through D_1 and R_{14} creates a voltage drop that turns on the transistor. Under short-circuit conditions, the drop across R_{12} cancels the drop across D_1 and R_{14}. This protects Q_1 by allowing it to conduct only approximately 5 A. Integrated circuit IC_4 is internally current-limited to approximately 1.5 A.

The upper portion of the schematic shown in Fig. 15-16 is devoted to the two adjustable 20-V power supplies. The transformers, bridge rectifiers, and filter capacitors C_1 and C_2 develop about 25 V of unregulated direct current. Zener diodes ZD_1 and ZD_2 regulate this to ±18 V with respect to ground. The regulated 18 V is used to energize the dual operational amp. It is also used to energize the voltage divider made up of potentiometers R_3, R_4, and R_5. Resistor R_4 is the front-panel control for adjusting the positive 0- to 20-V output. When S_2 is in the NORMAL (N) position, the voltage at the wiper arm of R_4 is applied to the inverting input of the op amp at the top of the schematic. The output of the op amp drives the ground (G) terminal of IC_2. Thus, changing the setting of R_4 will adjust the output voltage of IC_2.

In Fig. 15-16 IC_3 is the negative regulator. Resistors R_{10} and R_{11} form a voltage divider across the negative output. The voltage from the wiper

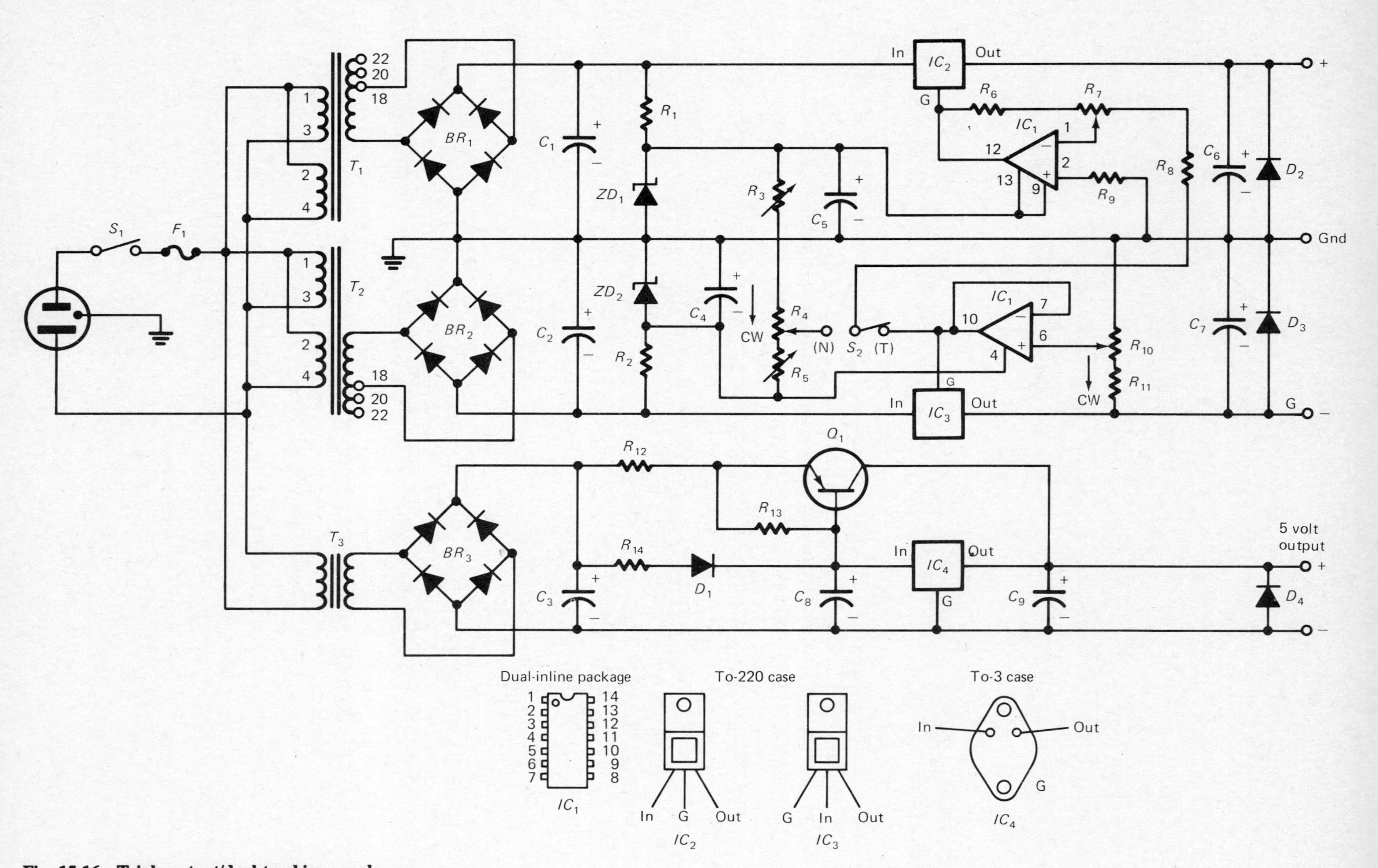

Fig. 15-16 Triple output/dual-tracking supply.

arm of R_{10} drives the noninverting input of the op amp. The output controls the ground pin of IC_3. This circuit can be adjusted for an output of from −5 to −20 V with respect to ground. If S_2 is in the TRACKING (T) position, R_{10} becomes the master control and both power supplies will track from 5 to 20 V. The error in the tracking mode is less than 150 mV.

CONSTRUCTION DETAILS

The IC regulators and the transistor must be provided with adequate heat sinking. Mount the devices onto the heat-sink surface using mica washers, insulating bushings, and silicon grease. Make absolutely certain that the devices are insulated from the heat sink. Appendix B shows how to mount devices on a heat sink.

Parts List

Part Numbers	Description
BR_1, BR_2	200-PIV 1.5-A bridge rectifiers
BR_3	200-PIV 10-A bridge rectifier
C_1, C_2	1.5-mF 35-V electrolytic capacitors
C_3	8-mF 15-V electrolytic capacitor
C_4–C_9	4.7-μF 35-V electrolytic capacitors
D_1–D_4	200-PIV 2.5-A silicon diodes
F_1	2-A 120-V 3AG slow-blow fuse
IC_1	LM474CN dual op amp or equivalent
IC_2	7805 5-V regulator or equivalent
IC_3	7905 5-V negative regulator or equivalent
IC_4	LM309K 5-V regulator or equivalent
Q_1	2N6594 45-V 12-A PNP silicon transistor
R_1, R_2	330-Ω ½-W resistors
R_3	10-kΩ printed-circuit potentiometer
R_4, R_{10}	10-kΩ 1-W linear panel potentiometers
R_5	2.4-kΩ printed-circuit potentiometer
R_6, R_8	10-kΩ ½-W resistors
R_7	1-kΩ printed-circuit potentiometer
R_9	4.7-kΩ ¼-W resistor
R_{11}	2.7-kΩ ¼-W resistor
R_{12}	0.1-Ω 5-W resistor
R_{13}	6.8-Ω ½-W resistor
R_{14}	0.22-Ω 1-W resistor
S_1	2-A 120-V SPST switch
S_2	1-A 50-V SPDT switch
T_1, T_2	1-A 50-V Stancor P-8623 power transformers or equivalent
T_3	7.5-V 4-A Stancor P-5015 power transformer or equivalent
ZD_1, ZD_2	18-V 1-W 1N4786A zener diodes or equivalent
Misc.	Chassis, cabinet hardware, output jacks, heat sinks, fuse holder, line cord, circuit board, IC socket, wire, terminals, knobs
Optional	Voltmeters, ammeters, panel lamp, decals

You may wire the power supply using a circuit board or insulated tie points. Make sure that potentiometers R_4 and R_{10} are mounted on the front panel. All other adjustable resistors are of the printed circuit type and are adjusted with a screwdriver. Be very careful to observe the proper polarity with all diodes and electrolytic capacitors. Capacitors C_8 and C_9 should be mounted as close as possible to IC_4, and their negative leads must share a common tie point with the ground (G) lead. If IC_2 and IC_3 are more than 3 in. from their main filters, C_1 and C_2, their input leads will also have to be bypassed to ground with 4.7-μF capacitors. This is to ensure the stability of the IC regulators.

You will need an accurate voltmeter for testing and adjusting the power supply. Test the fixed 5-V section first. Next, place the switch in the NORMAL position. Turn the front-panel positive-voltage adjust knob fully counterclockwise (ccw). Carefully adjust R_3 with an insulated screwdriver until the positive output is exactly 0 V. Now turn the front-panel knob fully clockwise (cw) and adjust R_5 for an output of exactly 20 V. You may have to repeat the two adjustments to make the positive output range exactly from 0 to 20 V. The final adjustment is made by placing the switch in the TRACKING position. Adjust the front-panel potentiometer R_{10} for a negative output of 15 V. Finally, adjust trimmer R_7 to make the positive output also equal to 15 V. Verify that the positive power supply tracks the negative power supply over the range of 5 to 20 V.

Although the schematic does not show it, you may wish to add some built-in meters to your power supply. Since the fixed 5-V power supply is predictable, no voltmeter is required; however, two voltmeters are a nice feature for the adjustable power supplies. You may also wish to add some current meters and an on-off indicator lamp.

Using the power supply is straightforward. Always double-check your connections before turning it on. The fixed 5-V power supply is completely independent. This means that you must remember to ground one of its leads to the circuit you are working on (this would usually be the negative lead). The two adjustable power supplies share the common ground. One ground connection from either of them will usually be adequate. A load can also be connected from the negative adjustable output to the positive adjustable output for achieving up to 40 V. Since there are so many combinations, diodes D_2 through D_4 are included to prevent reverse polarity damage to the outputs.

APPENDIX A

Electronic Wiring and Soldering

A1 CHASSIS WIRING

To Install a Part:

1. Cut the leads to the proper length.

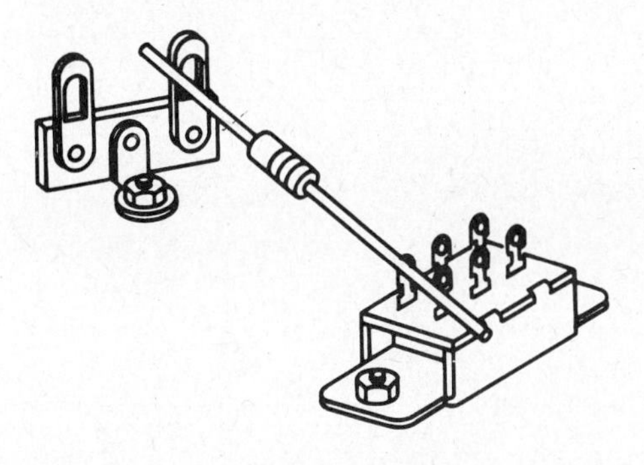

2. Fasten the lead ends.

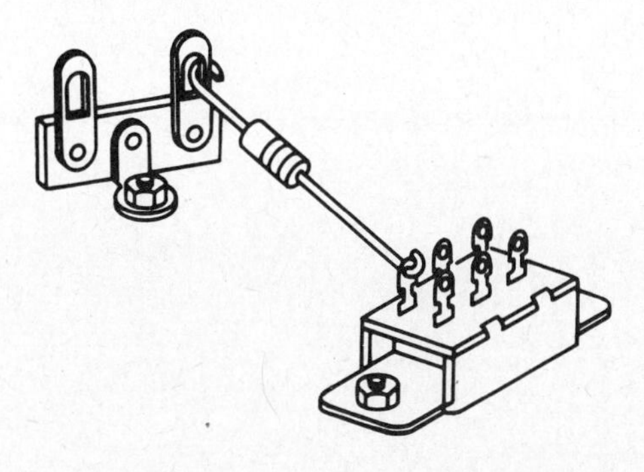

This material excerpted from the Heathkit Builder's Guide by permission of the Heath Company.

Note: Use sleeving when it is called for to provide insulation.

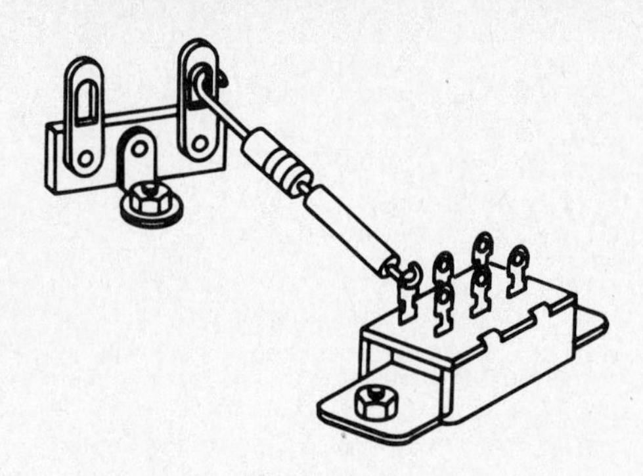

To Solder a Connection:

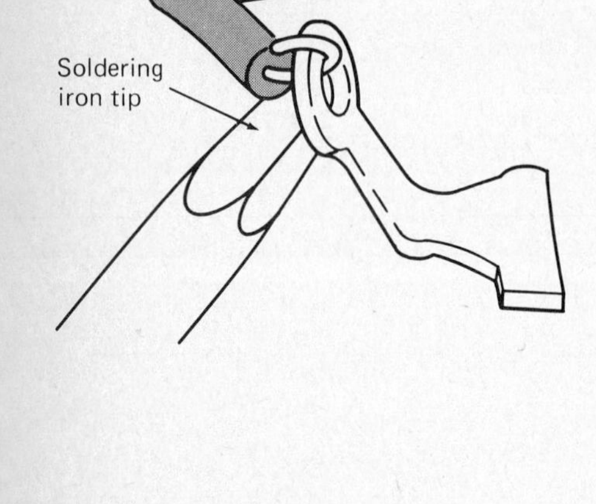

1. Prepare the wire and crimp it around the connector. Touch the tip of iron to both the wire and the connector for 2 or 3 s.

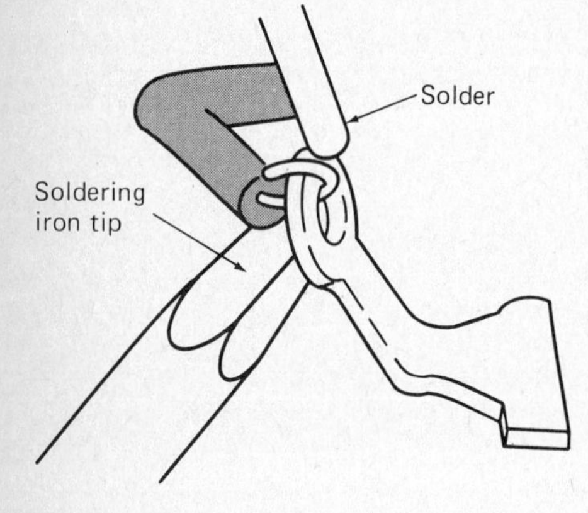

2. Apply only enough solder to thoroughly wet both the tip and the connection.

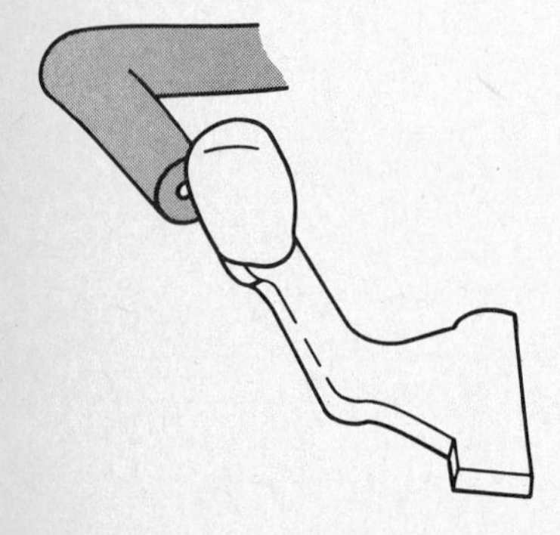

3. Let the connection harden before moving the wire. The connection should be smooth and bright.

4. Check the connection. Poor connections look crystalline and grainy, or the solder tends to blob. Reheat the connection if it does not look smooth and bright.

A poor connection

REMEMBER:

Keep the soldering iron tip clean. Wipe it often on a wet sponge or cloth; then apply solder to it to give the entire tip a wet look. This "tinning" process will protect the tip and enable you to make good connections. When the solder tends to "ball" or not stick to the tip, the tip needs to be cleaned and retinned. Use rosin-core radio-type solder (60:40 or 50:50 tin-lead content) for all soldering.

A2 PRINTED CIRCUITS

To Install a Part:

The following example uses a resistor, since resistors are usually installed first.

1. Position the circuit board with the plain side (not the foil side) up.
2. Hold the resistor by the body as shown and bend the leads straight down.

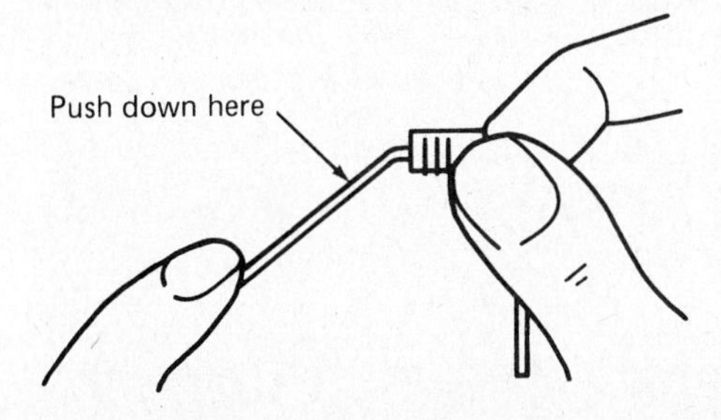

3. Push the leads through the holes at the proper location on the circuit board. The end with color bands may be positioned either way.
4. Press the resistor against the circuit board. Then bend the leads outward slightly to hold the resistor in place.

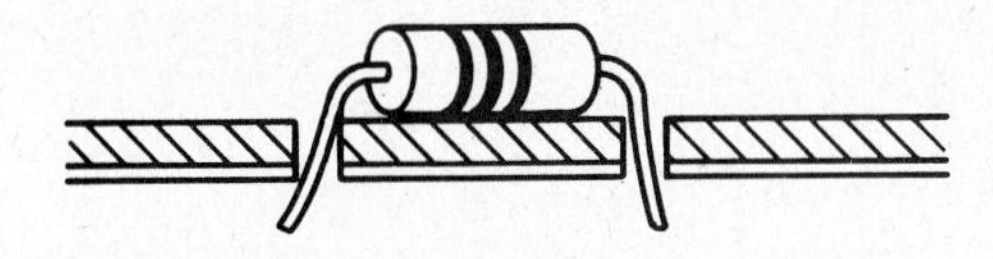

To Solder a Connection:

1. Place the soldering iron tip against both the lead and the circuit board foil. Heat both for 2 or 3 s.

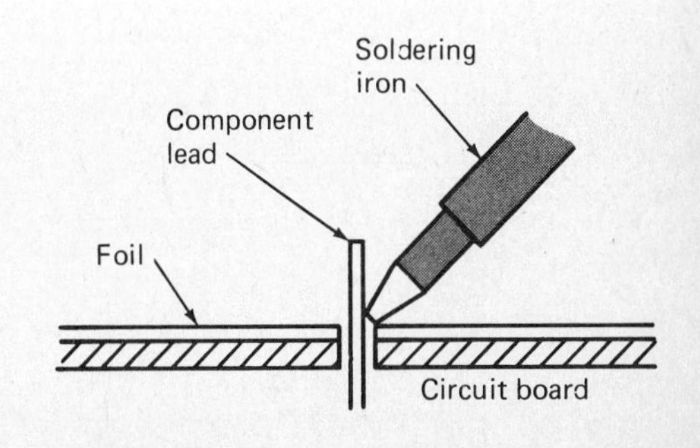

2. Then apply solder to the other side of the connection. *Important:* Let the heated lead and the circuit board foil melt the solder.

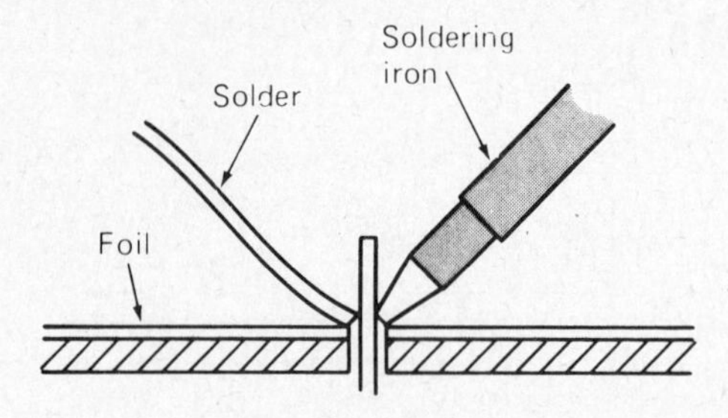

3. As the solder begins to melt, allow it to flow around the connection. Then remove the solder and the iron and let the connection cool.
4. Hold the lead with one hand while you cut off the excess lead length close to the connection. This will keep you from being hit in the eye by the flying lead.

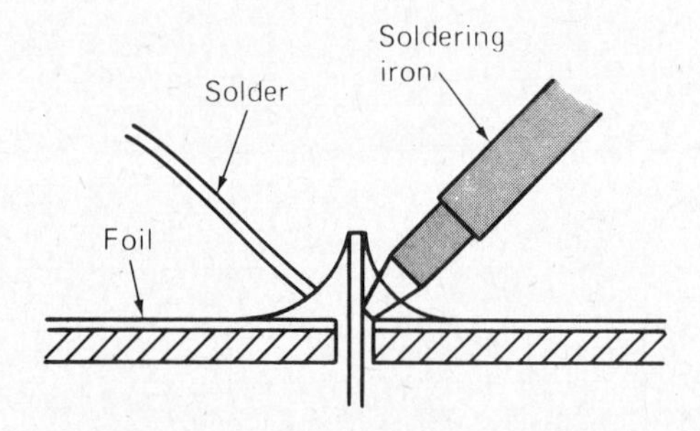

To Check a Connection:

Be sure the solder made a good electrical connection. **When both the lead *and* the circuit board foil are heated at the same time, the solder will flow onto the lead and the foil evenly. The solder will then make a good electrical connection between the lead and the foil. When the *lead* is not heated sufficiently, the solder will not flow onto the lead as shown.**

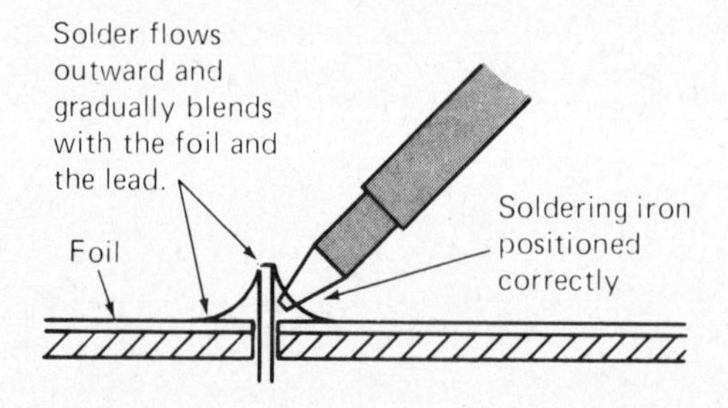

Reheat the connection and, if necessary, apply a small amount of additional solder to obtain a good connection. When the *foil* is not heated sufficiently, the solder will blob on the circuit board as shown. Reheat the connection and, if necessary, apply a small amount of additional solder to obtain a good connection. *Be sure you did not make any solder bridges.* Due to the small foil area around the circuit board holes and the small areas between foils, you must use the utmost care to prevent solder bridges between adjacent foil areas.

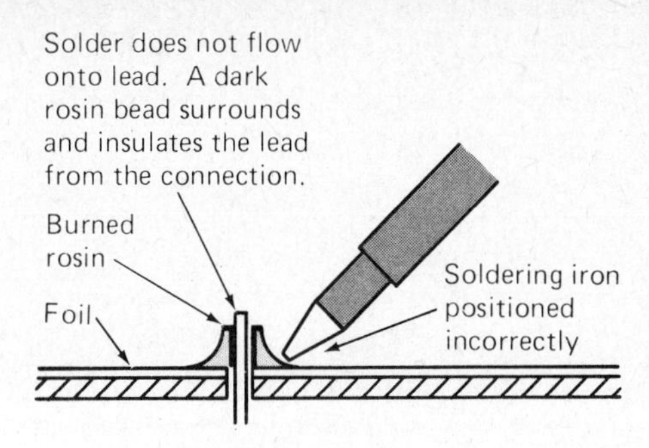

A solder bridge may occur if you accidentally touch an adjacent connection, if you use too much solder, or if you "drag" the soldering iron across other foils as you remove it from the connection. Always take a good look at the foil area around each lead before you solder it.

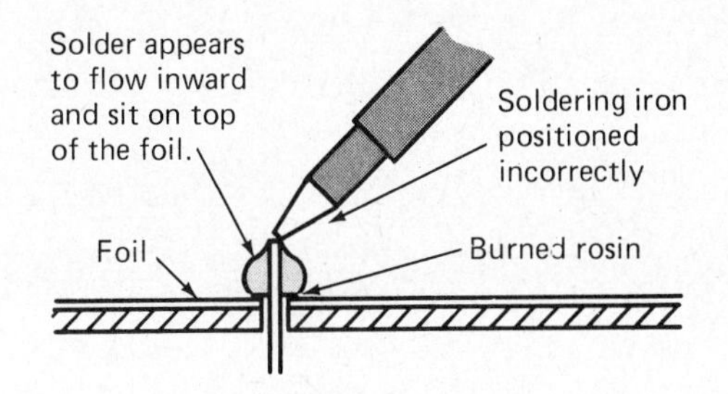

Then, when you solder the connection, make sure the solder remains in this area and does not bridge to another foil. This is especially important when the foils are small and close together.

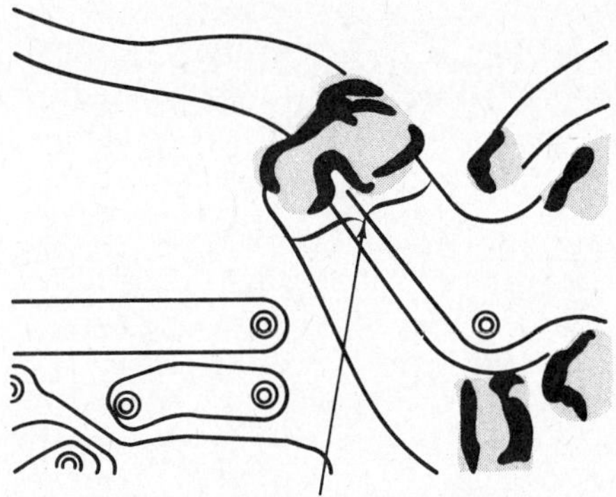

A solder bridge between two adjacent foils

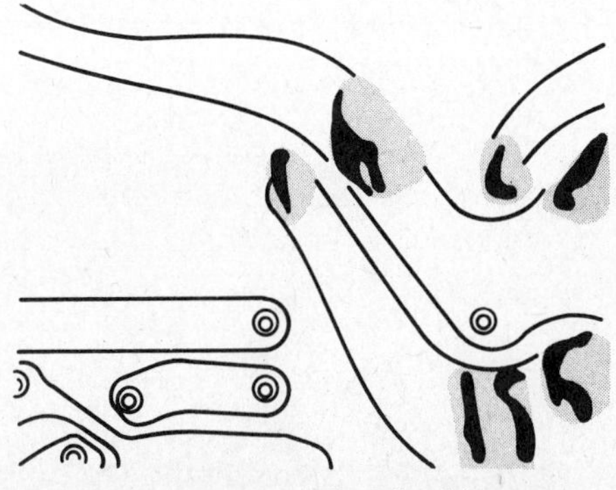

How the connection should appear

A3 PRINTED-CIRCUIT DESOLDERING

It is sometimes necessary to remove a defective part from a printed circuit board. This can be difficult to do when the part has several leads. Several tools and aids have been developed to make the job easier. There are two popular vacuum tools for this job. The vacuum desoldering pencil melts the joint, and then the bulb is released to draw the solder off of the board (Fig. A3-1). After all the leads have been desoldered, the part can be removed. A separate vacuum desoldering bulb (Fig. A3-2) can be used with a separate soldering pencil to accomplish the same job.

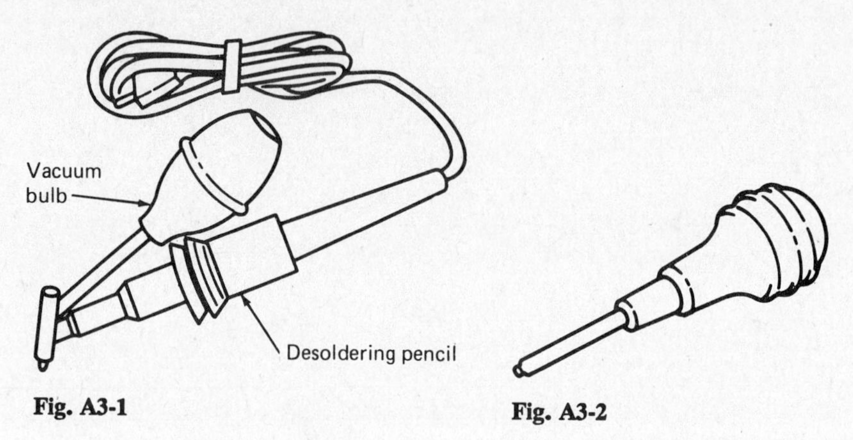

Fig. A3-1 **Fig. A3-2**

Some technicians prefer to heat all connections of a component at the same time, which also allows removal of the part. Special desoldering tips are available to accomplish this. Different tip styles are needed for the various transistor and IC parts (Fig. A3-3).

Yet another technique is to use finely braided wire. The wire and the tip are both applied to the connection. Capillary action causes the

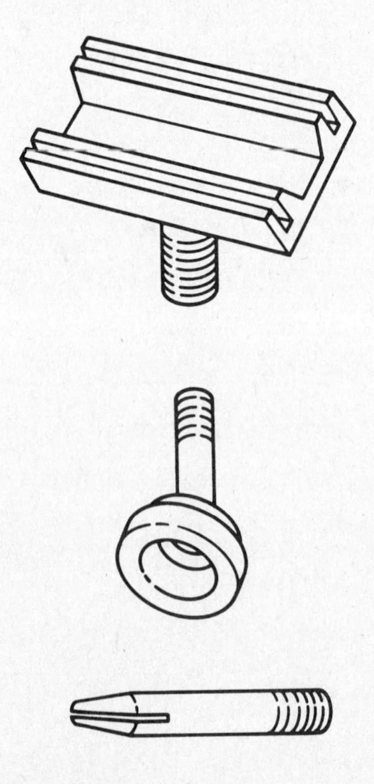

Fig. A3-3

solder to flow off of the board and into the braided wire. Special wire made just for this purpose is available.

As circuits become more complicated, so do circuit boards. Many circuit boards are double-sided, with traces on both sides of the board. There are also multilayer boards with traces inside the board. Double-sided and multilayer boards are difficult to desolder. Since the holes for the component leads are plated through the board, the solder adheres to the sides of the hole.

Vacuum desoldering stations are recommended for removing components from circuit boards with plated-through holes. They contain a vacuum pump and circuits to control the temperature of the tip. A hand-held unit is connected to the station with a vacuum hose and a cable. The vacuum can be released with a finger control or a foot switch.

Figure A3-4 shows the hand-held portion of a vacuum desoldering station. The tip is applied to the circuit board as shown in Fig. A3-5. A back-and-forth motion is used. When the solder melts, the component lead moves freely. At this moment, the vacuum is released. The solder is drawn up into the tip and air enters the hole to cool the board and the component lead.

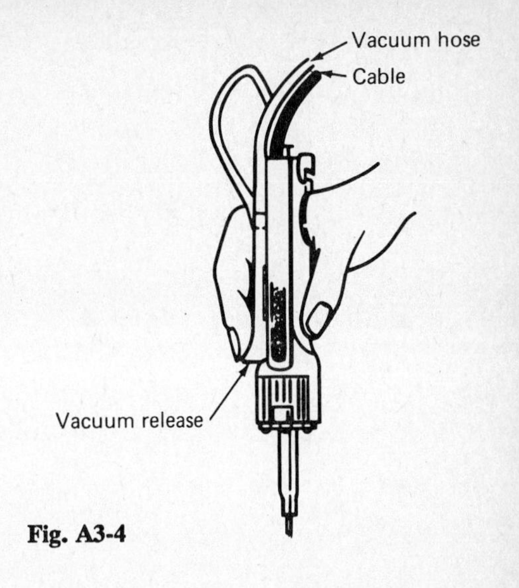

Fig. A3-4

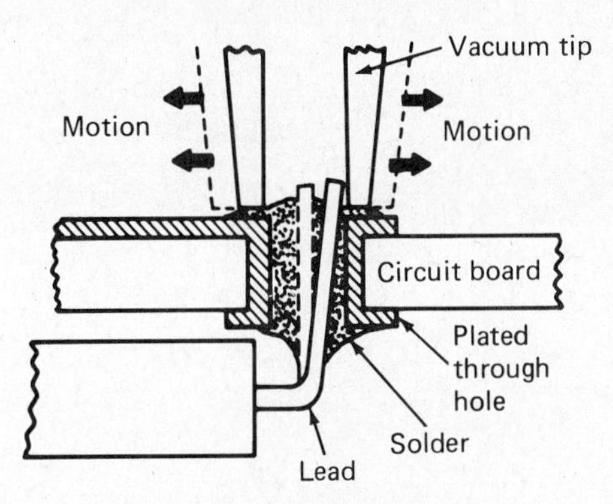

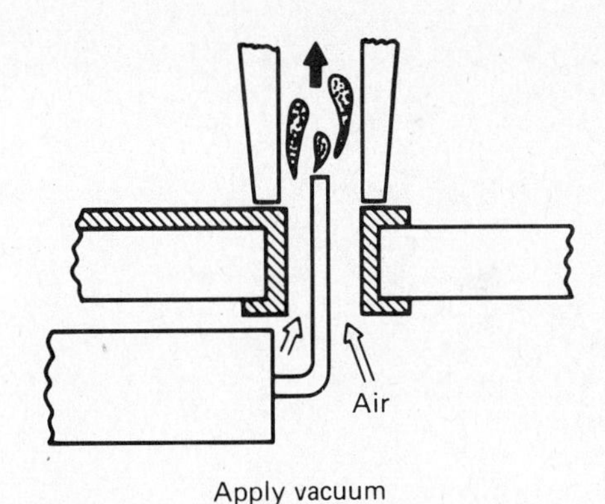

Fig. A3-5

APPENDIX B

Thermal Design and Heat Sinks

Power transistors, thyristors, rectifiers, and some ICs can run very hot. In some cases, the internal (junction) temperature may reach a point where the device is damaged or destroyed. Care must be taken to prevent this from happening.

Figure B-1 shows a derating curve for a 200-W transistor. It is capable of safely dissipating its rated power only when its case temperature is 25°C (77°F) or lower. Notice that the power rating drops to 115 W at 100°C and to 0 W at a case temperature of 200°C. Obviously, the case temperature must be maintained below 200°C if the device is to serve any useful purpose.

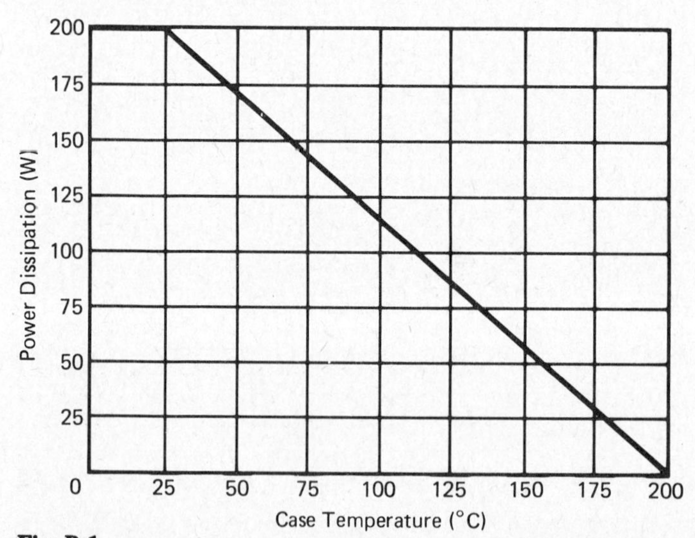

Fig. B-1

A 200-W power transistor will often be packaged in the large, metal TO-3 case, which has a thermal resistance of 34°C/W. A check of the manufacturer's specification sheet shows two interesting facts:

$$\theta_{JC} = 0.875°C/W$$

$$\theta_{CA} = 34°C/W$$

where θ_{JC} = thermal resistance of device from junction to case
θ_{CA} = thermal resistance of case to ambient (surrounding air)

Most silicon devices are rated for a maximum *junction* temperature of 200°C. You now have enough information to calculate how much power the device can safely dissipate. Assume an ambient (air) temperature of 25°C. The allowable temperature rise is therefore 175°C (200 − 25). The thermal "circuit" contains two resistances, θ_{JC} and θ_{CA}. The thermal resistances act in series just as they do in a series electric circuit. It is safe to use just θ_{CA} in this case, however, because it is so much larger that it effectively swamps out the other thermal resistance. Based on a 175°C temperature rise

$$\text{Maximum dissipation} = \frac{\text{max. temp rise}}{\theta_{CA}} = \frac{175°\text{C}}{34°\text{C/W}}$$

$$= 5.15 \text{ W}$$

This means that the 200-W transistor mounted in the TO-3 case cannot safely dissipate much more than 5 W if the surrounding air temperature is 25°C. If the air temperature is higher, *less* than 5 W can be dissipated safely. In practice, when a device must dissipate more than several watts, a *heat sink* is used. The heat sink may be the metal chassis, a large area of foil on a printed circuit board, the cabinet, or a separate casting or extrusion for carrying the heat away from the device. Figure B-2 shows a typical heat sink made from extruded aluminum. It measures 11.4 × 7.8 cm (4½ × 3¹⁄₁₆ in.) and is equal in cooling capacity to a flat sheet of aluminum 25.4 × 20.3 cm (10 × 8 in.) assuming the heat-sink is *mounted in free air with its fins vertical.* Heat sinks of this type are often mounted on the rear panel of electronic equipment. They may also be mounted inside the equipment and force-cooled with a fan.

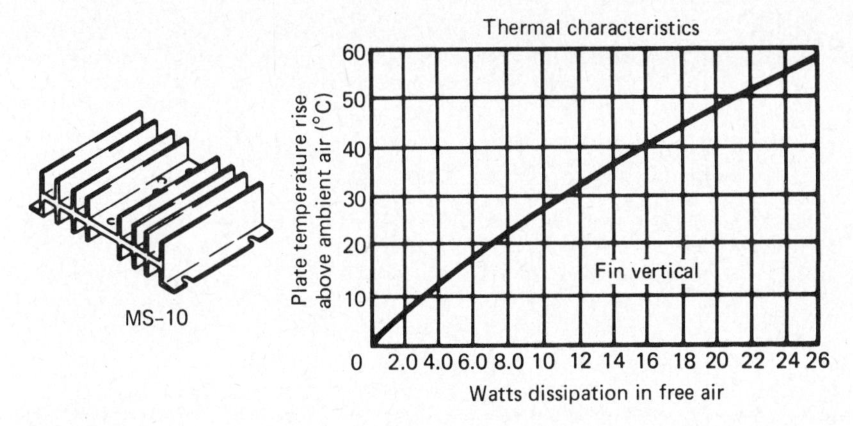

Fig. B-2

Heat-sink manufacturers rate their products according to thermal resistance. You can extract this rating from the curve shown in Fig. B-2. It shows a temperature rise of 40°C when the dissipation is 16 W. The thermal resistance θ_{SA} (sink to ambient) is

$$\theta_{SA} = \frac{40°\text{C}}{16 \text{ W}} = 2.5°\text{C/W}$$

What happens when you mount the TO-3 power transistor on the heat sink? You should eliminate the case-to-ambient thermal resistance and replace it with the sink-to-ambient thermal resistance, which is much lower. This will improve the safe dissipation of the transistor. However, quite often a metal-to-metal mount is not possible. The collector of the power transistor is electrically tied to the case. A direct mount would cause a short circuit because the collector would be grounded (unless the collector is normally connected to ground). In most cases, an insulating washer must be used. Washers have thermal resistance which must be taken into account. This new thermal resistance, called θ_{CS} (case to sink), is typically 0.4°C/W for a mica washer. We are now in a position to calculate the *total* thermal resistance from the junction to the ambient. Remember, it acts as a series circuit.

$$\theta_{JA} = \theta_{JC} + \theta_{CS} + \theta_{SA} = 0.875 + 0.4 + 2.5$$
$$= 3.78°\text{C/W}$$

One more calculation will show the improvement in dissipation capability offered by the heat sink. Once again, use the assumption of a 25°C ambient temperature and maximum safe temperature of 200°C, for a total temperature rise of 175°C.

$$\text{Maximum dissipation} = \frac{\text{max. temp rise}}{\theta_{CA}} = \frac{175°\text{C}}{3.78°\text{C/W}}$$
$$= 46.3 \text{ W}$$

Over 46 W can now be safely dissipated. It should be obvious how important heat sinks are when device dissipation must be high.

When mounting devices, special care must be taken to avoid short circuits and high thermal resistance. Figure B-3 shows the general scheme for mounting a TO-3 package. Notice the placement of the mica insulator and the insulating bushings. They are very important because they prevent shorts. Also notice that *silicon grease* is to be applied to both sides of the mica insulator. This ensures minimal thermal resistance. Figure B-4 shows mounting details for the TO-220 package, and Fig. B-5 shows stud rectifier mounting.

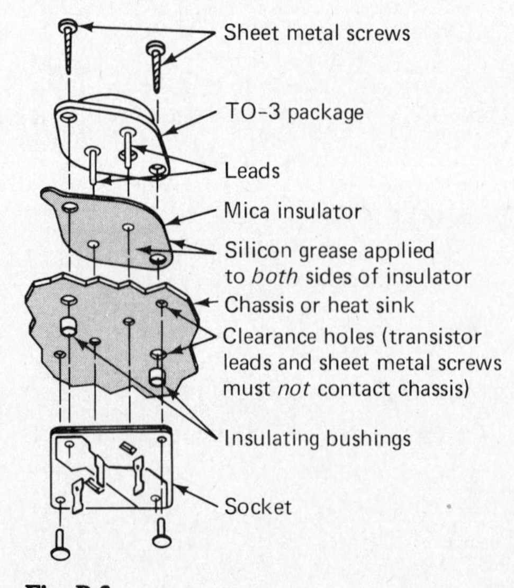

Fig. B-3

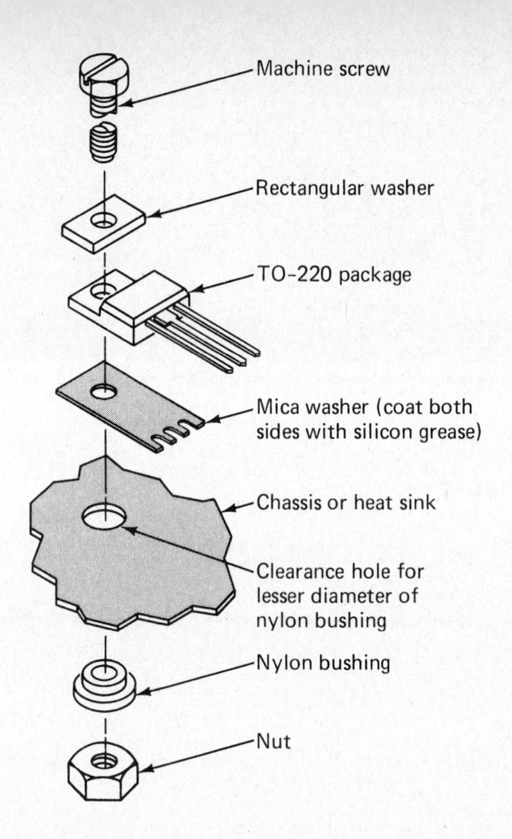
Machine screw
Rectangular washer
TO-220 package
Mica washer (coat both
sides with silicon grease)
Chassis or heat sink
Clearance hole for
lesser diameter of
nylon bushing
Nylon bushing
Nut

Fig. B-4

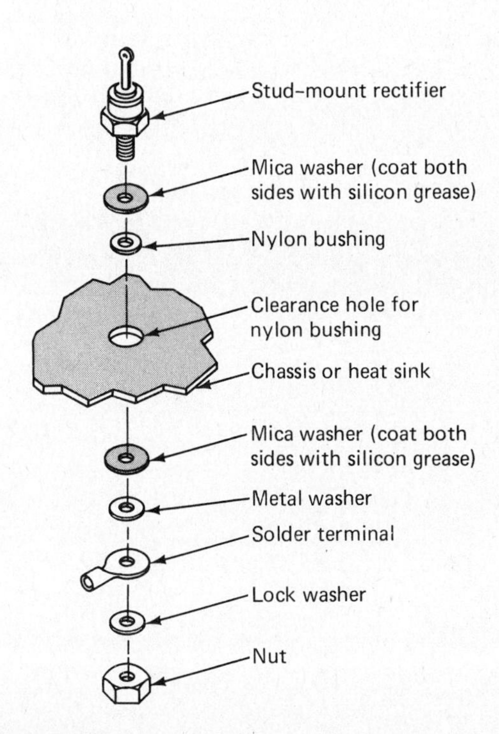
Stud-mount rectifier
Mica washer (coat both
sides with silicon grease)
Nylon bushing
Clearance hole for
nylon bushing
Chassis or heat sink
Mica washer (coat both
sides with silicon grease)
Metal washer
Solder terminal
Lock washer
Nut

Fig. B-5

APPENDIX C

Linear-Integrated-Circuit Specifications

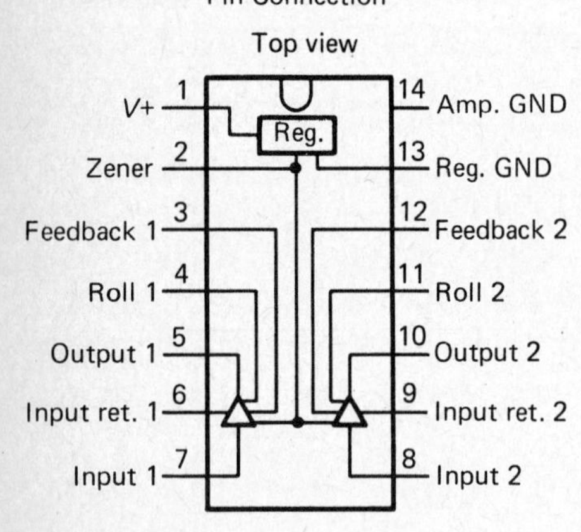

DUAL LOW-NOISE PREAMPLIFIER

GENERAL DESCRIPTION

A dual low-noise preamplifier consisting of two identically matched 68-dB gain amplifiers fed from an internal zener-regulated power supply. Operation requires only a single external power supply and a minimum number of external frequency-shaping components.

FEATURES

- Low audio noise
- Wide power-supply range
- Built-in power-supply filter
- Low distortion
- High channel separation

APPLICATIONS

- Stereo tape player/recorder
- Stereo radio receiver
- Movie projector
- Phonograph
- TV remote-control receiver
- Microphone amplifier

ABSOLUTE MAXIMUM RATINGS

Power-supply voltage.................................... 16 V dc
Storage temperature............................... −55 to +150°C
Operating temperature............................. −30 to +85°C

Adapted by permission of Radio Shack, a division of Tandy Corporation.

QUAD OP AMP

GENERAL DESCRIPTION

The 324 series consists of four independent, high-gain, internally frequency-compensated op ams designed specifically to operate from a single power supply over a wide range of voltages. Operation from split power supplies is also possible, and the low power-supply current drain is independent of the magnitude of the power-supply voltage.

Application areas include transducer amplifiers, dc gain blocks, and all the conventional op-amp circuits which now can be more easily implemented in single power-supply systems. For example, the 324 series can be directly operated off the standard +5-V dc power-supply voltage used in digital systems, and it will easily provide the required interface electronics without requiring the additional ±15-V dc power supplies.

QUAD OP AMP

Pin Connection

Top view

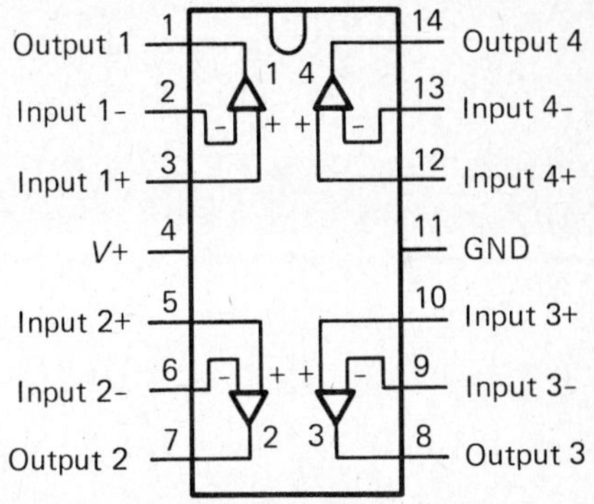

Dual-in-line and flat package

FEATURES

- Internally frequency-compensated for unity gain
- Large dc voltage gain: 100 dB
- Wide bandwidth (unity gain): 1 MHz (temperature-compensated)
- Wide power-supply range: single power supply 3 to 30 V dc or dual power supplies ±1.5 to ±15 V dc
- Very low power-supply current drain (800 μA), essentially independent of power-supply voltage (1 mW per op amp at +5 V dc)
- Low input biasing current 45 nA dc (temperature-compensated)
- Low input offset voltage 2 mV dc and offset current 5 nA dc
- Input common-mode voltage range includes ground
- Differential input voltage range equal to the power-supply voltage
- Large output voltage swing 0 to ±1.3 V dc

ABSOLUTE MAXIMUM RATINGS

Power-supply voltage. . . . . .32 ± 16 V dc
Differential input voltage. . . . . .32 V dc
Input voltage. . . . . −0.3 to +32 V dc
Power dissipation, molded DIP. . . . . .570 mW
Cavity DIP. . . . . .900 mW
Output short circuit to GND (one amplifier). . . . . .Continuous $+V \leq V$ dc and T_A = 24°C
Input current ($V_{in} < -0.3\ V_{OL}$). . . . . .50 mA
Operating temperature. . . . . .0 to +70°C
Storage temperature. . . . . −65 to +150°C
Lead temperature (soldering, 10 s). . . . . .300°C

QUAD COMPARATOR

Pin Connection

Top view

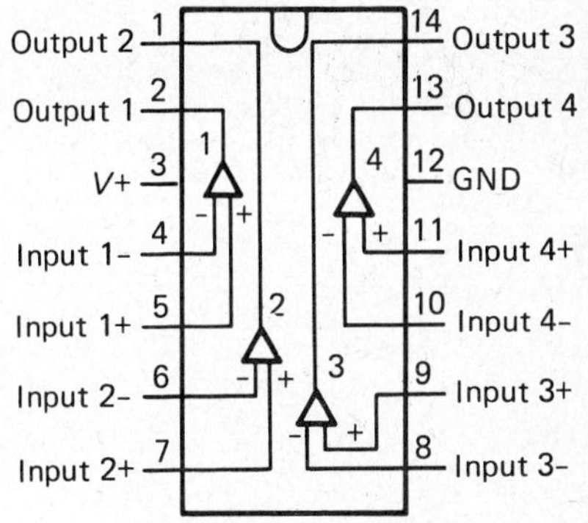

Dual-in-line and flat package

Schematic Diagram

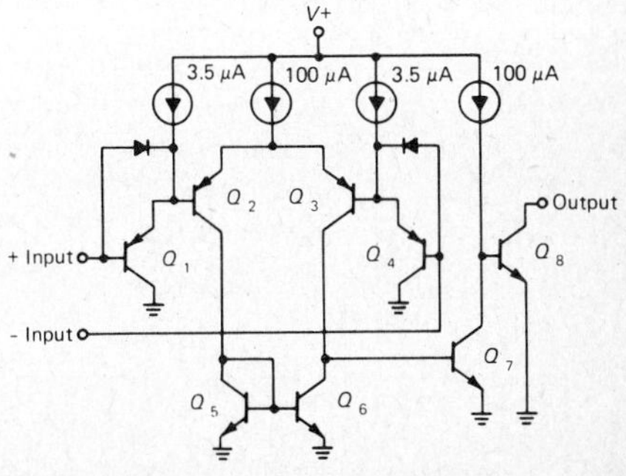

QUAD COMPARATOR

GENERAL DESCRIPTION

The 339 series consists of four independent voltage comparators designed specifically to operate from a single power supply over a wide range of voltages. Operation from split power supplies is also possible, and the low power-supply current drain is independent of the magnitude of the power-supply voltage. These comparators also have a unique characteristic in that the input common-mode voltage range includes ground even though operated from a single power-supply voltage.

FEATURES

- Wide single power supply: voltage range 2 to 36 V dc or dual power supplies ±1 to ±18 V dc
- Very low power-supply current drain (0.8 mA), independent of power-supply voltage (1 mW per comparator at +5 V dc)
- Input common-mode voltage range includes ground
- Differential input voltage range equal to the power-supply voltage
- Low output 1 mV at 5 μA; saturation voltage 70 mV at 1 mA
- Output voltage compatible with TTL (fanout of 2), DTL, ECL, MOS, and CMOS logic systems

ABSOLUTE MAXIMUM RATINGS

Power-supply voltage + V .... 36 or ±17 V dc
Differential input voltage .... 36 V dc
Input voltage .... −0.3 to +36 V dc
Power dissipation, molded DIP .... 570 mW
  Cavity DIP .... 900 mW
Output short-circuit to GND .... Continuous
Input current (V_{in} < −0.3 V dc) .... 50 mA
Operating temperature .... 0 to +70°C
Storage temperature .... −65 to +150°C
Lead temperature (soldering, 10 s) .... 300°C

DUAL 2-W AUDIO AMPLIFIER

GENERAL DESCRIPTION

The 377 is a monolithic dual-power amplifier which offers high-quality performance for stereo phonographs, tape players, recorders, and AM/FM stereo receivers, etc.

The 377 will deliver 2 W per channel into 8- or 16-Ω loads. The amplifier is designed to operate with a minimum of external components and contains an internal bias regulator to bias each amplifier. Device overload protection consists of both internal current limit and thermal shutdown.

DUAL TWO-WATT AUDIO AMPLIFIER

Pin Connection
Top View

Pin name	Pin	Pin	Pin name
Bias	1	14	V+
Output 1	2	13	Output 2
GND	3	12	GND
GND	4	11	GND
GND	5	10	GND
Input 1	6	9	Input 2
Feedback 1	7	8	Feedback 2

Dual-in-line package

Schematic Diagram

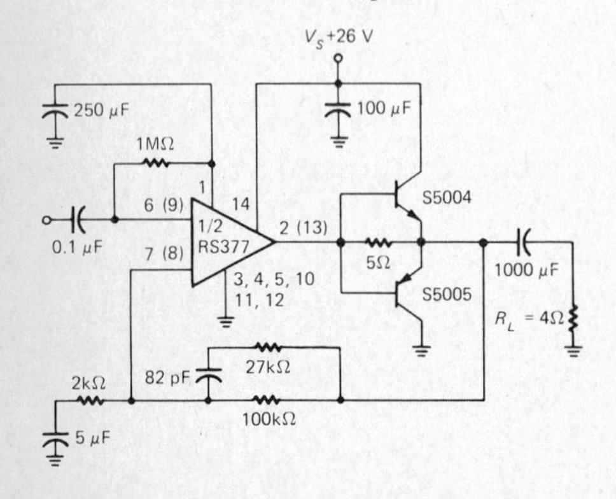

FEATURES

- A_{VO} typical 90 dB
- 2 W per channel
- 70-dB ripple rejection
- 75-dB channel separation
- Internal stabilization
- Self-centered biasing
- 3-MΩ input impedance
- 10- to 26-V operation
- Internal current-limiting
- Internal thermal protection

APPLICATIONS

- Multichannel audio systems
- Tape recorders and players
- Movie projectors
- Automotive systems

- Stereo phonographs
- Bridge output stages
- AM/FM radio receivers
- Intercoms
- Servo amplifiers
- Instrument systems

ABSOLUTE MAXIMUM RATINGS

Power-supply voltage.................................26 V dc
Input voltage...0 to 26 V
Operating temperature..............................0 to +70°C
Storage temperature.............................. −65 to +150°C
Junction temperature...................................150°C
Lead temperature (soldering, 10 s)........................300°C

TIMER

GENERAL DESCRIPTION

The 555 is a highly stable device for generating accurate time delays or oscillation. Additional terminals are provided for triggering or resetting if desired. In the time-delay mode of operation, the time is precisely controlled by one external resistor and capacitor. For astable operation as an oscillator, the free-running frequency and duty cycle are accurately controlled with two external resistors and one capacitor. The circuit can be triggered and reset on falling waveforms, and the output circuit can source or sink up to 200 mA or derive TTL circuits.

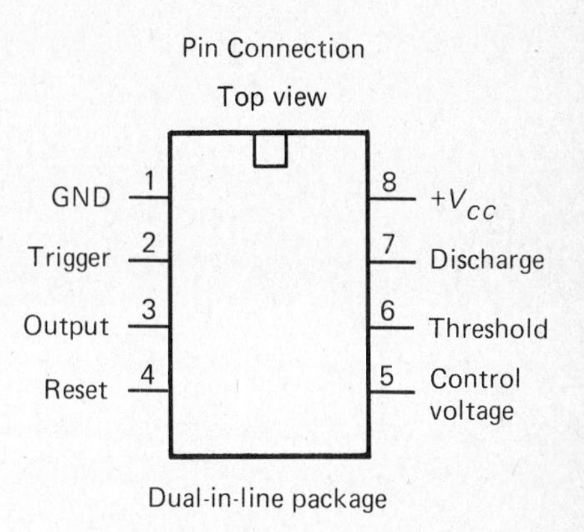

FEATURES

- Timing from microseconds through hours
- Operates in both astable and monostable modes
- Adjustable duty cycle
- Output can source or sink 200 mA
- Output and power supply TTL-compatible
- Temperature stability better than 0.005 percent per Celsius degree
- Normally on and normally off output

APPLICATIONS

- Precision timing
- Pulse generation
- Sequential timing
- Time-delay generation
- Pulse-width modulation
- Pulse-position modulation
- Linear ramp generator

ABSOLUTE MAXIMUM RATINGS

Power-supply voltage.............................. +18 V dc
Power dissipation......................................600 mW
Operating temperature..............................0 to +70°C
Storage temperature.............................. −65 to +150°C
Lead temperature (soldering, 10 s)........................300°C

DUAL TIMER

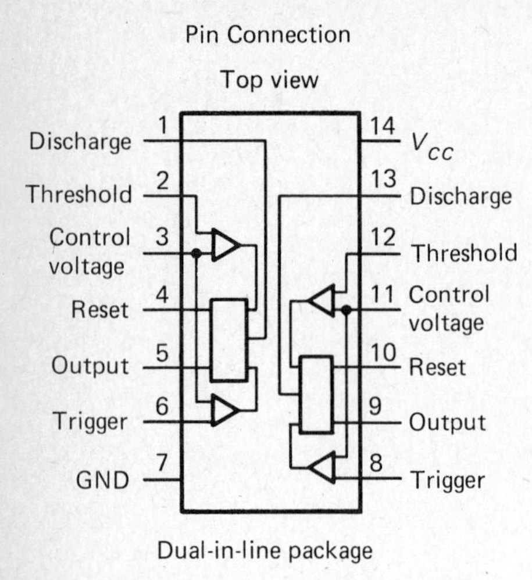

DUAL TIMER

GENERAL DESCRIPTION

The 556 dual timing circuit is a highly stable controller capable of producing accurate time delays or oscillation. The 556 is a dual 555. Timing is provided by an external resistor and capacitor for each timing function. The two timers operate independently of each other sharing only V_{CC} and ground. The circuits can be triggered and reset on falling waveforms. The output structures may sink or source 200 mA.

FEATURES

- Timing from microseconds through hours
- Operates in both astable and monostable modes
- Replaces two 555 timers
- Adjustable duty cycle
- Output can source or sink 200 mA
- Output and power supply TTL-compatible
- Temperature stability better than 0.005 percent per Celsius degree
- Normally on and normally off output

APPLICATIONS

- Precision timing
- Pulse generation
- Sequential timing
- Time-delay generation
- Pulse-width modulation
- Pulse-position modulation
- Linear ramp generator

ABSOLUTE MAXIMUM RATINGS

Power-supply voltage.................................. +18 V dc
Power dissipation...600 mW
Operating temperature...................................0 to 70°C
Storage temperature.............................. −65 to +150°C
Lead temperature (soldering, 10 s)..........................300°C

VOLTAGE-CONTROLLED OSCILLATOR

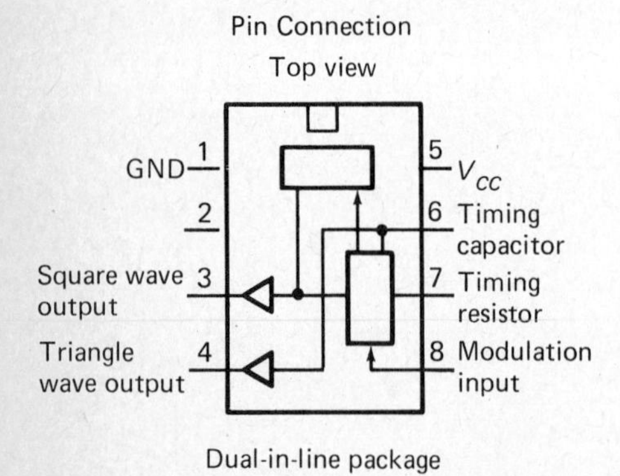

VOLTAGE-CONTROLLED OSCILLATOR

GENERAL DESCRIPTION

The 566 is a general purpose VCO which can be used to generate square and triangular waves, the frequency of which is a very linear function of a control voltage. The frequency is also a function of an external resistor and capacitor.

FEATURES

- Wide power-supply voltage range, 10 to 24 V dc
- Very linear modulation characteristics
- High-temperature stability
- Excellent power-supply voltage rejection
- 10:1 frequency range with fixed capacitor
- Frequency-programmable by means of current, voltage, resistor, or capacitor.

APPLICATIONS

- FM modulation
- Signal generation
- Function generation
- Frequency-shift keying
- Tone generation

ABSOLUTE MAXIMUM RATINGS

Power-supply voltage.................................26 V dc
Power dissipation....................................300 mW
Operating temperature...............................0 to 70°C
Lead temperature (soldering, 10 s).........................300°C

TONE DECODER

GENERAL DESCRIPTION

The 567 is a general-purpose tone decoder designed to provide a saturated transistor switch to ground when an input signal is present within the passband. The circuit consists of an *I* and *Q* detector driven by a VCO which determines the center frequency of the decoder. External components are used to independently set center frequency, bandwidth, and output delay.

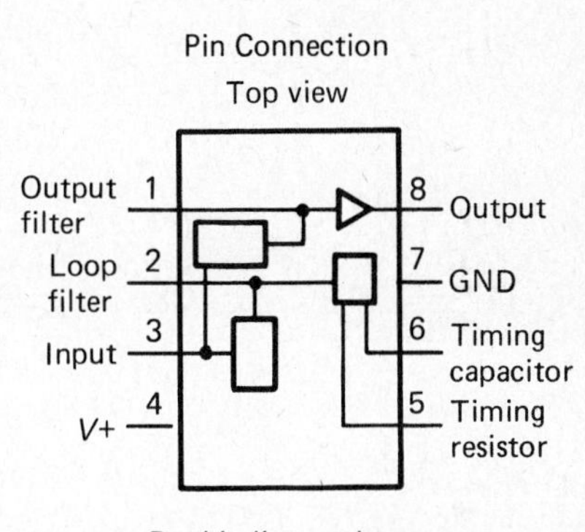

FEATURES

- 20:1 frequency range with an external resistor
- Logic compatible output with 100-mA current-sinking capability
- Bandwidth adjustable from 0 to 14 percent
- High rejection of out-of-band signals and noise
- Immunity to false signals
- Highly stable center frequency
- Center frequency adjustable from 0.01 Hz to 500 kHz

APPLICATIONS

- Touch-tone decoding
- Precision oscillator
- Frequency monitoring and control
- Wide-band frequency-shift keying demodulation
- Ultrasonic controls
- Carrier-current remote controls
- Communications paging decoders

ABSOLUTE MAXIMUM RATINGS

Power-supply voltage.................................10 V dc
Power dissipation....................................300 mW
V_8...15 V
V_3... −10 V
V_3...V_8 + 0.5 V
Storage temperature............................. −65 to + 150°C

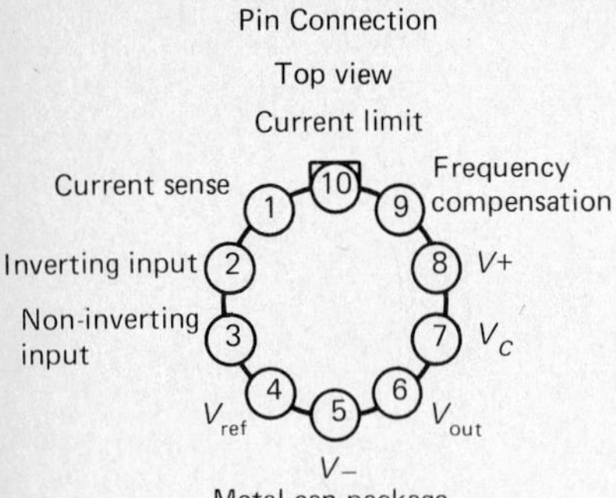

Metal can package

Note: Pin 5 connected to case.

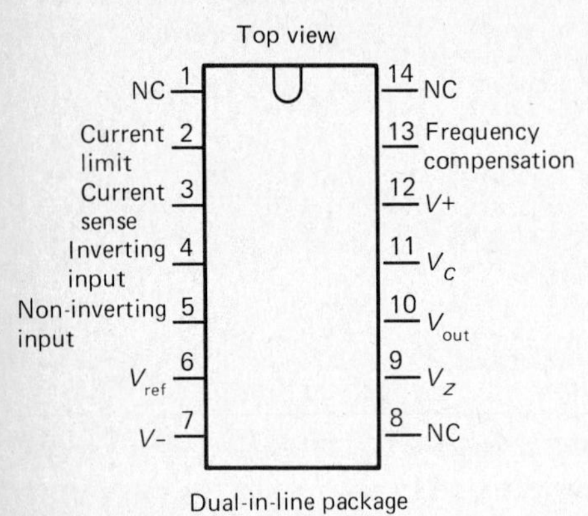

Dual-in-line package

VOLTAGE REGULATOR

GENERAL DESCRIPTION

The 723 is a voltage regulator designed primarily for series regulator applications. By itself, it will supply output currents up to 150 mA; but external transistors can be added to provide any desired load current. The circuit features extremely low standby current drain, and provision is made for either linear or foldback current limiting.

FEATURES

- 150-mA output current without external pass transistor
- Output currents in excess of 10 A possible by adding external transistors
- Input voltage 40 V max.
- Output voltage adjustable from 2 to 37 V
- Can be used as either a linear or a switching regulator

The 723 is also useful in a wide range of other applications such as a shunt regulator, a current regulator, or a temperature controller.

ABSOLUTE MAXIMUM RATINGS

Pulse voltage from $+V$ to $-V$ (50 ms)........................50 V
Continuous voltage from $+V$ to $-V$..........................40 V
Input-output voltage differential.............................40 V
Maximum amplifier input voltage, either input................7.5 V
  Differential..5 V
Current from V_Z..25 mA
Current from V_{ref}..15 mA
Internal power dissipation, metal can.....................800 mW
  Cavity DIP..900 mW
  Molded DIP..600 mW
Operating temperature..............................0 to +70°C
Storage temperature, metal can.................. −65 to +150°C
  DIP.. −55 to +125°C
Lead temperature (soldering, 10 s)..........................300°C

OPERATIONAL AMPLIFIER

GENERAL DESCRIPTION

The 741 series are general-purpose op amps which feature improved performance over industry standards. They offer many features which make their application nearly foolproof: overload protection on the input and output, no latch-up when the common-mode range is exceeded, and freedom from oscillations.

ABSOLUTE MAXIMUM RATINGS

Power-supply voltage................................ ±18 V dc
Power dissipation...500 mW
Differential input voltage................................ ±30 V
Input voltage.. ±15 V
Output short-circuit duration.........................Indefinite
Operating temperature..............................0 to +70°C
Storage temperature............................ −65 to +150°C
Lead temperature (soldering, 10 s)..........................300°C

LED FLASHER/OSCILLATOR

GENERAL DESCRIPTION

The 3909 is a monolithic oscillator specifically designed to flash LEDs. Making use of the timing capacitor for voltage boost, it delivers pulses of 2 V or more to the LED while operating on a power supply of 1.5 V or less. The circuit is inherently self-starting and requires addition of only a battery and capacitor to function as an LED flasher.

It has been optimized for low power drain and operation from weak batteries so that continuous operation life exceeds that expected from battery rating.

Application is simplified by inclusion of internal timing resistors and an internal LED current-limiting resistor.

Timing capacitors will generally be of the electrolytic type, and a small 3-V rated part will be suitable for any LED flasher using a supply up to 6 V. However, when picking flash rates, it should be remembered that some electrolytics have very broad capacitance tolerances, for example −20 to +100 percent.

FEATURES

- Operation over 1 year from one G-size flashlight cell
- Bright, high-current LED pulse
- Minimum external parts
- Low voltage operation, from just over 1 V to 5 V
- Low current drain, averages under 0.5 mA during battery life
- Powerful; as an oscillator directly drives an 8-Ω speaker

ABSOLUTE MAXIMUM RATINGS

Power dissipation	500 mW
V^+ voltage	6.4 V
Operating temperature	−25 to +70°C

TEMPERATURE CONTROLLER

GENERAL DESCRIPTION

The 3911 is a highly accurate system for temperature measurement and/or control for use over a temperature range of −25 to +85°C. Fabricated on a single monolithic chip, it includes a temperature sensor, a stable voltage reference, and an op amp.

The output voltage of the 3911 is directly proportional to temperature in kelvins at 10 mV/K. Using the internal op amp with external resistors, any temperature scale factor is easily obtained. If the op amp is connected as a comparator, the output will switch as the temperature transverses the set point, making the device useful as an on-off temperature controller.

An active shunt regulator is connected across the power leads of the 3911 to provide a stable 6.8-V voltage reference for the sensing system. This allows the use of any power-supply voltage with suitable external resistors.

OPERATIONAL AMPLIFIER

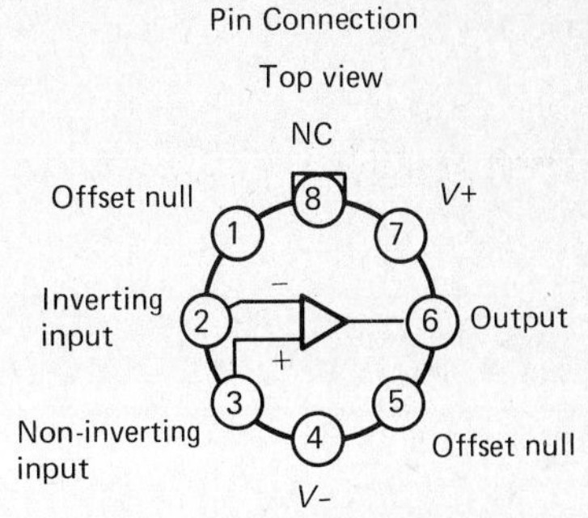

Metal can package

Note: Pin 4 connected to case.

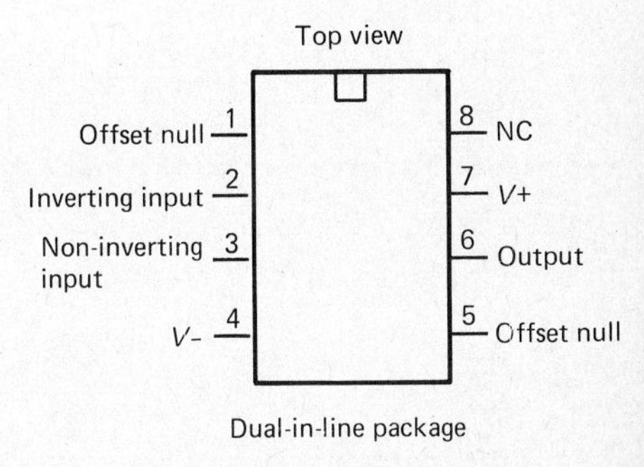

Dual-in-line package

LED FLASHER/OSCILLATOR

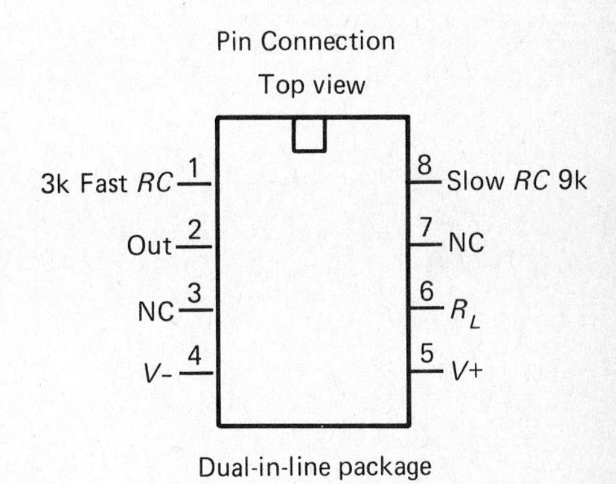

Dual-in-line package

TEMPERATURE CONTROLLER

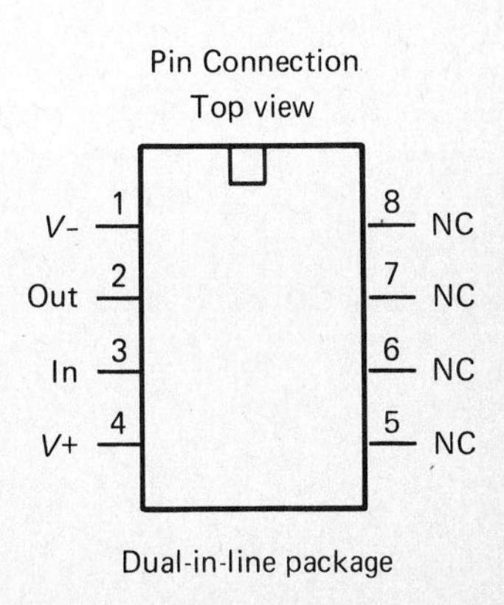

Dual-in-line package

FEATURES

- Uncalibrated accuracy ±10°C
- Internal op amp with frequency compensation
- Linear output of 10 mV/K (10 mV/°C)
- Can be calibrated in kelvins or Celsius or Fahrenheit degrees
- Output can drive loads up to 35 V

ABSOLUTE MAXIMUM RATINGS

Power-supply current (externally set)........................10 mA
Output collector voltage $+V$..............................36 V
Feedback input voltage..............................0 to +7.0 V
Output short-circuit duration............................Indefinite
Operating temperature............................ −25 to +85°C
Storage temperature............................ −65 to +150°C
Lead temperature (soldering, 10 s)........................300°C

5-V VOLTAGE REGULATOR
12-V VOLTAGE REGULATOR
15-V VOLTAGE REGULATOR

5-V VOLTAGE REGULATOR (7805)
12-V VOLTAGE REGULATOR (7812)
15-V VOLTAGE REGULATOR (7815)

GENERAL DESCRIPTION

Pin Connection
Bottom view

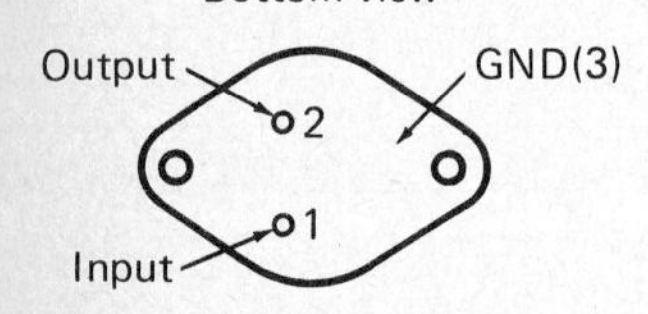

Metal can package
Aluminum TO-3 (KC)

The 78XX series of three-terminal regulators is available with several fixed output voltages, making them useful in a wide range of applications. One of these is local on-card regulation, eliminating the distribution problems associated with singlepoint regulation. The voltages available allow these regulators to be used in logic systems, instrumentation, hifi, and other solid-state electronic equipment. Although designed primarily as fixed voltage regulators, these devices can be used with external components to obtain adjustable voltages and currents.

The 78XX series is available in two different packages which will allow over 1.5-A load current if adequate heat sinking is provided. Current limiting is included to limit the peak output current to a safe value. Safe area protection for the output transistor is provided to limit internal power dissipation. If internal power dissipation becomes too high for the heat sinking provided, the thermal shutdown circuit takes over, preventing the IC from overheating.

FEATURES

- Internal thermal-overload protection
- No external components required
- Output transistor safe-area protection
- Internal short-circuit current limit

Top view

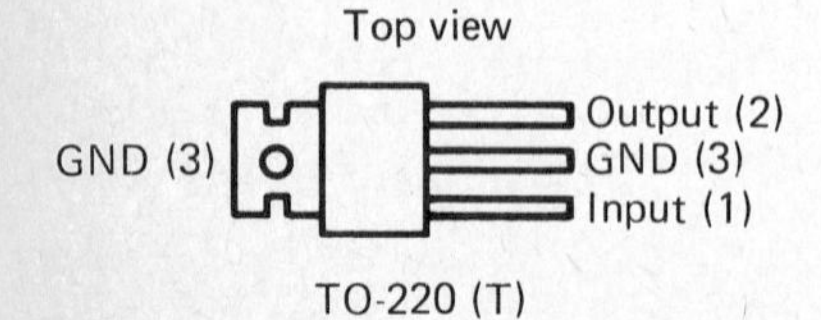

TO-220 (T)

ABSOLUTE MAXIMUM RATINGS

Input voltage:
  Output voltage options 5 through 18 V..................35 V dc
  Output voltage option 24...............................40 V dc
Internal power dissipation......................Internally limited
Operating temperature range..........................0 to +70°C
Maximum junction temperature............................150°C
Storage temperature range...................... −65 to +150°C
Lead temperature (soldering, 10 s)......................300°C

MONOLITHIC JFET INPUT OPERATIONAL AMPLIFIER

GENERAL DESCRIPTION

The 13741 is a 741 with BI-FET input followers on the same die. Familiar operating characteristics (those of a 741) with the added advantage of low input bias current make the 13741 easy to use. Monolithic fabrication makes this drop-in-replacement op amp economical and easy to use.

FEATURES

- Low input bias current 50 pA
- Low input noise current 0.01pA / $\sqrt{\text{Hz}}$
- High input impedance 5×10^{11} Ω
- Familiar operating characteristics

ABSOLUTE MAXIMUM RATINGS

Power-supply voltage.................................. ±18 V dc
Power dissipation (TO-99, H package)......................500 mW
Operating temperature................................0 to +70°C
$T_{j(max)}$..100°C
Differential input voltage................................ ±30 V
Input voltage.. ±16 V
Output short-circuit duration..........................Continuous
Storage temperature............................ −65 to +150°C
Lead temperature (soldering, 10 s)........................300°C

MONOLITHIC JFET INPUT
OPERATIONAL AMPLIFIER

Pin Connection

Top view

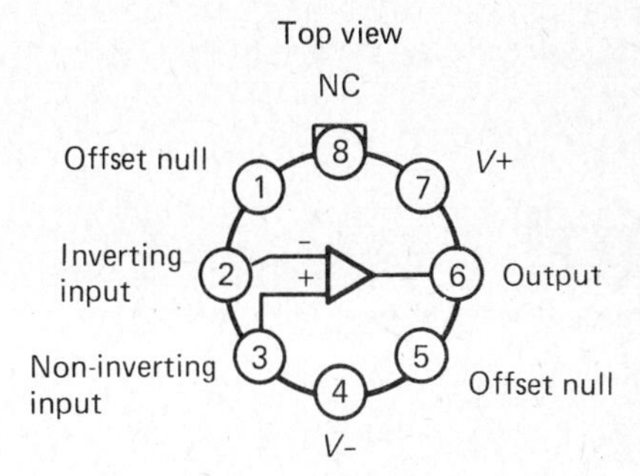

Metal can package

Note: Pin 4 connected to case.